Working in Social Work

Working in Social Work

THE REAL WORLD GUIDE TO PRACTICE SETTINGS

Jessica Rosenberg

FOREWORD BY TERRY MIZRAHI

Routledge
Taylor & Francis Group
New York   London

Routledge
Taylor & Francis Group
270 Madison Avenue
New York, NY 10016

Routledge
Taylor & Francis Group
27 Church Road
Hove, East Sussex BN3 2FA

© 2009 by Taylor and Francis Group, LLC
Routledge is an imprint of Taylor & Francis Group, an Informa business

Printed in the United States of America on acid-free paper
10 9 8 7 6 5 4 3 2 1

International Standard Book Number: 978-0-415-96551-4 (Hardback) 978-0-415-96552-1 (Paperback)

Library of Congress Cataloging-in-Publication Data

Rosenberg, Jessica (Jessica Millet)
    Working in social work : the real world guide to practice settings / Jessica Rosenberg.
        p. cm.
    Includes bibliographical references and index.
    ISBN 978-0-415-96551-4 (hardback : alk. paper) -- ISBN 978-0-415-96552-1 (pbk. : alk. paper)
    1. Social service--Vocational guidance--United States 2. Social workers--United States. 3. Private practice social work--United States. I. Title.

HV10.5.R67 2009
361.3'20973--dc22   2009011053

Visit the Taylor & Francis Web site at
http://www.taylorandfrancis.com

and the Routledge Web site at
http://www.routledgementalhealth.com

For my father,
Stanley Millet

Contents

Foreword

Rosenberg's book, a vital introduction to career paths in social work is being published in 2009, in the heart of one of the worst economic recessions in U.S. history. For our noble profession, now in its second century, it is the worst of times and the best of times. The worst for humanity, as many Americans—individuals, families, communities, and organizations from all backgrounds and circumstances—find themselves in dire straits; the best for the profession as, ironically, the need for professional social workers is greater than ever. The worst for those whose industries and sectors have been downsized or for those who, after choosing careers such as business or finance, have become disillusioned with a commercial career track; the best because many young people (in age and spirit) are heeding the message of hope of President Obama and his wife, Michelle, and are pursuing careers of service and change.

The book is a down-to-earth, composite of the breadth and depth of social work. It may surprise many readers who have a narrow or even stereotypical view of what social work encompasses to learn that social work is vibrant and diverse. The book reveals the complexity and challenges for our profession, which many seek in a workplace setting over a lifetime. The book's inspiring mini-autobiographies written by the "unsung" heroes and heroines in the major sectors of social work practice, demonstrate that there is a place for everyone.

As someone who has been in the profession for more than 40 years and who has been a leader of social workers in the U.S. and internationally, I was re-energized by the narratives of these experienced social workers who exemplify what I label the 3 "C's." These social workers from 13 different fields of practice exhibit "commitment," "competence" and "confidence." Commitment shines through; they all have compassion and empathy; they all have "good hearts." These are reflected in the values and ethics of fairness, social justice, opportunity, and service that are the hallmark of our dignified profession. But these traits and characteristics are only the foundation for a career in social work. Competence is needed to complement commitment. Social workers acquire the professional knowledge and skill to translate their commitment into "the doing" needed to be effective practitioners. By obtaining their BSW and MSW degrees and additional credentials where available, they use their knowledge and skills to influence the attitudes and actions of countless others. And perhaps most exciting is the confidence that exudes from these pages as these experienced social workers present their stories with pride. The 3 C's are alive and well in our profession, sometimes against all odds.

These exemplars do not represent the best; rather I see them as typical of the hundreds of thousands of social workers across the country who are making a difference, and collectively changing the lives millions of people every day. More importantly, not only do these social workers affect individual circumstances, but they and others like them have responsibilities for and impact institutional and system change as well. In the vernacular of social work this is called "macro" as well as "micro" level change. Social workers work at both ends of the spectrum, sometimes simultaneously. In our jargon it is called the "person-in-environment" perspective.

Each of the 13 practice settings is described by a well known expert in the field who highlights the context in which these exemplar social workers do their jobs. In a succinct and cogent manner, the reader has a glimpse of the history, contemporary situations, and anticipated future directions for this field or specialization. These overviews state with clear conviction that social work often struggles against the lack of resources, gaps in services, inequitable or inadequate policies by government at all levels, and uninformed or prejudicial attitudes about people in need. Over time, social work has become more sophisticated in linking policy with practice, and the personal to the political. And over time, social workers have understood the importance of being at the right tables—inside the agency, in the community, and in the political and policy arena.

Finally, I want to acknowledge the commonalities across fields of practice. In each of these diverse settings, the social work role includes key core components— building relationships, developing and utilizing resources, applying behavioral and organizational theory, understanding cultural competency, and promoting advocacy at the individual case and collective class level.

You can read this book cover to cover or selectively. You will get a rich sense of the social work profession as a whole and learn where you can find your niche. While the profession struggles to shape the policies and programs to help people maximize their potential, you will become more informed about its diversity and depth.

Terry Mizrahi

Dr. Mizrahi is a professor at the Hunter College School of Social Work of the City University of New York where she chairs the Community Organization & Planning concentration and teaches social policy and health and mental health policy. She is the director of the Education Center for Community Organizing which provides information, workshops, and technical assistance to community leaders and community-based professionals in New York City and beyond.

She completed a Fulbright Fellowship in Israel in 2006 at Hebrew University where she taught a seminar in comparative community development and organized two major national conferences. In 2004, she was a Kreitzman Fellow at Ben Gurion University in Israel. She continues to informally consult with the Ministry of Social Affairs after producing for them a report on best practices on client and citizen participation in improving policies in the US. She also consults with the Jerusalem Intercultural Center and the Interdisciplinary Forum on Community Development.

Dr. Mizrahi is co-editor-in-chief of the *Encyclopedia of Social Work,* 20th edition which was released for publication by NASW and Oxford University Press in March 2008. She is the author of 5 books and monographs and 70 articles, book chapters, reviews, and manuals. Her areas of research, training and consultation include professional socialization, coalition building, community organizing practice, and health policy. She completed a study on social work leadership in hospitals and the leadership of Deans of Schools of Social Work in promoting interdisciplinary collaboration.

Her publications include *Women, Organizing and Diversity: Struggling With the Issues* (co-author); *Getting Rid of Patients: Contradiction in the Socialization of Physicians; Community Organization and Social Administration* (co-editor and author); and *Strategic Partnerships: Building Successful Coalitions and Collaborations* (co-author). She is under contract from Columbia University Press to write a book to be titled *Health and Mental Health Policy for Social Workers.*

Dr. Mizrahi served as elected national president of the National Association of Social Workers (NASW) from 2001–2003, the largest professional organization in the world with 155,000 members. She was secretary of the Association for Community Organization and Social Administration (ACOSA) and is a founder of the Journal of Community Practice. She is recipient of the Hunter Presidential Awards for Excellence in Applied Research 2008 and Community Leadership in 1994 and Lifetime Achievement Award from ACOSA in 2004.

Preface

Social work is an extremely broad field and this defining feature is both its greatest strength and weakness. With so many possible career paths, social workers have tremendous flexibility and the profession offers career choices that include a multiplicity of roles, functions, and settings. At the same time, the wide-ranging scope of the profession makes it extremely difficult to achieve clarity about what social workers do. The social work profession has struggled with this problem for much of its history and the prevalent public confusion about what social workers do led the National Association of Social Workers (NASW) to launch a public education campaign some years back.

As a new social worker working in community mental health in the late 1980s, I found that I was largely uninformed about social work across fields of practice. What does a child welfare social worker do? What are the benefits of going into private practice? I knew I wanted to make some career changes, but I had no idea what direction to pursue and little sense of what would be a good fit for me. I was reminded, years later when I became a social work professor, of having been at a loss regarding my own career choices when I was new to the field.

The social work profession has changed considerably since I was a new social worker and social work services continue to emerge and evolve in response to societal developments. For example, the demand for social work with the military has increased exponentially since the wars in Afghanistan and Iraq and social work in health care is shifting from an inpatient service delivery system to a community-based model of care because of a complex mix of factors, including advances in medical technology, the needs of an aging society, and the fiscal constraints imposed by managed care. The experience of the new social worker has changed as well. When I graduated from social work school, there was a longer grace period during which a new social worker adjusted to the field and learned his or her craft. Many of us met with a senior social work supervisor for weekly training sessions. Those days seem like a luxury gone by in today's hectic and fast-paced world. The productivity demands have gone up and social workers are expected to be prepared to shoot out of the starting gate. There is a much greater need to be independent because the opportunity for social work supervision has declined. In many settings, social workers no longer report to supervisors who are themselves social workers, and thus there is less opportunity to be socialized into the profession.

One of the things that I recognized early on in the classroom is that it is not only the profession that is changing; there are considerable differences between today's students and the students of my generation as well. Many of my students come to class with a take-charge attitude about their careers. They have lots of questions and, at times, they can be a little challenging in their pursuit of answers. In class, students often want to know, right up front, the ins and outs of the social work field: what to expect, what social workers do, the job market, salaries, and the pros and cons between respective practice settings. In short, they want to know the nitty-gritty about the profession. Responding to their questions is no easy task. Yet as a professor, it became clear to me that it is more important than ever for students to have as much preparation as possible in order to effectively meet the challenges of professional practice. In the appendix, readers will find two additions that can be quite useful: The first is a chart that provides an at-a-glance comparison of fields of practice. The second is an extensive list of useful social work internet sites.

I searched for an introductory textbook for my students, one that would provide an accessible and reader-friendly snapshot of the profession across fields of practice. My idea of what such a book should contain was in part shaped by my previous position as assistant director of the New York City Chapter of the National Association of Social Workers. As editor of the chapter's newsletter, *Currents*, I was charged with putting out monthly newsletters about the social work profession. I started conceptualizing theme issues that profiled a specific field of practice each month, highlighting prominent leaders in the field, the voices and experiences of frontline social workers, practice concerns, and pragmatic issues about salaries and the job market. What students needed, it occurred to me, is something similar: a book that pulls together a lot of information in order to provide an accessible and contemporary picture of the profession. This is that book—a book that grew out of my desire to respond to my students, who often put me on the spot in class with their directness and assertiveness, their desire to be in charge of their careers, and their insistence on getting "the real story."

STRUCTURE OF THE BOOK

The book comprises 13 chapters. Each chapter covers a different field of practice:

1. Social Work in Addictions
2. Social Work With Older Adults
3. Social Work With Child Welfare
4. Social Work in Criminal Justice
5. Domestic Violence and Social Work
6. Social Work in Health Care
7. Social Work With Housing and Homelessness
8. Social Work in the International Arena
9. Social Work and Mental Illness
10. Social Work With the Military
11. Social Work With Palliative and End-of-Life Care
12. Social Work and Private Practice
13. Social Work in School

CHAPTER STRUCTURE

Each chapter presents a true picture of what to expect as a frontline social worker in the given practice setting, consistently formatted in the following sections for ease of reference and comparison across settings:

Field Overview and Forecast
Critical Issues
First-Person Narrative
Resources to Learn More

The Field Overview and Forecast section is designed to provide an overview of the field and to identify emerging issues and employment trends. Each overview covers the following areas:

Scope of Services
The Social Worker's Role
Credentialing
Emerging Issues and Employment Trends

The Critical Issues section of each chapter consists of an interview with an established authority in his or her respective field. The interviewee was chosen on the basis of his or her expertise about the trends and critical issues that inform the respective field, and considerable effort was made to include experts from across the country so that geographic representation and perspective is conveyed in the book. The interviewees include some of the most important leaders in the profession, including Dr. Terry Mizrahi, co-editor-in-chief of the *Encyclopedia of Social Work*, 20th edition, and past national president of the National Association of Social Workers; Dr. William Bell, CEO of Casey Family Programs and past commissioner of the New York City Administration for Children's Services; Ms. Kristin Day, chief social worker for the Veterans Association; and Dr. Stacey Desmond, president of the National Organization of Forensic Social Work.

Each First-Person Narrative is a vignette written by a social worker who practices in the respective field. The Critical Issues section is designed to focus on policy and professional trends; the intent of this section is to describe the challenges and joys in direct practice. The contributors of the narratives relate their paths in social work, as well as their frustrations and rewards in their respective fields. In the process, ethical dilemmas and organizational challenges are identified and discussed. As with the interviews, the contributors of the Critical Issues vignettes were carefully chosen to represent social work practice from diverse geographic areas in order to provide an accurate portrayal of the variety of practice settings. The locales for these narratives range from rural school social work in Vermont to working with the mentally ill homeless on the streets of New York City, and from working with battered women in Louisville, Kentucky, to the experiences of an international social worker in Darfur, Sudan. Students who have read early draft versions of this book often say that the narratives are among the most enjoyable and illuminating parts. In conceptualizing these sections, I am indebted to the many excellent publications of the National Association of Social Workers that tell the real-life stories of frontline practitioners.

The Resources to Learn More section is tailored specifically to each practice setting, including relevant books and other traditional print materials, information about specialty credentials, educational programs and centers, as well as hard-to-find Internet sites.

While the world of social work continues to evolve and the issues facing frontline social workers present numerous challenges, the field has never been more exciting and promising. Social workers are gaining in public recognition, respect, and in financial remuneration for their services. Social workers save lives every day, and their passion to make the world a better place and their belief in the possibility of a better future for their clients are a constant beacon of light that shines bright in the hearts of new social workers everywhere. I hope this book serves as a road map to help new social workers find their way along an exciting and worthwhile path.

Acknowledgments

First and foremost, I am especially grateful to my editor, Dana Bliss, who gave clear and helpful guidance from the very beginning. His input significantly improved the quality of this book and his support brought a nascent idea to fruition. My husband, Sam Rosenberg, patiently read every draft and consistently provided me with thoughtful and constructive criticism. His input strengthened the book considerably. I am indebted to the invaluable assistance of several of my colleagues in the Social Work Department at Long Island University. My chair, Dr. Samuel Jones, was extremely helpful and generous with his feedback. Dr. Amy Krentzman shared her considerable technical expertise and knowledge of the social work field with me, and Dr. Susanna Jones was always a source of great intelligence and support. Our department administrative assistant, Ms. Naterena Parham-Cofield, with great patience and good humor, provided invaluable technical assistance. Writing a book is a long and lonely process, one that I could not have accomplished without my colleague Dr. Syed Ali, who was always there with a quick smile and a kind word when I felt discouraged.

This book was significantly strengthened by many excellent social workers who shared their own paths in social work. Their stories and expertise truly add the "real world" dimension to this book! These contributors include Terry Altilio, Krystal Ashling, William C. Bell, Patricia Brownell, Lynn Bye, Jennifer Clements, Fran Danis, Kristin Day, Stacey Hardy-Desmond, Rus Ervin Funk, Laura W. Groshong, Eileen Klein, Ken Lewis, Erin Majesty, Robin Sakina Mama, Stanley G. McCracken, Terry Mizrahi. Ken Onaitis, Dan Pitzer, Elise Rackmill, Julie Richards, Jenny Ross, James Shepard, Lynn Spevak, Madeleine Stoner, and W. Patrick Sullivan

A special note of appreciation to the social work students at Long Island University, whose thoughtful questions provided the inspiration for this book. I hope you find some answers here. Other colleagues in the field have been a source of ongoing learning and inspiration: Mitch Kahn, director of social work at Ramapo College of New Jersey and social worker par excellence, Dr. Robert Schachter of NASW-NYC, and Dr. Elizabeth Clark and her staff at the National Association of Social Workers. And finally to my children, Daniel and Adrienne, who are always my toughest critics and my biggest supporters.

1

Social Work in Addictions

SECTION ONE: FIELD OVERVIEW AND FORECAST

Scope of Services

Substance abuse is a serious and widespread problem in the United States, one that either directly or indirectly affects a large segment of society. In 2006, an estimated 22.6 million persons age 12 or older were diagnosed with a substance- or alcohol-abuse problem. If one adds to this number the multiple stressors related to having a friend or family member who is struggling with a drug or alcohol problem, it truly is a problem of epidemic proportions (Substance Abuse and Mental Health Services Administration, 2008).

Among the most troubling aspects of substance and alcohol abuse is the damage caused to children. Many children grow up in homes where drugs or alcohol are abused, with estimates suggesting that 1 in 4 children is impacted by familial alcohol abuse and that 1 in 10 children lives with a parent or another adult who is a drug abuser. As children grow older and start school, they are at increased risk of exposure to illegal drugs. According to a National Survey of American Attitudes on Substance Abuse conducted by Columbia University's National Center on Addiction and Substance Abuse (2000), 11 million high school students and 5 million middle school students regularly come into contact with illegal drugs, dealing, and drinking on school grounds.

Alcohol and drug abuse are major health and social problems that cut across age, race, gender, and class. Regardless of the practice setting, social workers will encounter clients and client systems where abuse of drugs or alcohol is a problem. The need for social workers in all practice settings with the necessary skills and knowledge to effectively work with clients who have an alcohol or drug problem cannot be overstated. It is extremely important that social workers seek specialized training in working with addictions, either while enrolled in their degree programs, in continuing education courses, or in supervision.

Settings

Addiction settings hire social work staff with varying levels of education, with some settings requiring a master's degree and others requiring a bachelor's degree. Frequently, specialized addiction certifications, such as a certified alcohol- or substance-abuse credential, are preferred and will significantly strengthen a resume.

In residential programs, such as a therapeutic community (TC) or a group home, social workers use generalist practice skills, primarily case management and counseling. Generally, these positions can be obtained with a bachelor's degree in social work and/or specialized addiction training, such as a certified alcohol and addiction credential.

Employment in inpatient centers, partial hospitalization centers, and outpatient treatment programs generally requires a master's degree. In these settings, social workers provide clinical treatment, often running therapy groups. Social workers in private practice frequently treat clients with addiction problems. The requirements for independent private practice vary from state to state, but the standard is that a master's-level social work degree with licensure at the clinical level is needed. At the macro level, social workers are employed as administrators and are hired to develop and implement programs, conduct research, and develop public policy. Advanced training and prior experience is usually required to move into an administrative position.

The Social Worker's Role

The social worker's role varies based on the practice setting. Since many clients with an alcohol or substance-abuse problem initially present themselves in non-addiction settings, such as a mental health center or a medical clinic, the social worker is often the first professional to identify and diagnose a substance-abuse problem. Frequently, the initial social work task is identification of the problem. The key social work skills are assessment, screening, and referral (Hanson, 2001).

Self-help or mutual aid has significantly shaped the social worker's role in working with addictions. The defining characteristic of self-help and mutual aid is that people with similar problems and experiences come together to provide help and support for each other. Sharing personal stories and learning coping skills is a key part of the recovery process (Seebohm, Henderson, Munn-Giddings, Thomas, & Yasmeen, 2006). Alcoholics Anonymous (AA), founded in 1935, is the prototype for mutual-aid groups, and numerous groups such as Gamblers Anonymous (GA), Narcotics Anonymous (NA), and Overeaters Anonymous (OA) subsequently modeled themselves on AA. Mutual-aid groups are widely viewed as an important method for building a positive community that promotes and supports recovery (Van Wormer & Davis, 2008).

In addictions treatment programs, the influence of the self-help and the mutual-aid movement can be found by the prevalence of treatment staff who are themselves in recovery. In particular, the development of the therapeutic community, which grew in prominence and popularity in the mid-1960s and 1970s with programs such as DayTop Village and Samaritan Village, is based on the principle of mutual aid and peer support. Within this context, social workers and other professionally trained staff who worked in addictions programs frequently found themselves on the defensive with clients and other staff who were recovered addicts and alcoholics, as their credibility was questioned because they could not provide personal stories of their own addiction and recovery. Staff members who were recovered addicts and alcoholics often resented professionally trained staff because they had the educational training and credentials that enabled them to move into better-paying, supervisory positions. Whereas tensions between staff who are recovered addicts and alcoholics and professionally trained social workers still persist in some agencies, the organizational culture of substance-abuse programs has evolved and is characterized by mutual respect for and appreciation of respective roles. This is partly the result of an increased emphasis on credentialing and professional training by accrediting bodies, as well as implementation of reimbursement policies for training, as more and more professionally trained staff enter this field.

Credentialing

There are a number of specialized credentials for working in addictions, and social workers who obtain dual credentials in social work and the addictions are significantly more competitive in the job market. At the national level, there is the National Certified Addiction Counselor Credential (NCAC) and the National Association of Certified Clinical Alcohol, Tobacco, and Other Drugs Social Worker (C-CATODSW), which is offered by the National Association of Social Workers. Many states offer their own credentials, and the requirements vary from state to state. Typically they include: (a) basic competency and ethical conduct requirements, (b) work experience requirements, (c) education and training requirements, and (d) passing a written examination and/or oral exam.

Emerging Issues and Employment Trends

Social work in the addictions is a growth area for social workers. According to a study of the social work workforce conducted by the Association of Social Workers (Whitaker, Weismiller, & Clark, 2006a), less than 3% of licensed social workers currently identify addictions as their primary practice area, with men more likely to work in addictions than women. However, the demand for social workers in this area is likely to outpace the supply. The Bureau of Labor Statistics (2008) projects that jobs for social workers trained to work with substance abusers is likely to increase at a faster rate than for other occupations. In particular, employment opportunities will exist for social workers to work with people who have been arrested and convicted of a drug-related offense. There is a growing trend (in part spurred by the overcrowding of prisons) to provide individuals convicted of a drug charge with treatment programs as an alternative to incarceration or as a condition of probation. Consequently, there will be an increased demand for social workers to work with substance abusers who have been court-mandated to obtain treatment.

Working in addictions is a field of practice that presents many challenges. Substance-abuse clients are one of the most difficult populations to work with.

They are difficult to engage, often resistant to treatment, and tend to go from one crisis to the next. Good clinical skills are important, as is a good sense of humor. However, for the savvy social worker, this is an exciting growth area with great potential.

ACTIVITIES TO LEARN MORE

- Attend a local Alcoholics Anonymous and a Narcotics Anonymous meeting. Afterward, ask yourself what it would be like to work with this population, and if you think you would find it rewarding and challenging.
- Log on and explore the NAADAC Web site at http://www.naadac. org. This is the largest national association for addictions professionals and provides a wealth of information about working in the field of addictions.
- Log on to the National Association for Social Workers Web site at www.socialworkers.org and read the publication "Choices: Careers in Social Work." Review the section about addictions.

SECTION TWO: CRITICAL ISSUES
Stanley G. McCracken, PhD

Stanley McCracken is a senior lecturer in the School of Social Service Administration. He is a licensed clinical social worker and a registered dual-disorder professional with over 30 years experience. His practice and teaching interests lie in the areas of mental health, substance abuse, co-occurring disorders, behavioral pharmacology, multicultural mental health, aging, and implementation of evidence-based practice.

Professor McCracken has published a number of articles and book chapters in such diverse areas as behavioral medicine, behavioral pharmacology, psychiatric rehabilitation, substance abuse, and evidence-based practice. He is coauthor of two books, *Practice Guidelines for Extended Psychiatric Care: From Chaos to Collaboration* and *Interactive Staff Training: Rehabilitation Teams That Work*. He also is coauthor of the Council on Social Work Education Gero-Ed Advanced MSW curriculum in mental health and aging.

When not at SSA, Professor McCracken spends a good deal of time providing staff training as well as clinical and program consultation to a variety of public sector and nonprofit service providers. Most of his current work is in assisting community programs to implement evidence-based practice.

My path to professional social work has taken a few twists and turns. In 1969, I entered the United States Army and served in Vietnam. After returning from the war, I wasn't sure what I wanted to do with my life, but after a few years, I decided to enroll in a master's of social work program, largely because I was influenced by an interest in Carl Jung, and because I enjoyed working with people. Upon graduation, I worked in behavioral pharmacology research and later in direct practice with substance abusers. I subsequently earned a PhD from the School of Social Service Administration at the University of Chicago.

How does social work with addictions differ today from in the past?
There have been significant changes in the evolution of social work practice with addictions. In the past, few social workers worked in substance abuse programs, and few social work students identified addictions as a career choice. Social work education, heavily influenced by the psychoanalytic movement, focused its clinical content largely on a psychodynamic orientation and, for the most part, paid scant attention to the treatment of addictions. Working in addictions was viewed by the social work profession as a step down from mental health and regarded as a lower status career choice. Those that chose to work in substance abuse programs often had a personal history of drug or alcohol abuse and were themselves in recovery. Some measure of mutual mistrust existed between professionally trained staff and those who had a personal past as an addict and came up through the treatment ranks. Today, working with addictions is widely recognized as a legitimate area of social work practice, and many schools of social work offer courses or have concentrations in substance abuse.

What kinds of settings do social workers in addictions work in?
We can conceptualize addictions treatment as taking place along a continuum, with a completely controlled environment, such as a closed unit at one end, and outpatient treatment in a private practice setting at the other end. The social work role differs depending on the setting. The residential programs are staffed mainly by preprofessionals who are not social workers. Hospital-based programs, day treatment, and outpatient programs employ MSWs and BSWs.

Medical detoxification is a short-term inpatient hospital stay in which clients who are physically addicted are medically assisted through the withdrawal process. In medical detoxification, the social work role is focused on gathering data, conducting assessments, and developing discharge plans. Medical detox units have highly stratified and hierarchical power structures, with physicians at the top, and social workers have to learn to negotiate both formal and informal power structures.

Inpatient rehabilitation programs are usually 21–28-day hospital stays, often on a closed unit. In these settings, the major treatment modality is group work and milieu treatment. In milieu treatment, therapy is going on all the time, often informally in the hallways and recreation room. Social workers will spend the majority of their day with clients, utilizing treatment techniques that include modeling and reinforcing client behaviors. In these settings, social workers are challenged by having limited opportunities for privacy, where they can go to an office and close the door. Social workers need to be self-aware of how they interact with their coworkers on the unit; everything is out in the open. Self-care strategies become paramount for social workers, since they have limited opportunities to get away to a private office and relax. In day-treatment programs, clients live independently, attending day programs 5 days a week for several hours a day. Group work is the preferred treatment modality, with a strong milieu component. Intensive outpatient therapy programs treat clients several times a week with a combination of group and individual treatment.

Residential care is provided along a continuum in the wet, damp, and dry housing model. In wet housing, residents may be actively using substances, but they must refrain from using on the premises. In damp housing, it is expected that addicts will relapse occasionally. In dry housing, sobriety is expected and required.

In your opinion, what is the most important policy or trend impacting social work in addictions?

Historically, managed care contains costs by limiting access to substance abuse services—a policy that is changing due to recent legislation. We know that addiction is a chronic lifelong disorder, that addicts traditionally were viewed as always recovering and never recovered, and yet we routinely talk about addicts graduating from treatment programs. If we know that 10% of our population has a long-term problem with chemical dependency, why is treatment funded on a short-term basis? The mental health system funds long-term services for clients, primarily for serious mental illness. In substance abuse, treatment is typically funded for a greater number of people, but for comparatively less time. This funding approach does not take into account that engagement with substance abusers is a long, slow process. Most substance abuse clients enter treatment unwillingly, often under pressure from a court order, an employer, their family, or due to a health issue or other serious consequence. When treatment is approved for a time-limited period, by the time the client is engaged, there is not enough time left for active treatment.

How has the self-help movement influenced social work practice with addictions?

There is a troubled history between the 12-step model and the social work profession. In the past, considerable differences existed between these two groups. The 12-step model rejected the use of psychotropic medication. The professional community refuted the confrontational style utilized in 12-step programs, and was uncomfortable with the self-help movement's emphasis on spirituality. Today there is much more integration between 12-step programs and the professional community, and a mutual appreciation for their respective areas of expertise. The 12-step model no longer rejects the use of medication, and professionals routinely refer substance abuse clients to AA and other 12-step programs. The importance of spirituality in recovery has gained widespread acceptance.

What are co-occurring disorders, and what are the challenges to integrating treatment?

The Substance Abuse and Mental Health Services Administration of the U.S. Department of Health & Human Services defines a person with a co-occurring disorder as an individual who has at least one diagnosable mental disorder and an alcohol or drug use problem. Research suggests that close to 50% of people with serious mental illness have a co-occurring substance abuse disorder. We know that substance abusers have a high rate of mental illness. However, despite the clear evidence that so many people have an ongoing concurrent struggle with substance abuse and mental illness, services and resources are structured and funded independently. This leads to a disintegrated system of care, which is reflected in an educational system in which training in mental health omits substantial content on substance abuse. Licensing laws reinforce this split; clinical licensing exams contain few questions about substance abuse and perpetuate a fiction that clinical social workers do not work with addicts.

In what way do you think stigma impacts social work practice in addictions?
The first thing social workers in this field must do is address their own countertransference. For example, if one's client is a woman who just gave birth to her second baby with fetal alcohol syndrome, one must examine one's feelings about the client in order to work with her effectively. Social workers have to recognize that substance abusers come from all walks of life and avoid stereotyping them. Another big issue in addictions is self-stigma, meaning that our clients internalize and mirror negative societal views of addicts. Often, by the time an addict sees a social worker, he or she has already been in treatment and has relapsed. Addicts often feel very discouraged by repeated failures to get straight. I tell clients, "You didn't fail; the system failed you by putting you in a program that you weren't ready for or committed to."

If you had a magic wand and could change one thing about social work in addictions, what would it be and why?
We need to do a better job of cross-training staff. There is a perception in social work that the counseling skills that are taught in social work programs somehow do not apply to working with substance abusers. It is a mistake to assume that one's clients do not have a substance abuse problem. We cannot intervene with a problem that has not been identified. We cannot continue to simply say that we lack the skills to work with substance abusers and then refer them out. Parallel or sequential treatment for mental health problems and substance abuse problems does not work because clients inevitably fall through the cracks. We have to recognize that core social work skills apply to working with substance abusers, and we then get additional specialized training and supervision so that we can do the work even better.

What are three key skills that social workers need to be successful in working in addictions?
Social workers need to be expert in engagement skills, in motivational interviewing, and in relapse prevention skills. Social workers need to know how to help clients to develop coping skills and problem-solving skills. There is a big emphasis in substance abuse treatment in providing clients with education and information, which, in my opinion, is overblown. Instead, we need to focus on teaching clients

how to navigate daily life, for example how to go to a family reunion and turn down a drink. It is very important to engage families, and to be able to work with client systems.

How would you describe the major opportunities available to social workers who work in addictions?
Being credentialed in addictions will make a social worker much more competitive in today's job market. I recommend getting an MSW plus an addictions credential. If one's school offers advanced training in addictions, than take advantage of it and get dual credentials. If not, keep track of any classes that focused on substance abuse and any clients seen that present with substance abuse problems. This experience can be used to qualify a social worker to sit for addiction certification examinations. Having the knowledge base and skills in working with addictions is a plus wherever one works, because even in nonaddiction settings, one will have clients with substance abuse problems. Within the addictions field, the practice settings that are rapidly growing include treating older adults and working in the criminal justice system.

DID YOU KNOW?

- According to a 2006 survey by the Substance Abuse and Mental Health Services Administration (SAMHSA), the criminal justice system was the principal referral source to substance-abuse treatment programs for all admissions aged 18 to 25.
- The percentage of substance-abuse treatment admissions for methamphetamine/amphetamine abuse has more than doubled since 1995.
- The most recent data from SAMHSA reports that more than 1.7 million hospital emergency room visits during 2004–2005 were associated with drug or alcohol abuse.

Source: Substance Abuse and Mental Health Services Administration.

SECTION THREE: FIRST-PERSON NARRATIVE

The Accidental Career: A Social Worker in the Addictions Field
Dan Pitzer, LCSW, LCADC, CEAP

Dan Pitzer is a licensed clinical social worker (LCSW) in New York and New Jersey. He is a member of the Academy of Certified Social Workers (ACSW) and a licensed clinical alcohol and drug abuse counselor (LCADC) in New Jersey. He is a credentialed alcohol and substance abuse counselor (CASAC) in New York.

Mr. Pitzer has a master's degree in social work and a post-master's certificate in substance abuse counseling from New York University (NYU). He served as a family therapist at Beth Israel Hospital's Stuyvesant Square Inpatient Rehabilitation Program and as acting manager of the Member's Assistance Program at LOCAL 32-B-J. He has held several positions in the fields of developmental disabilities and HIV/AIDS.

Mr. Pitzer currently serves as assistant vice president and senior counselor at the Employee Assistance Program at Merrill Lynch. He is a treating clinician for the National Football League (NFL) Program for Substances of Abuse. Since 2000, he's served as coordinator of the Annual Addictions Institute of the New York City Chapter of the National Association of Social Workers (NASW). He is also a member of a work group coordinated by George Washington University Medical Center and the Network of Employers for Traffic Safety to develop screening and brief intervention procedures for alcohol misuse in the workplace. Mr. Pitzer lives in New Jersey with his wife, Michele, and son, Daniel James.

"Dan, would you like a job in the rehab?" This is how my social work career in addictions started. Not from a lifelong dream to work with addiction, but because of a job opening. I was offered a job by a classmate in my MSW program, and that started me down a road to a career in addiction treatment that has been more rewarding and fulfilling than I could have ever thought. The road has not been smoothly paved, however. For a social worker employed in hospital-based addiction treatment, the potholes are many.

I arrived at a local New York City hospital whose addiction program had once been at an uptown location that catered to the famous and famously addicted, that was now downtown and serving primarily Medicaid-covered addicted individuals. I was placed in the 28-day rehabilitation unit as an aftercare counselor, and eventually was promoted to family therapist.

The culture at the time was that the addiction counselors were mostly recovering people who became counselors during their recovery, and primarily used their own experience to help others. Most had either high school or bachelor's educations and many had the credentialed alcoholism and substance abuse counselor certification from New York State, a credential that did not require a college education, but did require many hours of experience in the field. This credential had just been created from two separate certifications, the certified alcoholism counselor (CAC) and the certified substance abuse counselor (CSAC).

These two certifications were frequently obtained by recovering people beginning to work in the field, and the credentialing process was much less stringent than the eventual CASAC. Many CACs and CSACs had been grandfathered in during the inception period of the CASAC. Integrating into the culture of recovering people doing the clinical work without graduate training was a bit of a challenge for a new MSW without a CASAC.

Resentments abounded during my first months on the job, and they came in many forms. I was seen as the MSW who was not in recovery (but they had no idea of my history), who got a job on the rehab floor, where they wanted to be. The rehab floor was where very intense clinical work was done; the counselors with the best clinical skills were handpicked to be there, and I was resented for taking a potential position away from them. In addition, I was a white male with a mostly African American and Latino patient population and a mostly African American staff. The odds were stacked against me, and the staff felt that the patients would eat me alive.

The patients challenged me, but I was able to employ clinical skills to succeed. Self-disclosure is a big clinical issue, particularly with addicted patients, as most want to know if you have shared their experience. One female patient said to me, "I need to know if you can FEEL me." The truth was that I had voluntarily stopped drinking 2 years before, but did not identify as a recovering alcoholic, and getting into my story was not the point of treatment. I was able to redirect the question back to her motivation for asking it, and processed that, leading to exploration of those feelings she most desperately wanted me to feel. I think that a direct yes or no answer from me would have shut down any such opportunity.

That tactic was difficult in the beginning, but became easier with more experience, as my self-confidence grew. I had learned a great deal about drugs and alcohol in my previous position as a case manager, which was also my field placement; but this was the first time I was delving into intense inpatient treatment, and the intensity of that work has not been matched in any position since. Working for eight months as an aftercare counselor enabled me to learn the ropes of the rehab, connect patients with a myriad of resources, fill in running groups when needed, and sharpen my clinical skills to prepare me for my promotion to family therapist.

Besides having to interview for a job I was already doing for several months (while a coworker was on medical leave and then resigned), the family therapist position was the most nerve-racking clinical experience I'd had to date. In order to survive the intense feelings, I had to thrive on the intensity, pushing patients and families further and further to explore the pain caused by addictive behavior. Having patients in an inpatient setting, you have the resources to "go for broke," since they have support around them 24 hours a day, and "go for broke" we did.

The idea was that after we worked with the families in group psychoeducation, we would bring them into the group with the patients as part of their primary treatment group. This is taken from the St. Mary's Minnesota Model and is rarely done in addiction treatment today, with a private family session being the preferred modality.

In one instance, a 10-year-old child told his mother that he had a dream about her funeral. I encouraged the child to describe the details of the funeral, including the coffin and the dress, to his mother, which was horrifying to others but cathartic to the child. It got a point across about how the child was living on a day-to-day basis with the fear of losing his mother.

At another family session, a mother in her 50s with a 20-year-old son said that she was so hurt by his stealing from her and that she had done so much to protect him. She disclosed in the morning family group that she had shot her former boyfriend to death when she found out he was abusing her son (the patient) and had served 5 years behind bars, and she would do it again. Her son's drive to feed his addiction was as strong as his mother's drive to protect him, which led him to betray her in the face of her dedication.

Group members benefited by vicariously experiencing the family members' pain, and identifying with their own experience, a very powerful tool. Being a social worker in this setting, I had the clinical training necessary to facilitate such powerful groups, and the family therapist position required a master's degree, so it was a good fit.

As social work students, we often have specific ideas about which settings and populations we want to work with or, usually, those we do not want to work with. Students and experienced social workers alike have often said to me that they do not want to work with addicted individuals because they do not want to work with people who do not want help, or who are not ready to change. My response is that, as social workers, we are both agents of change and responsible for meeting people where they are at the given time on the continuum of change. Addiction permeates all practice areas, and even if social workers are not involved in direct treatment, they are often dealing with undiagnosed addiction, substance use, substance abuse, medical problems secondary to substance abuse, and family dynamics structured around addictive behavior.

I found it more difficult working with addicted clients on the "outside" while in the role of a case manager, therapist, or employee assistance professional. Recognizing, confronting, and motivating an individual for change is a difficult process, and in my experience it is more difficult than having clients in a protected environment and working directly on the addiction issues.

Being a social worker in a hospital, in the department of chemical dependency, was an eye-opening experience, filled with challenges both expected and unexpected. There was the bias issue with the staff culture and also the political structure of the hospital. The Department of Chemical Dependency was in the Department of Medicine instead of the Department of Psychiatry. This meant a lesser emphasis on clinical skills as an MSW than the psychiatric social workers would have, and the department was also very pro-methadone. I operated in an environment that was a medical model, with methadone replacement therapy for opiate dependence seen as an effective treatment for addiction and not an addiction in itself. There is much debate in the field over methadone maintenance treatment, and most programs have a firm stance on one side or the other.

I obtained my CASAC after 1 year, taking postgraduate courses for the education requirement, and I became involved in the NASW Addictions Committee, which made me aware of best practices, as well as political context, in the addiction treatment world. I eventually chaired the committee and coordinated the annual addictions conference they sponsor for several years. Keeping a focus outside the walls of the hospital and outside of my role in subsequent positions has been key to enhancing my biopsychosocial focus on addicted individuals and families, as well as to furthering my education and skills.

Often, when social workers are completing their training and they are considering which path to choose, the path chooses them. In my case, the path chose me in the form of an open position, and it started me on a long career in addiction and addiction-related treatment that has proven extremely rewarding. The ability to view addiction from a biopsychosocial perspective leads to endless possibilities for intervention, with not only the client but the family and significant others as well. Looking at alternative therapies for addiction is generally the job of a social worker, since the majority of professionals who have been in the field as a result of their own recovery focus only on the "disease model," which advocates 12-step (Alcoholics Anonymous) membership and a commitment to total abstinence. This approach works, and has worked for many people, but many others, such as those who "do not want help," are not far enough on the continuum of change to be ready for total abstinence or identifying as having an incurable disease.

Motivational interviewing and cognitive behavioral therapy are treatments that focus on eliminating dangerous behaviors caused by substance abuse, with the social worker joining the client in a discovery process of what is the best path for him or her. Social workers are also trained to tease out the psychiatric disorders that may go along with substance abuse and are either exacerbated or masked by addictive behavior. Social workers can assist the patient in the process of recovery and learning how to stop the destructive addictive behavior, at which point we can treat the underlying psychiatric symptoms. This is a two-pronged approach that is very effective, in most cases.

Overall, my experience in addiction treatment as a social worker has been stimulating, rewarding, and challenging. Addiction permeates all modalities and populations we treat, and as professional social workers, we have the necessary skills and tools to help make a difference in this ever-changing field.

IS ADDICTIONS THE RIGHT FIELD FOR YOU?

- Dan had to field tough questions from clients who challenged him about whether or not he had ever abused substances. How would you handle this?
- Would you feel comfortable working in a field that is largely founded by people in recovery?
- Dan is nonjudgmental toward his clients, even when they relapse. How would you react to working with a population where relapse frequently occurs?

SECTION FOUR: RESOURCES TO LEARN MORE

Web Sites
- Alcoholic Anonymous: http://www.aa.org
- Alcoholism Center for Women: http://www.alcoholismcenterforwomen .org
- Adult Children of Alcoholics: http://www.adultchildren.org

- Narcotics Anonymous (NA): http://www.na.org
- National Association of Children of Alcoholics (NACoA): http://www.nacoa.org
- National Clearinghouse for Alcohol and Drug Information: http://ncadi.samhsa.gov
- National Council on Problem Gambling: www.ncpgambling.org
- National Institute on Alcohol Abuse and Alcoholism: www.niaaa.nih.gov
- Recovery USA: http://www.recoveryusa.net
- Substance Abuse and Mental Health Services Administration (SAMHSA): http://www.samhsa.gov

Journals
- *Alcoholism Treatment Quarterly*, Taylor & Francis
- *Journal of Social Work Practice in the Addictions*, Taylor & Francis
- *International Journal of Mental Health and Addiction*, Springer
- *The Journal of Studies on Alcohol and Drugs*, Center of Alcohol Studies, Rutgers University

Books
- *Alcohol, Other Drugs, and Addictions: A Professional Development Manual for Social Work and Human Services*, by Allan Edward Barsky (2005, Wadsworth/Thomson Learning)
- *International Aspects of Social Work Practice in the Addictions*, by Shulamith Lala Ashenberg Straussner and Larry Harrison (2002, Haworth Press)
- *Social Work With Addictions*, by James G. Barber (2002, Palgrave Macmillan)

Professional Associations
- Association for Addiction Professionals: http://www.naadac.org

Policy Statements
- Alcohol, Tobacco and Other Substance Abuse. In *Social Work Speaks*, 7th ed., NASW Policy Statements, 2006–2009

Practice
- About Addictions: http://www.helpstartshere.org

Standards
- The NASW Practice Standards Substance Use Disorders

Credentials
- Certified Clinical Alcohol, Tobacco, and Other Drugs Social Worker (C-CATODSW) (NASW credential)
- National Certified Addiction Counselor (National Association for Addiction Professionals)

Educational Programs/Centers
- Addiction Technology Transfer Center (ATTC)
- Boston University School of Social Work, Center for Addictions Research and Services (CARS)
- Columbia University, The National Center on Addiction and Substance Abuse (CASA)
- University of Northern Texas, Department of Rehabilitation, Social Work, and Addictions

2

Social Work With Older Adults

SECTION ONE: FIELD OVERVIEW AND FORECAST

Scope of Services

One of the most significant trends shaping America's population is the dramatic rise in the number of older adults. The general trend of an aging population is clear. The number of older adults is expected to steadily increase, and gerontologists predict that, by the year 2020, one in six Americans will be age 65 or older (Council on Social Work Education, 2006). The fastest growing segment of the population today is the "oldest old," those aged 85 years and over (Administration on Aging, 2007).

Within this context, the proportion of older Americans that are from diverse ethnic and racial groups is expected to grow at an even more accelerated pace. By the year 2050, population studies project that the percentage of the older population that is non-Hispanic white is expected to decline from 84% to 64%. At the same time, the percentage of older Americans who are African American is projected to increase to 12% from a current 8%. Hispanics are expected to experience the greatest growth. Presently, Hispanics comprise 6% of the older population. In 2050, it is predicted that Hispanics will account for 16% of older adults (Administration on Aging, 2007).

Many older adults contend with poverty and attendant problems such as limited access to housing and health services. Older adults from diverse backgrounds and women are particularly vulnerable. According to the Administration on Aging (2007), about 3.6 million elderly persons (10.1%) were below the poverty level in 2005 (the most recent year for which data is available), and another 2.3 million of the elderly were classified as "near poor." One of every 12 (7.9%) elderly whites was poor in 2005, compared with 23.2% of elderly African Americans and 19.9% of elderly Hispanics. With respect to gender, older women had a poverty rate of 12.3% compared with 7.3% for older men. Social work services are expected to be in high demand to meet the multiple needs of a growing elderly population.

Settings

Social work services with older adults cuts across a spectrum of settings that range from institutionally based care to community-based care. The need for community-based services, including case management, crisis intervention, mental health care, adult day care, senior centers, and transportation and housing assistance, is likely to continue to grow in part because of societal trends in which there is a preference for community living over institutional care. The goal of community-based social work services with older adults is to enable seniors to "age in place," in their homes and communities with dignity, a goal consistent with social work's guiding principle of self-determination (Sackman, 2005).

Employment settings for social workers vary in the proportion of BSW and MSW staff, with a higher proportion of BSWs employed in nursing homes and case-management agencies. A growing number of private practitioners who have an MSW offer specialized services to older adults and their families (Whitaker, Weismiller, & Clark, 2006a).

The Social Worker's Role

Social workers who work with older adults spend the majority of their time engaged in providing direct services to clients, with the most frequent tasks reported as screening/assessment, intake, data gathering and referral, individual counseling, treatment planning, and crisis intervention (Whitaker et al., 2006a). The psychosocial problems that social workers in this field are most likely to address are depression, isolation, physical decline, and financial problems.

An emerging professional role for licensed social workers is geriatric case management. A geriatric case manager (GCM) works privately with families, assesses an individual's social and medical needs, and develops and coordinates a treatment plan. In a survey of geriatric case managers conducted by the American Association of Retired Persons (AARP), over one third of the respondents had a social work license (Stone, Reinhard, Machemer, & Rudin, 2002). On average, geriatric case managers had a caseload of 17 clients per month and provided services to clients for an average of 1 year or less. The AARP survey found that geriatric case managers charge an average of $175 for an initial consultation, $168 to develop a treatment plan, and that fees averaged $74 an hour.

Credentialing

Although many employers may not require specialized credentials, obtaining these credentials can significantly strengthen employability. The National Association of Social Workers (NASW) offers three specialty credentials in gerontology, one at the BSW level and two at the MSW level. These are newly developed credentials, reflecting the increasing professionalization of this field of practice.

The Social Worker in Gerontology (SW-G) credential requires a BSW degree, no less than 2 years (equivalent of 3,000 hours) of experience working with older adults under social work supervision, 20 contact hours of continuing education relevant to work with older adults, or proof of an aging/gerontology concentration via transcripts or certificate, current BSW licensure or a passing score on an Association of Social Work Boards (ASWB) exam or 1 additional year of experience and 10 additional contact hours of continuing education.

The Advanced Social Worker in Gerontology (ASW-G) requires an MSW degree, no less than 2 years (equivalent of 3,000 hours) of experience working with older adults, 20 contact hours of continuing education relevant to work with older adults, or proof of an aging/gerontology concentration via transcripts or certificate, current MSW licensure or a passing score master's-level or advanced generalist-level license, or a passing score on the ASWB (Association of Social Work Boards) master's-level or advanced generalist-level exam.

The Clinical Social Worker in Gerontology (CSW-G) requires an MSW degree, no less than 2 years (equivalent of 3,000 hours) of experience working with older adults, 20 contact hours of continuing education relevant to work with older adults, or proof of an aging/gerontology concentration via transcripts or certificate, and have a current clinical-level license.

Social workers interested in pursuing a career as a geriatric case manager should also consider getting certified as a geriatric case manager. There are two major certification programs: The National Academy of Certified Case Managers (CMC) and the Commission for Case Management Certification (CMC). To obtain these certifications, applicants must meet an educational requirement (for social workers this can be at both the BSW and the MSW levels), have supervised work experience, and pass a qualifying exam.

Emerging Issues and Employment Trends

The demand for social workers in the field of aging is predicted to far outweigh the supply, with current studies projecting that 70,000 social workers will be needed by 2010 to serve the growing elderly population of the United States. Yet fewer than 3% of today's social work students want to work with older adults (Volland & Sisco, 2005).

Significant challenges face social workers who work in the field of aging. Findings from a NASW workforce study (Whitaker et al., 2006a) indicate high job turnover among social workers who work in this field, with almost half of the licensed social workers who work in aging employed with their current employer for less than 5 years. Social workers who work with older adults report higher caseloads than for other fields of practice, particularly among social workers who work in nursing homes. Problematic working conditions were also among the findings of a focus group with social workers in the field of aging held by the New York City chapter of NASW (2005). The focus group, composed of 11 gerontological social workers, identified low salaries, high caseloads, and high job turnover as challenges for the field.

The future demand for skilled social workers to work with older adults is expected to be strong (Hooyman, 2008). Given this reality, several leading organizations, including the Council on Social Work Education, the New York Academy of Medicine, and the Gerontology Society of America are developing programs that will prepare social work students to have the knowledge and skills to provide services to older adults and their families. The John A. Hardford Foundation Geriatric Social Work Initiative (GSWI) has invested over $31 million dollars to develop educational initiatives to help schools of social work train future social work students to work with older adults.

ACTIVITIES TO LEARN MORE

- Log onto the National Association of Social Workers Web site at www.nasw.org. Go to the Center for Workforce Study. Read the Specialty Practice Report on Aging.
- Compare the respective criteria for the Professional Geriatric Care Managers (PGCMs) credential offered by the National Association of Professional Geriatric Care Managers and the specialty certifications for gerontology offered by the National Association of Social Workers.
- Look up the local city or state agency responsible for aging services in your community and research the programs that they offer.

SECTION TWO: CRITICAL ISSUES
Patricia Brownell, PhD, LMSW

Patricia Brownell is associate professor of social work at the Fordham University Graduate School of Social Service (GSSS). She has a master's of social work degree and a PhD in gerontology from Fordham University's Graduate School of Social Service. She is a Hartford Foundation Geriatric Social Work Faculty Scholar, a Ravazzin Center Fellow, United States Representative to the International Network for the Prevention of Elder Abuse (INPEA), and faculty director of the Fordham University GSSS Institute for Women and Girls. She currently serves as president of the National Association of Social Workers—New York City Chapter, is immediate past president of the State Society on Aging of New York, and represents INPEA on the NGO Committee on Ageing of the United Nations and on the Sub-Committee on Older Women (SCOW) of the NGO Committee on the Status of Women (CSW).

Dr. Brownell's areas of research include gerontology, elder abuse, and domestic violence. Dr. Brownell has been active in the fields of domestic violence, aging, and public welfare for over 30 years.

Please tell me a little about yourself. What are some of the factors that motivated you to become a social worker? What drew you to gerontology as an area of focus? Was it a particular issue or concern?
I was inspired to become a social worker because of a very positive and life-changing experience with a social worker. When I was a young adult, I was

living in New York City, and my mother came for a visit. While she was here, she had a stroke that left her partially paralyzed. As you can imagine, this threw my family into a terrible crisis and a period of great uncertainty. My mother was hospitalized and, following her discharge, she wanted to return to the Midwest. The hospital social worker was incredibly supportive during this difficult time, helping us cope and adapt to this crisis. Ultimately, with the social worker's assistance, my mother returned to independent living in her home, which is what she wished to do. The social worker was so critical to the process that I was inspired to apply to a graduate social work program and become a social worker.

I got my master's degree in administration and policy and planning, and then my doctorate in gerontology from Fordham University Graduate School of Social Service. During those years, I worked for the New York City Human Resources Administration in a number of different programs and capacities, including child welfare, domestic violence, and aging services. I've been a professor of social work at Fordham University for 13 years.

What are the major societal trends that will shape the future demand for social work services with older adults?
The aging of the population will have a huge impact on the social work profession. Aging is a global phenomenon, with a worldwide decline of fertility rates in developed countries. At the same time, advances in medical technology have led to increased longevity in many parts of the world.

Increased longevity impacts the health and quality of life for many seniors. As people live longer, there is an inevitable trend toward chronic illness. At one time, an acute episode of pneumonia may have been life threatening. However, today the same illness is not necessarily fatal. In the future, many people will live with debilitating and chronic ailments that will impact their quality of life, and these people are likely to require family support services. For example, Alzheimer's is an illness for which families will likely need to receive caregiver supports. In these situations, social workers are extremely well trained to help families cope, adapt, and negotiate complex systems.

The majority of older adults prefer to live independently and to remain in the community. Societal trends support independent living because community-based care is much less expensive than institutionally based care. Family members do find it challenging to care for older loved ones with chronic disabilities. The National Family Caregiver Support Program, established in 2000 as an amendment to the Older Americans Act, provides funding to communities to develop a range of support services to help family caregivers.

Diversity is a very significant trend shaping social work services for older adults. The United States is a culturally diverse nation, and the proportion of older adults from diverse ethnic and racial backgrounds is growing. Social workers have to be knowledgeable about the cultures of the families that they serve, and they will need to have diverse linguistic skills so that they can communicate effectively and appropriately with older clients and their families.

What kinds of social work services will be needed to work with older adults?
The New York Academy of Medicine suggests that a major challenge facing older adults and their caregivers is the fragmentation and complexity of the existing aging and social service systems. Social workers providing services to older adults need the skills to help clients negotiate these very complicated systems.

For example, consider the following scenario: An older man is living independently in the community. His spouse and a number of his friends have passed away, while others have moved away. He becomes increasingly isolated. After some routine medical care, he is referred to a senior center, where he becomes active, makes friends, and eats his meals. Then he has a bad fall, breaks both hips, and is hospitalized. During the hospitalization, his funds become so depleted that he "spends down to Medicaid" because he no longer has the private or family finances to pay for health care services that Medicare won't cover. While in the hospital, he gets an eviction notice from his landlord. Medically, he is unable to return home without home care services, yet Medicare does not agree to reimburse him at the needed level. He winds up rehospitalized, and upon discharge he is referred to a subacute unit of a nursing home because of muscular atrophy.

This scenario is not uncommon and requires coordination of services across many complex systems. Social workers helping these kinds of clients and families need to be highly skilled and knowledgeable in negotiating and accessing services.

Geriatric social workers need to have a versatile skill set that can be targeted to the differing needs and preferences of the frail and the well elderly. Well older adults enjoy good health, and can be active and vital members of the community. For example, a well older adult might seek to become active in his or her faith communities, become civically engaged as a volunteer, or seek paid employment. Older adults can seek a number of vehicles to maintain health and vitality. They may seek self-actualization through therapy or play sports, all of which may all be appropriate goals in working with well older adults. For a frail older adult who is living with an acute or chronic ailment, a different range of services would be indicated, and a different skill set that includes assessment, advocacy, case management, counseling, and interdisciplinary consultation and collaboration would be more appropriate.

The Council on Social Work Education (http://www.cswe.org) identifies major domains that constitute foundational knowledge, values, and competencies necessary in geriatric social work. These four central areas are:

1. Values, ethics, and theoretical perspectives
2. Assessment
3. Intervention
4. Aging services, programs, and policies

A fifth area, leadership, reflects the importance of social workers to become active in advocating for services and programs that assist older adults and their families, as well as ensure that adequate resources are appropriated to ensure a professional level of care and good quality of life.

In what ways do social workers provide an important safety net of services to the most vulnerable older adults?
Social workers can protect the older vulnerable client through Adult Protective Services, which is a nationally mandated program that all 50 states provide. Adult protective services are designed for adults age 18 and older who are unable to protect themselves from harm, abuse, or neglect and may be indicated for older clients who are reluctant to accept services, perhaps due to cognitive deficits. Adult protective services include counseling and case management services, crisis intervention, and working with the legal system.

What is ageism and how does it impact social work services for older adults?
Elder abuse is a serious problem that includes the physical, emotional, sexual abuse, neglect, abandonment, and financial exploitation of the elderly. Assessment skills are key, and social workers need to be alert to the signs and symptoms of ageism. The International Longevity Center defines ageism as common and harmful prejudices that "result in widespread mistreatment, ranging from stereotypic and degrading media images to physical and financial abuse, unequal treatment in the workforce, and denial of appropriate medical care and services" (http://www.ilcusa.org).

Older adults engage in ageism when they adopt a perspective that they are too old to enjoy life, to learn, or to seek new experiences. Social workers also may subscribe to ageist attitudes, such as believing that being old is depressing. We know this is not true. Social work education challenges these false assumptions.

What are the reasons for the high turnover among social work staff in agencies serving older adults?
There are serious workforce issues in aging because aging services are not funded at a level that adequately reimburses social work services. Social work salaries in aging often lag behind those in other service delivery areas in part because not all aging service delivery systems recognize the training and education of a master's level social worker. Many social work positions are filled by social workers at the bachelor's level, which keeps salaries low.

Medicare and Medicaid reimbursement rates for social work services are insufficient, and this may serve as a disincentive for social workers to work with this population. Agency-based work with older adults may also be less attractive to social workers because there are often limited opportunities for career development, especially if the tasks and supervision do not provide the required clinical experience toward clinical licensure.

Why don't more social work students want to work with older adults?
Social work students can be adversely influenced by their own ageist attitudes. Research suggests that students with limited exposure to older adults are less likely to choose gerontology as a career option. The John A. Hartford Foundation works to promote social work education at the master's and bachelor's level through helping schools of social work develop curricula and field internships with older adults. Once students are exposed to older adults, many of them want to continue to work in this area. It's important that social work education continue to attract students

to gerontology through offering stipends and other funded opportunities, such as work study, as well as loan forgiveness for post-master's studies.

What are the rewards for social workers who work with this population?
This is an area where there can be a tremendous sense of satisfaction. Older adult clients and their families appreciate social work services, and often express gratitude to their social workers. Geriatric social workers articulate a sense of pride and accomplishment in their work.

One central truth is that we are all aging. Working with older adults helps students and professional social workers to dispel the myth that getting old prohibits learning and growing. This is a powerful lesson that can be applied to one's own life in a positive manner.

As president of the New York City chapter of the National Association of Social Workers, what role do you see for a professional association in improving social work services for older adults?
The National Association of Social Workers (NASW) has a major role to play in addressing and focusing on workforce issues in aging. The opportunities for professional development in aging lag behind other service delivery systems. As president-elect of the NASW-New York City Chapter, I think it is important to work with the leadership and membership to advocate for policies that promote funding for social work services for older adults and families. Professional associations are central to helping legislators and the public understand that social workers provide an important, skilled, and valuable component of services for older adults.

DID YOU KNOW?

- Research suggests that social work services decrease health care costs and improve quality of life for older adults (Rizzo & Rowe, 2006).
- The National Center on Elder Abuse estimates that elder abuse affects 1–2 million Americans age 65 or older.
- According to the American Geriatrics Society, the misuse of alcohol, drugs, and prescription and over-the-counter medications poses a serious health risk for older adults, especially for older men.

SECTION THREE: FIRST-PERSON NARRATIVE

Gerontological Social Work: Making a
Difference in the Lives of Older Adults
Ken Onaitis, LMSW

Ken Onaitis, LMSW, practices social work at the Carter Burden Center for the Aging, where he is director of elder abuse and police relations. In addition to his primary responsibility of directing CEMAPP, the Community Elder Mistreatment and Abuse Prevention Program, and acting as liaison to the 19th Police Precinct, he coleads a support group for adult children whose parents have Alzheimer's. Mr. Onaitis is co-coordinator of the New York City Elder Abuse Network (NYCEAN). He serves on the Executive Committee of the New York State Coalition on Elder Abuse, the Advisory Board for the annual New York State Adult Abuse Training Institute, and the Advisory Board for the Elder Abuse Center Planning Project. He holds a bachelor's degree in business administration, an MSW in social work from Fordham University, and a postgraduate certificate in aging from the Brookdale Center on Aging of Hunter College.

It is a Monday morning in July. Here in New York City, it is already hot, especially in the subways. Thankfully, at the end of my 45-minute commute, I will walk into my office on the lower level/basement of an air-conditioned building. I begin shifting my focus from the weekend to my professional life as a gerontological social worker. I think of the upcoming week. It is summer, so the number of meetings is reduced, but client activity remains high. A home visit to Ms. D. tomorrow? Was there a crisis over the weekend?

As I approach my desk, the telephone's flashing red light catches my eye. Voicemails, as usual. I sip my coffee and ease into the day by logging onto the computer to check e-mails, but today I feel my anxiety rapidly rising. A new computer program was installed last week, creating chaos. I wonder if the techs have worked the bugs out over the weekend.

I put down my coffee and start listening to the voice mails. SM, a client I met for the first time last week, left a message on Friday evening. She had received a letter from her landlord asking her to telephone him. She was aware that the landlord knew of the trouble she was having with her roommate and feared she was going to be evicted. *Please call immediately!* And, I have not written her progress note from the office visit last week. Since it is not safe to telephone her home, I called her cell phone. She is eager to talk, but the reception is bad. She will call back this afternoon.

My name is Ken Onaitis, LMSW (licensed master social worker in New York State), and I have been practicing social work for the last 10 years. Prior to receiving my MSW, I worked for several decades in the building industry, and very early in my career I was a welfare department caseworker. I returned to the social service field because I wanted a profession where I could grow emotionally and intellectually while serving people. I am pleased with my career change and have had the opportunity to serve people in a variety of settings, including a large government organization, a nursing home, a hospice in a medical setting, a clinic for people with chronic mental illness, and a victim rights organization.

Today I am employed in a small, thriving, community-based, nonprofit agency serving older adults in several neighborhoods in Manhattan. At the Carter Burden Center for the Aging (www.burdencenter.org), we are dedicated to supporting the efforts of older people to remain in their homes living independently, safely, and with dignity. Naturally, we help people with problems via case-management services, either in their homes or in our office. Simultaneously, our philosophy is to help people grow by supporting their focus on their positive attributes and strengths through our Luncheon Club (senior center) and our Cultural Connections Program. Linking all of our services is a strong volunteer program. In summary, our goal is to foster socialization, because isolation often contributes to physical and emotional problems as well as elder abuse.

Elder abuse is a major national problem, and it is my specialty. I am the director of Elder Abuse and Police Relations. My primary program is CEMAPP, Community Elder Mistreatment and Abuse Prevention Program. Funding for elder abuse is limited. I have a staff of one, a social worker, and we cover the northern half of the island of Manhattan from 59th St. to 237th St. Approximately 1 million people live in this geographical area, and 150,000, or 15%, are over the age of 60. We are a crisis intervention program serving older adults and their families. Prevention services are provided via education and training forums to consumers and professionals. The services are free.

Now from the macro level, a few words about elder abuse. Elder abuse is a foggy issue, an emotionally charged problem that knows no social, economic, or ethnic boundaries. It truly is a hidden problem. Shame and guilt continue to keep elder abuse victims from coming forward today, just as it held back domestic-violence victims 35 years ago.

Elder abuse is further complicated by the lack of a universal definition. In the criminal justice system, elder abuse is broadly defined as when an older person is the victim of a crime listed in their jurisdiction's penal code and is committed by a family member or a stranger. I have worked with three elder abuse programs and served clients under three different definitions of elder abuse. A lack of a clear definition can lead to underreporting, underfunding, and confusion among the public as to whether or not a situation is truly elder abuse. At CEMAPP, and the other eight NYC elder abuse programs funded by the New York City Department for the Aging, we define elder abuse as when an individual over 60 is the victim of financial, psychological, physical abuse, and active or passive neglect, regardless of the penal code. The abuser is someone the older adult trusts, usually a family member, neighbor, or "new best friend." Trust is the key word in this definition. Self-neglect, a significant social issue, is not defined as elder abuse. It is a related social problem because a person who neglects himself is often socially isolated, and thus more vulnerable to becoming a victim of elder abuse.

A final comment from the macro perspective. Because elder abuse is a hidden and ill-defined issue, a significant amount of my time is given to leadership roles in the community, trying to bring awareness to the issue, including: working and leading committees, planning conferences, giving presentations, and testifying before legislative bodies. While elder abuse prevention is an objective, making the community aware of our work with clients, i.e., "marketing," is a parallel objective. No clients, no program. In reality, 80% of client referrals come from family members and professionals in the community. Shame and guilt remain powerful disincentives blocking elder abuse victims from coming forward and asking for help.

Many program directors have to focus full time on their administrative and managerial responsibilities, but because of the small size of my program, I also continue to work directly with clients. My clinical responsibilities include emergency elder abuse consultations on the telephone, performing intake interviews, making home visits, and maintaining a caseload.

The voicemail this morning was from SM, who is 71, single, friendly, and a semiretired professional salesperson. She has lived in a one-room studio apartment for 40 years. Then she met a "new best friend" who was in a short-term housing crisis. SM offered CW, now 57, her sofa bed for a few nights. CW also brought her cat, which delighted SM. Six years later, she is still living there. CW does not leave the apartment, is depressed, and has dramatically gained weight, which has resulted in medical problems. In January, my client SM had a medical crisis from which she recently recovered. In April the cat died, and CW stopped bathing regularly. CW's abusive behavior toward SM, screaming and scratching, also increased. When CW hit her, SM called 911. The police removed CW to an emergency room, and SM assumed she would be kept in the psychiatric unit. CW returned to the apartment several hours later, and SM fled in fear to a friend's apartment. In May SM went to Housing Court to have CW evicted. CW did not respond to the court order but later agreed with SM to move by June 30. A friend suggested SM contact my agency for advice, but SM wanted to hope CW would move as she had promised. On July 1 SM called CEMAPP and I opened her case.

Last week, during the initial phone call from SM, I listened as she calmly described the situation. She said she was desperate to have her home back to herself and was ready to return to the legal system to have CW evicted, but she first wanted to find out if other resources were available to help CW. We explored the pros and cons of how various systems would interface with CW. These included housing, medical, mental health, and criminal justice. SM concluded that CW would not cooperate, and in a sorrowful voice concluded that Housing Court was definitely the next step. Then she paused and I kept quiet. I suspected she would like to talk further and suggested an office visit. She agreed and reiterated she did not want to make anyone homeless. She asked about meeting next week and was surprised when I offered her 1 o'clock the next day. She quickly agreed.

As I hung up the telephone, I thought about the conversation. It had been an unusual consultation for several reasons. First, an elder abuse victim only calls about 20% of the time. Second, SM was well informed about her options, and Housing Court was a viable one. Third, several crises had already occurred, and she sounded ready to take that next action step. Yet I felt I had violated the basic social work tenet—"start where the client is"—when I offered her an appointment the next day after she had suggested the next week. Was she ready to talk further, or did I want her to go directly to Housing Court because it would be a quick resolution of the elder abuse, and then I could successfully close the case? Or did she not want to seem "pushy" by asking for an appointment too soon? Was this a parallel of the dynamics between her and CW? I thought the odds of her keeping the appointment the next day were 50/50.

The next day at 1 o'clock, the phone rang and SM apologized, saying she would be 10 minutes late. I was relieved, yet anxious because of my self-reflection yesterday. SM arrived and, like most clients, eagerly began talking about her problem. She told her story, including her conclusion that Housing Court was necessary. Her reporting of the situation today was consistent with her description yesterday on the phone. Then she paused as if she had run out of breath. I had said little to this point, so I asked, "What do you hope to get from this meeting today?" She seemed surprised. She said she was tired of talking about the problem and just wanted to have it "go away." She asked, "What should I do?"

This was a critical moment in the interview. I had asked a straightforward question, and she responded with a direct question. Mentally, I explored my choices. I could say nothing and encourage her to break the silence with a nonverbal cue. I could redirect the interview by gathering data for paperwork. I could ask about how she had made difficult decisions with her past problems. I could ask her what her friends and family have told her to do. I could again summarize her situation and flip her question back to her.

I told her that from my experience working with hundreds of elder abuse clients, that at this point most clients know what to do. But that does not make it any easier to do. At CEMAPP, I told her, we will help you help yourself. I asked, "What about you?" She sat quietly and nodded "yes," then said that she had to give CW another chance. Her plan was to firmly tell CW to move and to help her financially, if necessary. If that failed, she would go back to Housing Court. As she was leaving, she thanked me for listening.

Suddenly the phone rings and I snap back to Monday after thinking about SM's visit last week, or as I see it, replaying the movie. It is SM. She is anxious about what to say to her landlord. Can she come in to talk tomorrow? I smile quietly and ask if 1 o'clock works for her.

A success! True, a small success, but the multilayers of an elder abuse problem mean that resolving abuse is usually not completed with one intervention. It is done with small steps, one success at a time. I am trying to care for myself, to prevent burnout, so I can continue practicing social work.

I start preparing for tomorrow. However, my day isn't over. I will spend my evening practicing another time-honored social work skill—group work. My agency is in a collaboration that offers a recreational and therapeutic program for older adults who are experiencing memory loss, known as a social-model adult day program. One of the services we offer is a support group for the adult children of parents with memory loss, primarily Alzheimer's disease. Like elder abuse, Alzheimer's knows no social, economic, or ethnic boundaries. As caregivers, these adult children face the constantly evolving task of trying to be responsible for their parent's well-being and safety while balancing their parent's right of self-determination. I colead the group with a registered nurse.

Facilitating the support group is a stimulating variation from my daily crisis intervention work, primarily because of the relationships that develop over the time that a member attends—an average is 3 years. The caregivers are traditionally female, ranging in age from 40 to 75, and are caring for their mothers.

In the last meeting, A, who is fighting her own cancer, told the group that she is frazzled because her mother will not eat and relies on her for her every need. B asked the group what questions to ask a lawyer about estate planning, especially power of attorney. C vented her anger at her brother for not helping or even supporting her. The group laughed and cried as D described what her mother said in her small moment of clarity last week. E wondered if her mother's recent screaming bout was the result of a change in her medication. The group told F that she deserved and needed a vacation because she is exhausted from visiting her mother every day in the nursing home. G fears her mother's excellent Jamaican home health aide will leave because her mother expresses overt prejudice against blacks.

As I head home on the subway afterward, my mind lingers on my work. I'm proud to say that I am a geriatric social worker, yet I realize our society does not see it as a "sexy" job. When I tell people at parties what I do for a living, they suddenly need a drink refill. However, I accept this because I find stimulation and satisfaction in my career working with older people and their families. Why? I thoroughly enjoy the opportunity to engage with all aspects of the legal, medical, and religious/spiritual communities through older adults. Older adults are often disenfranchised in our ageist society, so I often use my advocacy skills to help them. Because the number of older adults is increasing dramatically, I have a number of professional and career opportunities. My life is made richer by older adults, who expand my knowledge of historical events and past daily life as they talk about their personal experiences. Older adults offer wisdom and experience that I can incorporate into my own life.

Most of all, I am honored when an older adult says to me, "I have never been able to tell anyone this before."

IS WORKING WITH OLDER ADULTS THE RIGHT FIELD FOR YOU?

- Working with older adults is a field in which one needs a strong internal commitment to the work, since social recognition often lags behind. Ken describes his passion and his pride to be a gerontological social worker, and suggests these are essential ingredients for being satisfied with this field.
- Ken's work entails multiple roles: He is a clinician, community organizer, community liaison, public speaker, administrator, and advocate He is extremely versatile in his skill set and in his ability to function on the micro, mezzo, and macro levels. Would you like a position that offers such a wide range of functions?
- Working with older adults provides social workers with a tremendous opportunity to hear life stories that can expand one's historical perspective. Ken finds this aspect of his work fascinating and personally rewarding.

SECTION FOUR: RESOURCES TO LEARN MORE

Web Sites

- Ageworks: http://www.ageworks.com
- American Association of Retired Persons: http://www.aarp.org
- American Society on Aging: http://www.asaging.org
- Gray Panthers: http://www.graypanthers.org
- National Council of Senior Citizens: http://www.ncscinc.org
- National Council on the Aging: http://www.ncoa.org
- The Gerontological Society of America: http://www.geron.org
- The National Academy on an Aging Society (NAAS): http://www.agingsociety.org
- National Institute on Aging: http://www.nia.nih.gov
- New York Academy of Medicine, Geriatric Social Work Practicum Development Program: http://www.nyam.org

Journals

- *The Gerontologist*, The Gerontological Society of America
- *Journal of Gerontological Social Work*, Taylor & Francis

Books

- *Gerontological Practice for the Twenty-First Century: A Social Work Perspective*, by Virginia E. Richardson and Amanda S. Barusch (2005, Columbia University Press)
- *National Directory of Educational Programs in Gerontology and Geriatrics* (2000, Association for Gerontology in Higher Education; digitized Aug 22, 2007)

Policy

- Long-Term Care. In *Social Work Speaks*, 7th ed. NASW Policy Statements, 2006–2009
- Senior Health, Safety, and Vitality. In *Social Work Speaks*, 7th ed. NASW Policy Statements, 2006–2009

Practice

- Gerontological Social Work: http://www.naswnyc.org
- Seniors and Aging: http://www.helpstartshere.org

Standards

- NASW Standards for Social Work Services in Long-Term Facilities

Credentials

- Clinical Social Worker in Gerontology (CSW-G)
- Advanced Social Worker in Gerontology (ASW-G)

- Social Worker in Gerontology (SW-G) (NASW credentials)
- National Association for Professional Gerontologists Credentials:
  - Graduate level: gerontologist
  - Baccalaureate level: gerontological specialist
  - Associate/certificate level: gerontological coordinator
  - Professional/scholar: affiliate

Professional Associations
- American Society on Aging: http://www.asaging.org
- Association for Gerontology in Higher Education: http://www.aghe.org

Educational Programs/Centers
- Council on Social Work Gero-Ed Center
- The Geriatric Social Work Initiative (GSWI)
- Rutgers University School of Social Work, gerontological training programs
- University of South Carolina, College of Social Work, South Carolina Center for Gerontology, Certificate of Graduate Study in Gerontology Program
- University of Tennessee, gerontology programs

3

Social Work With Child Welfare

SECTION ONE: FIELD OVERVIEW AND FORECAST

Scope of Services

C hild welfare services include a wide range of social programs designed to promote the safety and well-being of children. These services consist of child protective services, family preservation and preventive services, foster care, group homes, residential facilities, adoption services, and kinship care services (Pecora, 2008). Child welfare, more than any other field of practice, is linked to social work by the public. To some extent, this association is accurate. There is an extremely strong ideological fit between the primary mission of child welfare and of the social work profession, as they both share a core commitment to promote and protect vulnerable children and families.

Social workers have long been in the front lines of child welfare services, dating back to the earliest day of the profession. Jane Addams (1860–1935), one of the principal founders of the Settlement House Movement and the winner of the 1931 Nobel Peace Prize, was a strong advocate for the well-being of children and families. One of the major activities of the Settlement House Movement was to develop educational programs for children living in poverty and to fight against child labor (Lieberman, 1995).

In 1853, Charles Loring Brace, the founder of the Children's Aid Society, established the Orphan Train Movement. The Orphan Train Movement, considered the forerunner of modern foster care, transported thousands of homeless and destitute children from the slums of New York City to rural farm families (Children's Aid Society, 2008). At the federal level, the Children's Bureau was created by President Taft in 1912 and headed by a social worker, Julie Lathrop, to focus on social problems affecting children. From its inception, the Children's Bureau developed programs to address infant mortality, monitor birth rates, and investigate and assist orphans and juveniles involved in the courts. Today the Children's Bureau, which is largely staffed by social workers, develops and funds programs throughout the United States to prevent and protect children from abuse and neglect, and finds permanent placements for children who cannot safely return to their homes.

Nonetheless, despite social work's long and extensive involvement with child welfare, a great deal of public confusion exists about child welfare social workers. This is largely the result of continuous negative media portrayals of child welfare social workers as intrusive and/or incompetent. When a tragedy such as a child fatality due to abuse or neglect occurs, the media coverage tends to vilify social workers, frequently without factual basis. More often than not, the media misidentify caseworkers who have no formal social work training and incorrectly label them as "social workers." This misrepresentation is damaging to the social work profession, and to the clients and the communities that need social work services.

Child abuse and neglect is a serious and widespread social problem. According to the Children's Bureau, in 2006 (the most recent year for which data is available), close to 1 million children were determined to be victims of abuse or neglect. Infants comprise the largest age group of abused or neglected children, accounting for almost 25% of all documented cases. Neglect is much more prevalent than is abuse, with more than 60% of all abuse and neglect cases determined to be neglect (Gaudiosi, 2006).

The most devastating consequence of abuse and neglect is a child fatality, which occurs at a rate of 2.04 deaths per 100,000 children. During 2006, an estimated 1,530 children died because of abuse or neglect. Nearly 80% of perpetrators of child maltreatment are parents, with women comprising the majority of abusers (U.S. Department of Health & Human Services, 2008).

Child abuse and neglect occur in families from all racial and cultural backgrounds and from all religious denominations. While research reveals that no differences exist among races regarding the prevalence of child abuse and neglect, the number of children of color represented in the child welfare system is disproportionately high. The overrepresentation of children of color in the child welfare system is considered to be the result of fundamental social inequalities. Poor and minority children are more likely than white children to come into contact with the child welfare system, and to be closely scrutinized, leading to an increased rate of removal and placement (Casey Family Programs, 2009).

Settings

The major settings of employment for child welfare social workers are not-for-profit individual and family services agencies, schools, or in publicly funded local or county social services (Bureau of Labor Statistics, 2008). Public child welfare agencies are charged with the mission of protecting and keeping children safe. They have the authority to conduct child abuse investigations, to remove children from their homes, and, when necessary, to place them in alternative care, such as foster care or residential placement. In a study of the social work workforce conducted by the National Association of Social Workers (Whitaker,

Weismiller, & Clark, 2006b), slightly more than half of all child welfare social workers work in a public sector agency. Social workers employed in a public sector agency tend to have good benefit packages, in part because the public sector is often unionized.

Private not-for-profit sector child welfare workers are employed in after-school settings, community-based programming for children and families, and in foster-care agencies that typically are contracted out by state and city agencies. Tensions between public and private not-for-profit child welfare agencies can exist because of competition over funding and because of differing missions. For example, Coltoff (2005), the CEO of the Children's Aid Society, cautioned against "myopic" thinking among city child welfare officials, who he described as overly focused on preventive programs to the detriment of foster-care families. In recent years, public/private partnerships between government-funded child welfare agencies and not-for-profit community programs have become an attractive and viable way to provide child welfare services. The Annie E. Casey Foundation, a leading privately funded philanthropic organization, seeks to strengthen the family foster-care system through developing family-focused and neighborhood-based services that bring government and not-for-profit agencies together as collaborative partners.

The Social Worker's Role

Social workers seek to promote and protect children through a myriad of interventions that may be directed toward individuals, families, and toward effecting community change. Family preservation and preventive programming is targeted toward helping families identified at high risk for abuse or neglect. Protective services social workers investigate abuse and neglect allegations and make removals when indicated. Residential placements, group homes, foster-care placements, and adoption planning are developed for children who cannot return to living with their families of origin. Child welfare social workers often interface with the legal system and may be called upon to testify in family court. Findings from a recent study of child welfare social workers indicate that direct practice with families and children is by far the most common role performed by child welfare social workers. In this study, the respondents reported that the bulk of their time is spent on information/referral, screening/assessment, and crisis intervention. Other activities include interdisciplinary teamwork and administration (Whitaker et al., 2006b).

Credentialing

The National Association for Social Workers (NASW) offers two specialty credentials in child welfare, one at the BSW level and one at the MSW level. At the BSW level, social workers can obtain the Certified Children, Youth, and Family Social Worker (C-CYFSW) credential. Requirements include current NASW membership; a BSW degree; 20 contact hours of population-specific education;

documented 1 year and 1,500 hours of paid, supervised, post-BSW children, youth, and family social work experience. Evaluations from an approved supervisor and a reference from a BSW or MSW colleague must be submitted. The applicant must have either a current NASW Academy of Certified Baccalaureate Social Workers (ACBSW) credential, hold a current state BSW-level license, or have passed an exam certified by the Association of Social Work Boards (ASWB).

At the MSW level, social workers can obtain the Certified Advanced Children, Youth, and Family Social Worker (C-ACYFSW) credential. Requirements include an MSW degree; 20 contact hours of population-specific education; documented 1 year and 1,500 hours of paid, supervised post-MSW children, youth, and family social work experience. An evaluation from an approved supervisor and a reference from an MSW colleague must be provided. The applicant must be licensed at the current state MSW-level license.

Emerging Issues and Employment Trends

Child welfare is one of the most complex and challenging fields of practice for social workers. Child welfare social workers are charged with the responsibility of protecting children, and are routinely called upon to make tough choices and difficult decisions. Complicating the work is that little social consensus exists regarding the best way to keep children safe. Public opinion tends to favor policies that enforce stricter removal of children from homes whenever a child fatality occurs that receives a lot of media attention. Conversely, child welfare experts are often oriented toward promoting preventive services that keep families together. Social workers in direct practice may find themselves caught between these two opposing trends. As difficult as child welfare social work is, there are few fields in social work that can bring as much satisfaction as child welfare. Social workers employed in this area express drawing tremendous personal satisfaction from helping families and children.

National attention is being focused on the child welfare field because of serious workforce problems leading to high staff turnover rates. Research identifies a number of factors related to staff turnover, including stress, salary, caseload size, and inadequate supervision (Strolin, McCarthy, & Caringi, 2005). Social workers also relate feeling frustrated by an overall lack of resources to meet the multiple needs of the families with whom they work (Whitaker et al., 2006b). A number of studies of the child welfare workforce point to a strong connection between level of education and work satisfaction: professionally trained social workers, either at the BSW or MSW level, report being much happier at work, greater occupational commitment, and higher levels of satisfaction with salary, caseload, paperwork, and safety in the field (Landsman, 2001).

In summary, professional training makes all the difference in the world in the child welfare field. Social work education is excellent preparation for effective child welfare practice. Proper training and credentialing significantly strengthens work satisfaction, increasing the likelihood of staying in the field.

ACTIVITIES TO LEARN MORE

- Log on to the National Association of Social Workers Web site at www.socialworkers.org. Go the Center for Workforce Studies and read the Specialty Practice Report on Children and Families.
- Locate the local city or state child protective agency in your community and find out what job opportunities are available for social workers.
- Go to family court and spend an afternoon there. Pay close attention to your surroundings. Many court sessions are open to the public, and you can view a few trials. Sit discreetly in the back row, where there are generally benches available for the public, and observe the court proceedings. Try to attend a session where a social worker is providing testimony.

SECTION TWO: CRITICAL ISSUES
William C. Bell, MSW

William C. Bell is president and chief executive officer of Casey Family Programs, which is the nation's largest operating foundation with a mission focused solely on providing and improving—and ultimately preventing the need for—foster care. Mr. Bell has nearly 30 years of experience in the human services field. Prior to joining Casey, he served 2½ years as commissioner of the New York City Administration for Children's Services (ACS). There, he managed child welfare services—including child protection, foster care, child abuse prevention, day care, and Head Start—with a staff of more than 7,000 and a budget of about $2.4 billion. Mr. Bell earned his master's degree in social work at Hunter College School of Social Work, where he is currently a doctoral candidate. He received his bachelor's degree in biology and behavioral science from Delta State University.

Please tell me a little about yourself and your path in social work. What are some of the factors that motivated you to become a social worker? What drew you to social work in child welfare? Was it a particular issue or concern?
My first job in the social service field was in 1983. I had relocated to New York City from Mississippi, and I took a position as a caseworker in a foster-care prevention program. Shortly after that, New York City implemented a number of new initiatives designed to safeguard and protect children following a highly publicized sexual abuse scandal in a Bronx day-care center. As a part of this initiative, there was a plan to place on-site social services in day-care centers to work with the parents and families of the children, and to educate them about best practices to protect their children from abuse or neglect. The social workers also worked with the day-care center staff in implementing programming that supported child

development, and they trained the staff about how to fulfill their role as mandated child-abuse reporters.

I was hired as part of this new program, and in order to be hired, I had to be given a special waiver because the position required an MSW. At the time, I had a college degree, but I hadn't completed any graduate education. My undergraduate degree was in pre-med, and I was planning to go to medical school. After working in the social service component of the day-care center for three years, I decided not to go to medical school, but instead to become a social worker. I became extremely attached to working with the families and the children, and I developed a lot of compassion for this population. I really wanted to make a difference in their lives. I believed that there was no greater way to achieve this than to work in the child welfare field. As a result, I went to social work school.

As CEO of Casey Family Programs, please describe your organization's mission and services.

The core mission of Casey Family Programs is to provide and improve foster-care services, and to reduce and ultimately prevent the need for foster care. Casey Family Programs was established in 1966 by the late Jim Casey, who founded United Parcel Services. Mr. Casey started Casey Family Programs because, as he looked at the young men who were working for him, he realized that even though they had good jobs and good benefits, many of them faced significant life challenges stemming from the lack of an intact family. Mr. Casey asked himself what he could do to make a difference in the lives of the young men who worked for him, as well as other young people whom he observed to be struggling with problematic life circumstances. In response, Mr. Casey created Casey Family Programs, which in its inception was a foster-care provider. For many years, the primary function of Casey Family Programs was to provide long-term foster care.

In the last 5 years, we began to enlarge the original mission of Casey Family Programs. While we still provide foster-care services, we are actively working to reduce and prevent the need for foster-care services. Within this context, we have initiated the 2020 strategy. We believe that we can safely reduce the number of children and youth needing foster-care services by 50% by the year 2020. We are committed to helping foster youth have the same life outcomes as all Americans. At present, foster-care youth lag far behind along several key indicators.

Foster-care youth should have similar achievement rates in education and employment as the general population. In order to achieve this mission, the 2020 strategy targets three main areas: education, employment, and mental health.

Research shows that children in foster care are generally one to two grades behind their age-matched peers who are not in foster care. The chance that a young person in foster care will graduate from high school is significantly lower than for the general population. We have data on the 25,000 young adults who age out of foster care each year. This data shows that only 3% of foster-care children expect to go to college. In comparison, 70% of young people in the general population expect to go to college.

The mental health outcomes for youth transitioning out of foster care are seriously problematic. A study conducted in 2004 of 700 young adults leaving foster care revealed that 54% reported a serious mental health concern. This population is twice as likely to suffer from posttraumatic stress disorders as are war veterans.

Improved life outcome for youth in foster care is clearly tied to greater stability in the home and in school.

You were the commissioner of the New York City Administration for Children's Services. What were the biggest frustrations and rewards of that position?
When I think about my former position as commissioner of New York City's Administration for Children Services, the most significant challenge I faced is that it is impossible to fulfill the obligation of caring for NYC's children absent the support and involvement of the community. To be effective, we need strong community collaboration in the mission to embrace and protect our children, as opposed to absolving this responsibility to a stand-alone entity and charging it with the sole obligation of caring for children.

In order to be successful as a city commissioner, one needs tenure and the time to implement change. The average tenure of a child welfare commissioner in the United States is 18 months, and that is not nearly long enough to get anything done. In New York City, we were fortunate that we could enact significant reforms because we had an extended period of time beginning in 1996 under Commissioner Scoppetta and continuing with my administration. This period of prolonged administrative stability provided us with the time to put into action important changes.

It's a big challenge to get key community constituents, such as the faith-based community and the media, to buy into the perspective that we are all responsible for the well-being of our children. We need the ability to work across of organizational and service delivery systems, such as substance abuse and mental health, to support children.

The key ingredient that any successful child welfare administration needs is political will. In New York City, then-Mayor Giuliani held Administration for Children's Services in high regard, and gave it comparable stature and importance with other city agencies like the police department, fire department, and the board of education.

The prior child welfare commissioner had to go through five levels of bureaucracy to get the mayor's ear. In contrast, Mayor Giuliani made the Administration for Children's Services' commissioner a member of his cabinet who attended morning meeting on a daily basis. Having child welfare elevated in this manner meant that other key members of city government accorded child welfare respect, so that when the commissioner needed to pick up the phone and call the police chief or the head of family courts or the school chancellor, they would respond. It enabled the commissioner to get the political respect to collaborate meaningfully across systems, to implement policies, and to build a stronger system.

The foster-care population in the United States has nearly doubled over the past 2 decades, with over 500,000 children currently residing in some form of foster care. Why are so many children in placements?

We, as a society, have not made the true commitment to reduce and ultimately to end foster care. Only when political will is aligned with leadership can we enact positive change. If one looks, for example, at New York City, Los Angeles County, and Chicago, Illinois, there was a reduction in foster-care placements from 43,000 children to approximately 17,000 children, without any corresponding abuse. Getting children safely out of placement requires true commitment.

Foster-care placement means upheaval. Children have to change schools, change peers, change homes. Their ability to keep pace academically and socially is seriously challenged. Imagine how disruptive it is to keep moving, to keep learning new rules. We need to maintain stability for children in foster care, or better yet, never having to place them to begin with. As a society, we haven't committed to get our children out of placement. We need preventive interventions, so that removal is not our first strategy.

African American children make up approximately two thirds of the foster-care population and remain in care longer. Why are children of color overrepresented in the child welfare system? What strategies do you recommend to address this?

There is no simple answer to this question. In 1980, 55% of the children in foster care in America were white. Today, over 60% of children in foster care are children of color. We have seen a demographic flip in the placement population over the last 20 years. The issue of disproportionate representation among children of color, and how we resolve it, is a problem that is larger than the foster-care system. We have to address poverty. Poverty is the central underlying causal factor when we look at who comes into contact with the foster-care system.

What kinds of supports do you believe are most important to provide to children in placements?

Children need permanency. Children need stability in schools and in their neighborhoods. We don't want to remove children from the neighborhoods that they know, and from all that is familiar to them. We need one foster-care placement, with one social worker, for the life of the child's time in placement. Stability is the most important thing that we can provide.

When we reduce worker turnover and reduce the number of placements, we see a corresponding improvement in the life outcomes for children in foster care. We know how to raise children and what children need to succeed in life, but we don't apply it to the 500,000 children in care. Our society has not yet made that commitment.

Many social workers in child welfare report that job safety is a major concern. What can agencies do to improve the personal safety of social workers in child welfare?

We have to demonstrate that we value the lives and safety of the public servants that serve to protect and improve the welfare of our children. There needs to be a strong relationship between law enforcement and child welfare. That is not to say that law enforcement should be conducting child welfare investigations, but we need law enforcement to protect social workers, especially when social workers conduct home visits during late hours and in dangerous neighborhoods.

Social workers also need training about how to protect themselves when going into someone else's home, especially for a sensitive issue, such as a possible child removal.

I recall an incident in New York City in which a social worker was held in someone's home at knifepoint. In order to escape, the social worker had to talk the woman down. Another time, a social worker conducting a home visit was attacked by a man and had to flee. We need to send social workers out in pairs and to protect them in situations that could be dangerous. Building ties with the community is important because when child welfare is positively viewed and accepted by the community—when the community values the work of child welfare and recognizes that we are there to protect families and not break them apart—it changes the dynamic of how people respond to you. It's important that the media refrain from a negative portrayal of child welfare as an entity to be feared by families.

Why is turnover high among social workers in child welfare? What kinds of challenges do organizations face in building a stable workforce? What strategies might be employed?
We need a commitment to maintain a manageable workload. Child welfare is a field of practice that is very challenging because the judgments that one makes change people's lives forever. We can make the work more attractive by paying a decent salary with a manageable workload, and sufficient time off to recoup and recover from the demands of making such difficult decisions.

I remember a case in the Bronx where the child protective service worker did everything in her power that she could with a very difficult family. The mother would not allow her daughter to attend school, and was leaving her child at home with a boyfriend known to be abusive. This caseworker had been working very closely with the mother, and on a Friday, she informed her that if the child wasn't in school the following Monday, then she would make a home removal. The first thing the caseworker did on Monday was to check the girl's attendance, and when she found out that the girl was absent from school, the caseworker went to the home to remove the child. When she got to the house, the emergency medical service was there, and the girl had been killed. How could this worker, who I believe was thorough and conscientious, have known that this terrible thing would have happened? She was a competent and compassionate caseworker, and in return for her dedication, all that she received was a battery of questions second-guessing her work, and essentially blaming her for this tragic outcome.

When a police officer pulls his or her weapon in the line of duty, regardless of whether it was ever fired or not, a police officer receives support and counseling. We need to think about employee assistance for child protective workers who have a child die on their caseload. They need time off and support, yet too often there is a knee-jerk response to blame them.

Child welfare workers need decent salaries, manageable caseloads, adequate training, and support. Most of all, we have to recognize that these people are human beings.

What are the most important qualities that a social worker working in child welfare should have?
The most compelling quality in the child welfare field that a social worker needs is compassion. Social workers in child welfare must be able to understand that families have needs. This compassion must be coupled with unrelenting motivation and action to address these needs of the families who are coming into the child welfare system. Without compassion, it is impossible to be effective. When compassion is directed toward the child, it naturally extends itself to the parents. Even when dealing with parents who may neglect or abuse a child, one must realize that these people are also human beings and that, often, they have a past that brought them to this place in their lives. I have met many adults who are involved in the child welfare system because of neglectful behavior toward their children. It is not unusual for these individuals to come from homes that lacked stability. Many of them are still emotionally searching for their own parents. If a social worker can't see the humanity in this population and walks in someone's home with the attitude that this parent doesn't deserve to have a child, it is not at all helpful.

DID YOU KNOW?

- The child welfare workforce struggles with one of the highest rates of job turnover of any field of social work practice (Strolin et al., 2005).
- An NASW survey study found that 78% of all licensed social workers provide services to clients age 21 or younger, regardless of the practice setting or focus (Whitaker et al., 2006b).
- According to the Child Welfare Information Gateway, approximately 905,000 children were found to be victims of child abuse or neglect in calendar year 2006. Of this number, 64.1% suffered neglect (http://www.childwelfare.gov).

SECTION THREE: FIRST-PERSON NARRATIVE

Public Child Welfare: Making the Difference in the Lives of Children and Families
Jennifer Clements, PhD, LCSW

Jennifer Clements is a licensed clinical social worker (LCSW) in the state of Pennsylvania. She is currently a member of the Association for the Advancement of Social Work with Groups and more recently was elected to their board of directors. Ms. Clements received her master's degree in social work and PhD degree from the University of Maryland–Baltimore. She served as a social worker for a large children and youth agency and was formerly the director of a private nonprofit treatment foster-care program in Baltimore, Maryland. In addition, she has provided outpatient mental health services though a private practice in Silver Spring, Maryland.

Ms. Clements currently serves as an assistant professor at Shippensburg University of Pennsylvania. Working in the Department of Social Work and Gerontology, she teaches a practice course on working with individuals, groups, and families. She especially enjoys teaching the special field class in child welfare practice.

I decided in college to become a social worker, a decision that I have always felt was a good one. My hope was that I could work with children, so when there was a child welfare internship offered for my field practicum, I jumped at the opportunity. I learned very quickly that working with children would actually be very little of the direct work of my internship. I spent more time with parents, grandparents, foster parents, and very occasionally kids. I liked the internship a great deal. It was challenging both emotionally and intellectually. The days passed very quickly, and it would usually be my stomach that told me lunch had passed rather than the clock. As my internship came to a close, I happily interviewed and was offered the opportunity to work at the same agency.

The agency I work for is considered public child welfare. There are about 300 social workers and support staff that work in this agency. I work in a unit of about five other social workers who all have either BSW or MSW degrees. In addition to the social work staff, there are two parent-aid caseworkers who work with us in pairs with the families. While I work for the county, we are a state-paid agency, so I feel that I make decent money with health care, retirement, and disability insurance funds. I work in an urban/rural child welfare agency. This makes my work unusual, as I often enter the state's largest city and, on the same day, I might travel down a 5-mile dirt road to arrive at someone's farm in the country. I like the diversity of the setting. There is never quite the same thing going on, which keeps my days surprising.

Because the agency is so large, we are designated to units that are responsible for specific work in the county. There is a protective unit, a foster-care unit, and an adoptions unit, but I work in the family-preservation unit. I began working in the protective unit, which was wonderful and important work, but after a while, I longed for more intensive and longer term work with the families that I had on my caseload. Family preservation is really the kind of social work that I hoped I would be doing. We believe in the family as a unit and believe that they have the strengths they need to be successful; they might just need a little support. The role of this unit is to work with families in crisis and to prevent placement of their children in foster care. I usually work with families for about 6 months, and the work is intensive. I usually see the family twice a week, sometimes more than that in the beginning stages of the work.

One of the more memorable families that I worked with lives out in the country. They moved here from across the United States to start their lives over. The family consists of a mother and her three kids. I am asked to meet with them because the mother had come into the agency to put her son in foster care. The day she came into the agency, she spoke with a protective worker. There is sometimes a waiting list for family preservation, but I am assigned to work with her right away. There is not much time to lose, so I call her and make an appointment for the next day to see her. I like to schedule the first appointments when all the family members will be there so that I can get a feel for how the family is functioning. This means later hours, but I feel like it gives you the best view of what all the issues are in the family. Observations are so important, and they often tell a very different story.

I hope that I can share the story of my work with this family so that you can place yourself in my shoes for a bit.

I decide to read the report before I go out to the mother's home. The family has only been in the area for about 4 months. The oldest son has some serious medical needs and goes into the city hospital to get treatment. He was burned by his father very badly, and as he grows, he needs skin grafts. The mother is having a lot of trouble getting into the city for the appointments. In addition, the oldest son is acting out at school, missing for hours at a time, and came home smelling of alcohol the other day. He is only 12 years old. The other two children are twin girls who are 5 years old. There is no other information in the report.

Sometimes I feel a little underinformed when I go out to visit the families' homes. You really don't know a lot of what is going on, except what might be in the report. I have learned a few things to keep me safe when I go out to a home. Mostly, I remember to ask the family if there is anything I should know about the area, like where I should park, specific directions or landmarks. My agency has several safety plans that include a sign-in and sign-out procedure, where you tell coworkers where you are going and what time you can be expected back. We often will go out in teams if there is an unknown family or an area that is not considered as safe as other areas we travel. Today, I travel alone, since the mother went through a lengthy prescreening at the agency, and I feel comfortable going out by myself today. You can't count on cell phones in some of the more rural areas that I travel. I learn this on my way to the family's home. I am lost, as usual, and there is no signal on my phone. I decide to take the long dirt road back to the main street and call from there when I pass Sam.

While I have never met Sam, he is easy to recognize because he is so badly burned. He is walking up the dirt road to his home as I pass him, and he waves and smiles. I roll down my window and ask for directions, which he gives by pointing to the house right in front of me. I park my car and we laugh as we walk up to the house together. The house is in very poor condition. Sally, the mother, shares that they rent from the farmer who owns several homes on the property. I can see down to the dirt because the floor has several openings. This seems dangerous, and when I ask Sally about this, she shares that the landlord will not fix the floor. She shares that she is not working and that the support she is getting from SSI (Social Security

Income) and food stamps is all the support she has coming into the home. There is no heat in the home because the electric was turned off last week. They could not pay the $200 bill; it is October and getting colder. Sam is due for an appointment in the city next week, which they will not be able to make because Sally's car is in need of repair. The kids are all sleeping on one mattress in one of the bedrooms, and the mother is sleeping on the floor. Sam is no longer smiling at me once he understands that I am a "social worker."

Sam leaves the house as his mother yells at him to come back. The girls are sitting on the only couch in the room as I introduce myself, and then Sally begins to cry. The girls, as if on cue, leave the room, and Sally and I begin to talk about what "family preservation" is and what my role will be for the next 6 months with them. Sally shares that she wants a job; she wants to get her car fixed; and she wants to get help for her son. I know some of the local resources in the area and that they can help her with mattresses, furniture, and food. She is excited but unsure about asking for help. I assure her that we all need help every now and then. We make an appointment together to go to the job center and the other local agencies to get some help.

I pick her up the very next day, and we apply for energy assistance. They approve her and pay her bill, which will help her get her electric put back on. We head over to a local church, and they mark off a mattress, couch, and dishes that they will deliver to her home tomorrow. Sally begins to cry and shares that she feels so uncomfortable asking for all this help. As we arrive at the job center, I assure her that she is eligible for help and that it is there for her and her family to help themselves. At the job center, she works on a resume and receives donations of professional clothing for interviews. Sally already seems energized, and as we pull out of the parking garage, she asks me to stop. She sees a help-wanted sign and asks for an application.

I worked with this family for about 5 months. In that time, Sally got a job and paid for the repairs on her car herself. She advocated with her landlord for home repairs, which he agreed to do. I worked with Sally on parenting skills, setting boundaries with her kids and rules that were developmentally appropriate. The girls entered counseling to talk about what had happened to their brother and their feelings about the move. The therapist used play therapy with them, which they greatly enjoyed and benefited from. Sam was a bit more of a challenge. We were able to get disability transportation services to get him to his doctor appointments. Really, the only way to connect with him was to go for walks. We would walk together all over the farm, and the walking helped him to share. He shared very little at first, and a lot of the time we would just walk in silence. After some time, he began to talk. We worked to build trust and rapport, and by the end of the time I had with them, he trusted me. He began therapy with a community social worker who was willing to come to the home, and that was successful. I get to see Sally a good deal since the closure of the case. Every time I leave the parking garage, she is there to take my money and ticket.

The hardest part about my job is to learn how to not take things home. I have to be honest and admit that I have not really been able to get that down to a science.

I cry sometimes on my way home about the frustrations of my work and the pain that my families deal with on a daily basis. I am clear about leaving the work at work. So when I am not on call, I keep my work life and personal life separate. I have developed a strong circle of social work friends that know and understand the stress of our work. They know when to ask, when to listen, and when to just chat about the latest movie. What keeps me going is my belief in the strength and resilience of the people I work with from day to day. I know that they have been surviving before me and will continue to survive after I am gone. I hope that the survival is just a bit easier and that they find the peace they are searching for.

IS CHILD WELFARE THE RIGHT FIELD FOR YOU?

- Are you comfortable making home visits?
- Are you able to work a flexible schedule that might include evenings?
- Jennifer relates that the hardest part of her job is not getting emotionally overwhelmed by the level of the distress and suffering she encounters in her work. What steps would you take to protect yourself emotionally and to ensure that you were not adversely affected by your work?

SECTION FOUR: RESOURCES TO LEARN MORE

Web Sites
- Children's Bureau: http://www.acf.hhs.gov/programs/cb
- Children's Defense Fund: http://www.childrensdefense.org
- Child Welfare Information Gateway: http://www.childwelfare.gov
- Child Welfare League of America: http://www.cwla.org
- Child Welfare Workforce: http://www.aecf.org
- Citizen's Committee for Children: http://www.cccnewyork.org
- Council of Family and Child Caring Agencies: http://www.cofcca.org
- Generations United: http://www.gu.org
- National Center on Substance Abuse and Child Welfare: http://www.ncsacw.samhsa.gov
- Research Forum at the National Center for Children in Poverty: http://www.researchforum.org

Journals
- *Child and Adolescent Social Work Journal*, Springer
- *Child and Family Social Work*, Wiley-Blackwell
- *Families in Society*, Alliance for Children and Families
- *Journal of Child and Family Studies*, Springer
- *Journal of Public Child Welfare*, Taylor & Francis

Books
- *Child Abuse and Culture: Working With Diverse Families*, by Lisa Aronson Fontes (2008, Guilford Press)

Policy
- Child Abuse and Neglect. In *Social Work Speaks*, 7th ed. NASW Policy Statements, 2006–2009
- Foster Care and Adoption. In *Social Work Speaks*, 7th ed. NASW Policy Statements, 2006–2009
- Public Child Welfare. In *Social Work Speaks*, 7th ed. NASW Policy Statements, 2006–2009

Practice
- Kids & Families: http://www.helpstartshere.org
- Supporting Professional Social Work in Child Welfare: www.socialworkers.org

Standards
- NASW Standards for the Practice of Social Work With Adolescents

Credentials
- Certified Advanced Children, Youth, and Family Social Worker (C-ACYFSW) (NASW credential)
- Certified Children, Youth, and Family Social Worker (C-CYFSW) (NASW Credential)

Educational Programs/Centers
- Boise State University School of Social Work, Child Welfare Center
- California Social Work Education Center, University of California, Berkeley, School of Social Welfare
- New York State Social Work Education Consortium
- University of Albany, State University of New York, School of Social Welfare, The New York State Child Welfare Workforce Initiative (CWWI)
- University of Minnesota, Center for Advanced Studies in Child Welfare
- University of Pittsburgh School of Social Work, Child Welfare Certificate Program

4

Social Work in Criminal Justice

SECTION ONE: FIELD OVERVIEW AND FORECAST

Scope of Services

*F*orensic social work is a broad field that includes any social work practice with individuals, families, groups, or communities that are involved with legal issues. At the micro level, this includes working with individuals and families who are involved in a criminal or civil dispute. At the macro level, this includes advocating for social justice issues such as prison reform, and working with the legislature to enact laws. Forensic social workers work with both victims and offenders, develop preventive services for persons at risk for incarceration, facilitate reentry for the formerly incarcerated, work with attorneys, provide expert testimony in courts, and support alternative programs to incarceration, such as drug courts.

Social workers have been working in the legal arena since the earliest days of the profession. In the 1870s through the mid-1920s, social workers worked closely with prisoners and young people who were institutionalized in reform schools. Social workers were involved in establishing juvenile courts, and they worked in these courts, presenting social histories of those charged with crimes, a role that social workers have to this day (Miller, 1995).

Although social workers have a long and substantial involvement with the legal system, forensic social work is a relatively newly defined area of specialization. It has taken the social work profession quite some time to catch up and claim one of the fastest growing areas of social work practice. Forensic social work is coming into its own as a well-defined and respected field of practice, but this did not happen overnight.

There is some speculation about why forensic social work has taken so long to get "on the profession's map." One theory is that professions naturally evolve into increased areas of specialization. Another factor may be that the profession has some ambivalence about this practice area because of the coercive nature of the criminal justice system, which is viewed as antithetical to the core social work values of self-determination and social justice (Miller, 1995; Alexander, Jr., 2008).

Nonetheless, forensic social work is one of the fastest growing social work practice areas, with great potential for the future.

Settings

One of the major areas for forensic social workers is juvenile justice and delinquency prevention. Society has demonstrated a clear trend toward more punitive treatment of children and youth offenders. As a result, there has been an increasing criminalization of young people and a concomitant overrepresentation of African-American youth in the criminal justice system (Correctional Social Work, 2006).

Social workers employed in the juvenile justice area have an important role. On a micro level, social workers are trained to work with young people and their families as counselors, to provide support and case management, and to help young people and families navigate through a confusing system during a time of crisis. On a macro level, social workers are instrumental in advocating for greater justice in the legal system. A significant issue is to ensure that children and youth involved in the criminal justice system receive different and age-appropriate treatment as compared with adults.

One of the largest arenas for forensic social work is in child custody and supervised visitation. Social workers conduct custody and visitation evaluations for family court. Social workers are obligated to represent the best interests of the child and will be called upon to provide written reports to the relevant parties, to the court, and to testify under oath. Social workers serve as expert witnesses and play a key role in custody decisions. Social workers who work in this arena should have excellent assessment skills as well as personal maturity (Louisiana State Board of Social Work Examiners, 1998).

Probation officers and correctional treatment specialists work with individuals who have been convicted of a crime but are not serving a sentence. The major tasks of these positions are to supervise and counsel offenders, develop rehabilitation plans, liaise with courts, write court reports, and provide expert testimony. A bachelor's degree in social work and completion of a training program provided by the state government is usually required.

The employment opportunities for probation officers are expected to be excellent (Bureau of Labor Statistics, 2008). In recent years, community courts have been established across the United States, and these are becoming increasingly popular as a means of alternative dispute resolution. Community courts are neighborhood-focused courts that seek to promote civic responsibility and that address low-level and quality-of-life crimes. Penalties for offenders include community service and may involve rehabilitation services. Many community courts employ social workers and offer treatment programs targeted to young people. The focus is on identifying needs and providing treatment, as opposed to punishment.

The Social Worker's Role

At the macro level, the strong social mission of the social work profession lends itself extremely well to advocacy efforts to change the many inequities in the criminal justice system. For example, social workers have been in the forefront to reform mandatory sentencing laws like the 1973 New York State Rockefeller Drug Laws, considered by many to be among the most draconian drug laws in the United States, and laws that discriminate against people of color and women (Bernabei, 2005). Treatment of mentally ill inmates is another social problem that social worker advocates are seeking to address. For those social workers interested in advocacy and legislative reform, forensic social work is an area where one can make a substantial contribution.

At the micro level, social workers can engage in forensic social work in an agency or in private practice. Providing expert testimony and writing court reports is a skill that is in demand. Developing a good referral source from an attorney would be essential in building this potentially lucrative practice niche. Many areas of child welfare, such as adoption services, fall under the rubric of forensic social work. As part of the process to adopt a child, prospective parents are often required to obtain a home study. These are conducted by social workers who visit the home and assess the home environment. Social workers who specialize in this area may work for an agency or may work independently.

Credentialing

Many universities are offering certificate programs in forensic social work. One of the first and most established is the Postgraduate Certificate in Forensic Social Work offered by the University of Nevada, Las Vegas. Other programs that are well regarded are offered by Georgia State University School of Social Work and Fordham University School of Social Services. Certificate programs are generally at the post-master's level. Social workers who would like to obtain advanced training in forensic social work should contact their local NASW chapter to find out what programs are available in their area.

Today's society is very litigious, and more and more people find themselves involved in court disputes, which are usually lengthy and expensive. A popular and attractive alternative to litigation is mediation. Instead of seeking legal counsel for dispute resolution, many parties are seeking the less complicated and less expensive option of mediation. Mediators engage in dispute resolutions in divorce cases, family disagreements, landlord/tenant disputes, and conflicts between business partners. Social workers are well suited to function as mediators because social work training emphasizes negotiation, listening skills, and consensus building. Mediators work independently in private settings, and they are also employed by the courts.

Some courts require specialized certifications; for example, the University of Maryland School of Social Work offers a certificate program in mediation developed to provide social workers and other mental health professionals with the requisite training to meet the educational requirements set by the Maryland court system (http://www.ssw.umaryland.edu). Similarly, Colorado State University School of Social Work, in collaboration with the Institute for Advanced Dispute Resolution (http://www.iadrglobal.org/), offers a certificate designed to train professionals to negotiate and resolve disputes (http://www.learn.colostate.edu). Social workers who are interested in becoming mediators should find out the requirements established by their local courts and look for local universities that provide appropriate certificate programs.

Emerging Issues and Employment Trends

There is a strong trend in the United States toward the criminalization of society. The United States has 2.3 million prisoners in jail, more than any other nation in the world. Prison sentences in the United States tend to be longer as compared with many other countries (Correctional Social Work, 2006). There are numerous, unintended consequences of this punitive and harsh legal system, and social workers are well positioned to address what is an often unjust and inequitable justice system. Social workers can work in alternative dispute resolution, develop preventive services for persons at risk for incarceration, and help facilitate reentry to society for those leaving prison. Career paths from advocacy to counseling, adoption to mitigation, and private practice to community justice are all viable career opportunities that are expected to expand.

ACTIVITIES TO LEARN MORE

- Join the National Organization of Forensic Social Work. This is a wonderful source of information. A student membership costs $40.00 per year. Once you are a member, make sure you join the online discussion list.
- Arrange a visit to a trial where a social worker is testifying. This information can often be provided by the local public defender's office.
- Find out what prisoner reentry services are offered in your area and what role social workers have in these programs.

SECTION TWO: CRITICAL ISSUES
Stacey Hardy-Desmond, PhD, LCSW

Dr. Hardy-Desmond is the president of the National Organization of Forensic Social Work (2008–2010) and the director of field education for the UNLV School of Social Work. As an educator-practitioner, she merges the fields of clinical psychology, social work, and law to emphasize experiential learning and development. Areas of practice and teaching focus include cultural competence, mental health, and clinical supervision, with a particular interest in social worker/lawyer collaborations.

Dr. Hardy-Desmond is one of the founders of the Forensic Social Work Certificate Program at UNLV, which was launched in fall 2005, and participated in structuring the joint MSW/JD program. Beyond these academic endeavors, Dr. Hardy-Desmond has a deep commitment to forensic social work practice and the contributions that the social work profession can make to the promotion of social justice on micro, mezzo, and macro levels.

Please tell me a little about yourself and your path in social work. What are some of the factors that motivated you to become a social worker? What drew you to forensic social work as an area of focus? Was it a particular issue or concern?

I majored in psychology as an undergraduate student. My university did not have a social work program, and I hadn't had much exposure to social work. I must admit that, at that time, I wasn't sure exactly what social workers do! After I graduated, I planned to go to graduate school, intending to enroll in a clinical psychology PhD program. However, at that time I was employed in a group home with a clinical director who was a social worker, and I will never forget her advice that I should interview as many professionals as I could before deciding what I wanted to study in graduate school. Taking this recommendation to heart, I talked with a number of professionals, including psychologists and social workers. Of everyone I spoke with, the social workers were the most enthusiastic and passionate about their work. It was clear they found social work to be an incredibly rewarding profession, and that they deeply cherished their work. When I went back and told my supervisor what I had learned, she just smiled. I think she had anticipated that after I spoke with professionals in the field, I would decide on my own to enroll in a graduate social work program. And she was right: I applied to UCLA and enrolled in the MSW program.

I fell in love with social work and came to accept it as my calling. I subsequently did complete a PhD program in psychology, and while I appreciate my education in clinical psychology, that educational experience served to strengthen my belief in the social work perspective. Upon graduating, I worked for the San Bernardino County Department of Mental Health for a number of years and taught at San Bernardino Community College. After that, I joined the faculty at the University of Nevada, Las Vegas School of Social Work, as the director of field education. However, even as an educator, I continue to work in direct practice and to see clients. I love being an educator, yet being actively involved in social work practice is also extremely important to me.

My experience working in the mental health field afforded me the opportunity to understand the extent to which legal issues impact mental health. In my social work practice, I saw many clients with legal concerns, such as divorce proceedings and child custody, yet I felt completely unprepared about how to help them through the legal system. I decided to go to law school so that I would be better able to understand and negotiate the legal context that affects many of our clients, and I earned a law degree from the University of Nevada, Las Vegas, in 2006. I learned a tremendous amount about myself during those years, as I taught social work during the day and attended graduate school at night. It was an amazing experience!

While in law school, it became increasingly clear that there is a tremendous need for partnerships between lawyers and social workers. Legal training does not prepare lawyers to understand, much less address, the client's psychosocial functioning. In contrast, social workers are well trained to assess relevant psychosocial dimensions that may influence the client's legal status. The differing skills sets of lawyers and social workers in an area with considerable overlap make these two professions extremely well suited to professional collaborations. Recognizing this tremendous potential and the mutual benefit from formal partnerships between law and social work, I developed a postgraduate certificate program in forensic social work at the University of Nevada, Las Vegas. I wrote the entire curriculum, and it was established in 2005. We believe that this program is the first postgraduate certificate program in forensic social work in the United States, setting the stage for other programs that have followed.

What is forensic social work?
The word *forensic* means "of the law" or "pertaining to the law." Forensic social work joins social work and the law, dealing with nexus and overlap of the two fields. It refers to an area of social work practice that deals with legal issues on a micro level, as in direct practice with clients, and on a macro level, working with communities, politics, and advancing the social justice mission of the social work profession.

Forensic social work is emerging as a large and well-respected specialization in social work. Many forensic social workers do not readily identify themselves as such because forensic social work is a relatively newly defined specialization. It is not uncommon that a forensic social worker gets the job first and then acquires the training later, and it is a struggle for social workers who have to get on-the-job training. There are not a lot of programs that provide training in forensic social work, although more are being developed. I believe that social work education will offer more training opportunities as forensic social work becomes more clearly defined and recognized as a practice specialization. It is very important that students and new social workers get the proper training and exposure to many different kinds of social work practice so that they can make informed choices in their career planning.

What do forensic social workers do?
In the mind of the public, forensic social work is most often identified with criminal cases. Although many forensic social workers work in the criminal area, the range of employment settings is much broader. Mediation and alternative dispute resolution is a huge growth area. Many people across the country have disputes, perhaps with neighbors, coworkers, or family members, and they want to avoid the expense and time associated with resolving complaints through the legal system. For example, here in Nevada, we have a neighborhood justice center that seeks to resolve civil disputes. Any citizen can seek mediation to resolve a conflict and avoid the considerable time and expense of going to court. It is not required to be a social worker to conduct mediations, but the social work skill set, which emphasizes consensus building and facilitating communication, makes social work a natural fit for this practice specialization. Alternative dispute resolution is quickly becoming an

accepted and attractive means of resolving conflicts, and it is a wonderful career choice for students and new social workers.

The political arena is a major setting for forensic social workers, particularly those that want to effect change at the macro level. In the political realm, forensic social workers work with the legislature to change laws and policies with the goal of promoting a more just society. Mitigation is a large area of forensic social work practice. Mitigation refers to the identification of extenuating factors or circumstances that may have contributed to the commission of a crime. Social workers work on developing mitigating evidence to help defense attorneys build their cases.

A well-known example of the importance of forensic social work with mitigation is the Wiggins case. In 2003, the U.S. Supreme Court ruled that Kevin Wiggins, a death-row inmate convicted of murder, had received ineffective counsel at his trial. At issue was his attorney's failure to provide mitigating evidence of Mr. Wiggins's horrific history of physical and sexual child abuse, and of his borderline IQ. The Supreme Court found that if the jury had known about Mr. Wiggins's history of trauma and borderline intellectual functioning, it might have affected their deliberations. In particular, Mr. Wiggins's attorney was cited for his failure to employ a forensic social worker to prepare a social history for the court. This Supreme Court ruling established the importance of social work evaluations in capital murder cases.

What kinds of clients and presenting problems do forensic social workers generally work with?
Public defenders employ social workers to assess the relevant psychosocial issues that affect legal deliberations. Social workers are often called upon to testify as expert witnesses in a variety of cases. I recently observed a case in which a social worker testified about the psychosocial context related to the defendant's indictment in a criminal case. In private practice, the potential exists for a very lucrative niche market in writing court evaluations. Attorneys often consult with and commission social worker to write court reports about a variety of issues, for example child custody and mental health cases. Social workers who develop a good reputation for writing effective court reports can establish a well-paying specialization.

Why is forensic social work considered an emerging area of social work practice when social workers have been working with the legal system for a long time?
Social work, like all professions, is evolving and is becoming increasingly specialized. For example, although child welfare has always had significant overlap with the legal system, e.g., in the termination of parental rights, social work has readily identified forensic practice as part of its mission. The profession's attitude is, "Let's leave it to the lawyers to recognize our role in the legal process." As we evolve as a profession, we understand that it is up to us to define our own areas of specialization and to clearly shape our contribution.

What are the major societal trends that will shape the future demand for forensic social work?

The increasing criminalization of people In our society is a trend that is shaping forensic social work. There is a broad societal view that the best way to address social ills is to put people in jail, throw away the key, and not think about them. This is not a viable plan because, when people go to jail, eventually most of them do come out. We have to be aware that these individuals need help. Many forensic social workers are employed in programs that facilitate reentry to society after prison, which is an important function of forensic social work and dovetails with our social justice mission.

While the trend toward increased criminalization and incarceration in our society has led to improved employment opportunities and job security for social workers, it is important to note that the social worker's role is to help persons at risk for incarceration. The rate of recidivism is high, and social work can help turn that around. Societal trends have led to the emergence of advocacy groups such as the Innocence Project, which is an organization that seeks to resolve cases of wrongful prison conviction. The Innocence Project builds cases and uses scientific data to exonerate people, many of whom have been unjustly imprisoned for years, with huge chunks of their life taken away from them. Social workers are on staff at the Innocence Project and other comparable advocacy groups. The social work profession's core mission of social justice resonates and informs forensic social work, and social workers work with the legal profession at the macro level to advance a social justice agenda.

What kinds of challenges do forensic social workers face?

Social work is generally misunderstood by the public. Many lawyers mistakenly have the idea that social workers only engage in child protective services, and the legal profession needs to become educated about the wide range of functions that forensic social workers provide. A number of years ago, our local public defender's office was being evaluated, and subsequent to the reaccreditation process, they were directed to hire social workers. At that time, they had no social workers on staff, and they came to our program for help in recruiting social workers. We started placing student interns there, and they now employ eight full-time social workers. Recently the director of the agency told me that he could not imagine how the agency could function without them. We social workers are often bad at marketing ourselves, and we need to enhance our ability to communicate what we do to the public.

What are some of the ethical dilemmas associated with forensic social work?

The most challenging ethical dilemma in this area of work relates to mandated child abuse reporting, as different standards for lawyers and social workers exist. If a social worker on a legal team discovers that a defendant is placing a child at risk of abuse or neglect, the social worker must report that. Lawyers, on the other hand, are under no obligation to report, and in fact this kind of information is likely to be protected by client confidentiality. Social workers who are members of a legal team struggle to resolve conflicting pressures about how to address child abuse and neglect and client confidentiality.

What kinds of skills do social workers need to be successful in forensic social work?
Social workers need to be skilled in professional competence. While educators teach cultural competence in terms of race, ethnicity, sexual orientation, and gender discrimination, we must also recognize that professions have their own cultures and that social workers need the skills in order to negotiate them. Working in a host environment, such as a medical or legal setting, needs to be approached as a cross-cultural experience. It is initially difficult for students and new social workers to adjust to working in a legal setting, and they need to develop the skills to build professional bridges and to work effectively with other professions.

What can social work students do to pursue a career in forensic social work?
More and more schools are offering programs and specialized certificates in forensic social work. Interested students should find out where these programs are and enroll in them. If that is not a viable possibility, students should seek to take courses that include content on forensic social work and to seek internships that provide field experience in this area. We encourage social workers to join the National Association of Forensic Social Workers. This is a wonderful way to learn about forensic social work, to network, to pursue ongoing continuing education, and to go to workshops and conferences.

DID YOU KNOW?

- Forensic social work is founded on principles of social justice.
- Forensic social workers literally save lies when they serve as mitigation specialists in death penalty cases.
- Forensic social work is a clinical specialization that can lead to a very lucrative private practice.

SECTION THREE: FIRST-PERSON NARRATIVE

Child Custody Evaluations by Forensic Social Workers
Ken Lewis, PhD

Ken Lewis, PhD, was a social work professor at several universities before devoting full time to custody evaluations. For the past 25 years, he has worked full time in the area of child custody, and he has been court appointed as a custody evaluator in more than two dozen states. His specialties are interstate custody and high-conflict cases, and he has presented workshops on "The Child-Centered Comprehensive Custody Evaluation" around the country. Dr. Lewis is the director of Child Custody Evaluation Services, Inc., in Philadelphia.

Imagine that you are a forensic social worker in the area of child custody. Imagine that a family court judge appoints you to recommend the best custody arrangement for a child whose parents are divorcing. Imagine that your responsibility includes where the child should go to school, how often the child should spend time with each parent, what telephone contacts should be allowed with the other parent, who should be the child's primary doctor, what religious activities should be allowed, how and where the child should spend summers, and a variety of other things that relate to the child's life. Wouldn't this be awesome responsibility?

This is the job of a child custody evaluator. It is child advocacy in domestic relations litigation. This is the job I chose, and I will tell you why.

I wanted to work with families in distress, but I didn't want to be limited to finding resources to help them through difficult times. I didn't want a job where I referred them to other agencies or other professional resources; I wanted to be a major resource myself. I wanted to be a child advocate, but I didn't want to work in the area of child abuse. I wanted to make a real difference in the lives of children of divorce and separation, but I didn't want to be a mediator for parents who fought over the custody of their children. I wanted to be independent from the parents and advocate directly for the child's best interests for the future.

Many years ago, before I accepted my first case as a custody evaluator, I had testified in court on several occasions. I was asked by the attorneys to testify on specific issues that would support their clients' positions. One attorney wanted me to research his client's proposed school system and testify that it would provide his client's child with an excellent education. In another case, the attorney wanted me to testify that his client's home was in an excellent neighborhood and could provide his client's child with a variety of cultural experiences. There was a third case where I was hired to provide testimony about one parent's ability to care for an infant child because an allegation was made that the parent was not capable.

I used social work skills in my interviews; I wrote my reports with precision and clarity; and I testified in a professional way. However, you will note in the above examples that my testimony was one-sided. I didn't have access to the other parent, so I was not able to make any comparisons. In the first case, I didn't compare the schools proposed by each parent; in the second case, I never visited the other parent's home environment; and in the third case, I was not able to compare both parents' childrearing abilities for the infant whose custody was being contested. I liked testifying in court, but I felt that I was being hired to be more like an advocate for the attorney than an advocate for the child.

You find in this work that the problem for judges in contested custody cases is that decisions are based on comparative evidence. In legal terms, the evidentiary burden is called "the preponderance of evidence," and the evidence can be produced by expert and lay witnesses. A further problem for a judge is when both sides of the case have experts who testify. Does the expression, "a battle of the experts," sound familiar?

Consequently, one-sided testimony was not fulfilling my desire to be an advocate for the child. It did, however, give me some awareness of how family courts operate; and it did provide me with experience testifying as an expert.

Years ago, when I accepted my first case as a custody evaluator, I was sure that I had found my calling. The judge directed both parents to split my fee and directed both parents to fully cooperate with me. Unlike the three cases above, I now had access to both sides of the custody litigation.

I spent 10 hours on my first case. I talked to both parents; I interviewed family members, neighbors, and school teachers; and I spent private time with the two children. When I wrote my report, I recommended custody and visitation based on what I really *felt* was best for those children. But to my surprise, one parent did not agree with my conclusions, and the case went to court. At trial, the disagreeable parent's attorney tore me apart.

When I testified, I explained that the reasons for my recommendations were based on my impressions and feelings after 10 hours of work in the case. I explained how I conducted my interviews, which gave ample opportunity for both parents to state their positions. I also explained how I felt about what the family members, neighbors, and teachers told me. Finally, I testified that the two children loved both parents and would not say where they wanted to live. I made my recommendation based on all of these factors. But, when the attorney asked me if I could support my conclusions with data, I was stumped. I felt totally inadequate, and I was discouraged and disappointed.

However, I learned from that experience that effective expert testimony requires evidence, not feelings and emotions. I learned that, in almost all cases, both parents love their children, but that love cannot be measured. I learned that evaluators should collect data (called "evidence" in court); then organize that data, and draw conclusions from it. The conclusions should form the bases of the recommendations.

Back in those days, there were no guidelines for custody evaluators; there were no "how-to" books or journal articles to consult. However, during the 1990s and into this decade, more and more mental health professionals have become interested in this work.

Social workers, psychologists, psychiatrists, counselors, family therapists, and child welfare professionals joined the field. Professional organizations developed child custody evaluation guidelines; papers were presented at workshops and at annual meetings; more than a dozen books were published; and some states passed legislation that set forth guidelines and regulations for custody evaluations. Several doctoral dissertations have assessed the methodologies used by evaluators, and there are even custody evaluation workshops and seminars at the family judges' conventions. Forensic social workers now have the advantage of learning from these resources and applying their social work skills to their work as custody evaluators.

Some forensic social workers are employed by agencies, either private or under the auspices of the local family court. Some forensic social workers are self-employed, taking their assignments by either consent between the parties or by direct court appointment. When self-employed, your resume is usually passed between the lawyers for both parents and, if agreeable, a consent order is then signed by the judge assigned to the case. If one lawyer objects, the other lawyer can petition the court for your appointment. In that case, the judge makes the determination of whether or not you will be appointed in that particular case.

This is a great time for a social worker to be appointed as a child custody evaluator. Social workers understand that a child's well-being involves more than just his/her relationship with one or both parents. A child lives in a larger social environment. Who better than a competent and well-trained social worker could make a comprehensive social and physical assessment of a child of divorce or separation, and present this assessment in court?

Here are some of the skills required for this work:

1. *Observations*: Spend equal time observing the children in the presence of each parent. During these observations, collect data that portrays each parent's parenting style. Organize the data to identify each parent's strengths and weaknesses.
2. *Interviews*: Interview the parents and collaterals to learn about the child's history. Important collaterals can be teachers, ministers, doctors, family members, neighbors, godparents, and others. Collaterals can provide relevant data that either confirms or denies the allegations that one parent may make against the other parent. Spend private time with the child to understand his or her feelings.
3. *Home study*: Observe children in their home environments. With older children, a walk around the block can be an opportune time to have them share their feelings with you. While it is usually not wise to ask directly about parental preference, listening to what they tell you about their experiences will often provide clues about which residence will serve their best interests. With a younger child, a private talk in his or her bedroom may illicit data that can guide you in your evaluation.
4. *Listening skills*: The social work skill of listening is unquestionably a requirement for custody evaluation work. Sometimes what is behind the words is more important than what is actually said, and can give a clue about what questions to ask next. Data derives from what is said and what is observed, not from what you think a person feels when that person is talking.
5. *Documents*: Review legal documents presented by the attorneys and review other documents provided by the parents, such as diaries, photographs, letters, etc. These documents will help you develop questions for your interviews. Be careful about self-serving documents because often the parents (and always the lawyers) attempt to persuade you through their maneuvers.

In summary, the skills of observing, interviewing, listening, and reading with understanding, when applied with compassion, are the building blocks of a comprehensive child custody evaluation. When the social worker conducts an evaluation and is called to testify, he or she is practicing forensic social work. What could be more satisfying than having a judge adopt your recommendations and pronounce a custody arrangement that serves the child's future best interests?

IS SOCIAL WORK IN CRIMINAL JUSTICE THE RIGHT FIELD FOR YOU?

- Forensic/criminal justice social workers frequently serve as expert witnesses and testify in court. Often, the attorney on the "opposition" side will try to tear down and discredit the social worker. How would you feel if this happened to you? What strategies did Ken utilize to cope with this?
- Ken states that he had to learn to put his emotions aside and deal with facts in order to be effective in his work. Would this be hard for you?
- Forensic/criminal justice social work can involve dealing with disputes, as in this vignette. Are you comfortable with conflict?

SECTION FOUR: RESOURCES TO LEARN MORE

Web Sites
- Center for Law and Social Policy: http://www.clasp.org
- Crimes against Children: http://www.fbi.gov
- Drop the Rock: http://www.droptherock.org
- The Legal Aid Society: http://www.legal-aid.org
- Legal Services For Children: http://www.Lsc-Sf.Org
- National Council of Juvenile and Family Court Judges: http://www.ncjfcj.org
- National Commission on Correctional Healthcare: http://ncchc.org

Journals
- *Journal of Forensic Social Work*: http://www.nofsw.org

Books
- *Forensic Social Work: Legal Aspects of Professional Practice*, by Robert L. Barker and Douglas M. Branson (2000, Haworth Press)
- *Social Work in Juvenile and Criminal Justice Settings*, by A. R. Roberts & D. W. Springer (Eds.) (2007, Charles C. Thomas)
- *Social Work and the Law: Proceedings of the National Organization of Forensic Social Work, 2000*, by Ira Arthell Neighbors, Anne Chambers, Ellen Levin, Gila Nordman, and Cynthia Tutrone (2002, Haworth Press)
- *The Role of the Helping Professions in Treating the Victims and Perpetrators of Violence*, by Morley D. Glicken and Dale Sechrest (2003, Allyn & Bacon)
- *The Witness Stand: A Guide for Clinical Social Workers in the Courtroom*, by Carlton Munson and Janet Vogelsang (2001, Routledge)

Professional Associations
- National Organization of Forensic Social Work: http://www.nofsw.org

Ethics
- National Organization of Forensic Social Work, Code of Ethics: www.nofsw.org

Policy
- Correctional Social Work. In *Social Work Speaks*, 7th ed. NASW Policy Statements, 2006–2009

Educational Programs
- Arizona State University, School of Social Work, Office of Forensic Social Work
- Fordham University Graduate School of Social Service, Interdisciplinary Center for Family and Child Advocacy
- Georgia State University, School of Social Work, forensic social work certificate
- UMassOnline, certificate in forensic criminology
- University of Nevada, Las Vegas School of Social Work, postgraduate certificate in forensic social work: http://socialwork.unlv.edu/
- University of Southern California, School of Social Work, Forensic Social Work Caucus
- University of Virginia, Institute of Law, Psychiatry and Public Policy
- Tarelton State University, Department of Sociology, Social Work, and Criminal Justice

5

Domestic Violence and Social Work

SECTION ONE: FIELD OVERVIEW AND FORECAST

Scope of Services

Domestic violence is defined as a pattern of abusive and coercive behaviors that takes place within the context of an intimate-partner relationship. Anyone can be the victim of domestic violence, and it occurs in both heterosexual and homosexual relationships. However, in the vast majority of domestic-violence cases, women are the victims and men are the perpetrators.

Domestic violence differs from assault in a number of important ways. First, domestic violence is not a random and isolated incident. Domestic-violence victims know their abusers, are generally in a "loving" and long-term relationship with their abusers, and are repeatedly victimized over time. Second, unlike assault, domestic violence is not confined to a single method of violence. Domestic violence includes a pattern of abusive behaviors: physical abuse, psychological trauma, sexual coercion, and economic control. The victims of domestic violence are particularly traumatized because the violence occurs at the hands of a person who was loved and trusted, happens over a prolonged period of time, and is experienced on multiple levels. The complexity of the context of domestic violence is critical for social workers to understand in order to develop interventions that successfully empower clients to extricate themselves from these abusive relationships (Davis, 1996).

Precise figures about the prevalence of domestic violence are not known. Findings from a study by the U.S. Department of Justice on Intimate Partner Violence (Rennison & Welchans, 2000) indicate that approximately 1 million incidents of domestic violence were reported in 1998. Of these, over 900,000 of the victims were women. Approximately 1,830 of these women were murdered. Other estimates of domestic violence are much higher, suggesting that 3 million women in the United States are physically abused by their husband or boyfriend per year (Family Violence Prevention Fund, n.d.). Since many incidents of domestic violence go unreported, there are no definitive figures on the extent of this serious problem. However, consensus exists that domestic violence is widespread and endemic to

American society and affects people from all walks of life, cutting across class, culture, race, and age (Wilt & Olson, 1996).

Settings

Since domestic violence is such a widespread problem, social workers employed in any direct service practice setting are likely to work with clients who are directly or indirectly victimized by domestic violence. This includes both victims and perpetrators of domestic violence, children who live in a home where there is domestic violence, and other family members and loved ones of someone who is involved in domestic violence. The direct practice settings where social workers are most likely to encounter clients affected by domestic violence are emergency rooms, shelters, schools, and legal settings such as courts or prisons, and on hotlines. Social workers in private practice see clients involved in abusive relationships. Child welfare social workers and social workers working with domestic violence have significant overlap in their practice because they both work with family violence. Any social worker doing a home visit, especially on an emergency basis, must be prepared to assess and address domestic violence. Domestic-violence shelters keep their locations secret in order to prevent women from being stalked and harassed by perpetrators. Social workers working in these settings must be very careful to strictly maintain the confidentiality of their clients. It can be a matter of life and death.

Many social workers want to work on domestic violence at the macro level. Social workers interested in advocacy can seek employment at one of the numerous organizations that are dedicated to ending domestic violence. Social workers employed in these organizations work at the legislative level, lobby for and develop public policy, organize conferences, conduct research and write reports, engage in community education campaigns, and serve as a clearinghouse for resources and information.

Social workers will find that domestic violence, which falls under the larger rubric of women's rights, is a major area of international social work. However, the vast majority of social workers are employed in direct practice. Finding employment in policy and advocacy work is generally more complicated. The world of advocacy is small and close-knit, and the best way to break into it is to get to know the people involved. Attending conferences and participating in professional association events can definitely help an enthusiastic social worker become known to the professional community, and to connect with potential employers.

The Social Worker's Role

Social stigma toward victims of domestic violence is prevalent, and most victims feel a strong sense of shame about being in an abusive relationship. It is unlikely that victims of domestic violence will readily disclose their situation, and many victims have been abused for years before they seek help. Their resistance to help and support is often reinforced by systematic attempts by the perpetrator to isolate the victim. For these reasons, victims of domestic violence are likely to present in any social service setting, and not just centers that are formally designated for domestic violence. Social workers working in a health or substance abuse setting may see a woman who has been abused for years, but who has never disclosed it to a professional. As such, it is imperative that all social workers in direct practice have excellent screening and assessment skills to appropriately identify domestic violence. Social service settings can provide opportunities to encourage victims to speak out by displaying posters on their walls and have informational material at hand in locally spoken languages in the waiting rooms (Mullender, 1996).

Social workers who work with victims of domestic violence have to be very careful not to allow their personal feelings about abuse affect their practice. Social work is primarily a female profession, and most victims of domestic violence are women. A strong statistical probability exists that the social worker either has been abused herself, or perhaps her mother, daughter, sister, or friend has been victimized. Social workers who have personal experience with domestic violence are strongly encouraged to work out their personal feelings in therapy or in supervision in order to provide appropriate services to their clients. It can take years to extricate oneself from an abusive relationship, and helping professionals have a tendency to become impatient and frustrated with victims. Society generally "blames the victims" for staying in abusive relationships, and social workers often "buy" into this negative ideology. It can be difficult to remain supportive of clients, and there is the likelihood that a host of negative feelings toward clients is elicited when the social worker repeatedly witnesses his or her client being battered and demeaned. However, social workers can do significant damage when they criticize their clients for failing to get out of abusive relationships. Ongoing training, continuing education, and supervision are strongly recommended for social workers in this area of practice.

Social workers provide services to perpetrators in a variety of settings, which are generally court-mandated. Men who are convicted of battering women are often referred by the courts to anger-management groups. While the data on the efficacy of educational and rehabilitative programs for offenders of domestic violence is somewhat mixed, intervention and education have been identified as helpful in preventing further occurrence of domestic violence (Mitton, 1999).

Credentialing

No advanced credentialing is necessary to work in this practice area. As noted, because of the highly charged feelings elicited by this work, continuing education and supervision are very important for social workers to properly manage these feelings.

Emerging Issues and Employment Trends

A number of trends are shaping the future of domestic-violence services: First, there is an increasing overlap between domestic violence and the criminal justice system as the penalties for offenders become stricter and more strongly enforced. For example, in 1996, New York became the first state to introduce an Integrated

Domestic Violence Court. Proponents of this system suggest that it provides greater protection for victims, leads to higher conviction rates and penalties for offenders, and increases compliance with court orders of protection (Domestic Violence Courts Program Fact Sheet, 2008). Social workers employed in this practice area are increasingly likely to have more client contact with offenders and more involvement with the legal system.

Second, domestic violence is primarily conceptualized as violence against women, and, as such, is understood as a fundamental violation of human rights. The expansion in international social work provides momentum to movements against violence toward women, both domestically and internationally, and provides an increased focus on immigrant women. Social workers are well positioned to take on leadership roles in this area. Cultural competence and linguistic skills are crucial for social workers seeking to move into the arena of international women's rights.

Third, most experts in domestic violence agree that the only way to stop violence toward women is through prevention. Early detection and intervention with boys and young men assessed at high risk for violence toward women is critical. There is sufficient evidence to suggest that children who experience violence at home are more likely to grow up into violent adults. Therefore, understanding and addressing family violence is critical toward ending domestic abuse. Coordination between child-welfare services and domestic-violence services at the policy and practice levels is important.

ACTIVITIES TO LEARN MORE

- Get trained by the National Domestic Violence Hotline as a hotline volunteer advocate. You will provide referrals, information, and guidance to telephone callers seeking help because of domestic violence and dating abuse.
- Read the statement on domestic violence in *Social Work Speaks*, 7th edition, NASW Policy Statements, 2006–2009.
- Go to www.socialworkers.org and type in "domestic violence" in the search box. Review the available resources and pay particular attention to the Universal Screening Risk Assessment Tool developed by Dr. Fran Davis.

SECTION TWO: CRITICAL ISSUES
Fran S. Danis, PhD, ACSW

Fran S. Danis, is associate professor and associate dean at the University of Texas at Arlington School of Social Work. She received her PhD from the Mandel School of Applied Social Sciences at Case Western Reserve University and her MSW from Stony Brook University in New York. She previously taught at the University of Texas at Austin and the University of Missouri–Columbia. As a social work practitioner, she founded a domestic- and sexual-violence community-based program in Denton, Texas; served as the chair of Texas Council on Family Violence, a state domestic-violence coalition; and was staff associate at the National Association of Social Worker/Texas. Her experience in the domestic-violence field includes direct services, policy development and advocacy, research, and evaluation. She has taught a social work course entitled, "Contemporary Issues in Domestic Violence" for the past 10 years.

Dr. Danis is a coeditor with Lettie Lockhart of *Breaking the Silence in Social Work Education: Domestic Violence Modules for Foundation Courses*, published by the Council on Social Work Education. They are currently working on a new edited book addressing intersectionality and culturally competent domestic-violence social work practice. Together they founded the Violence Against Women and Their Children annual symposium for the Council on Social Work Education.

Dr. Danis was also the principal investigator for the Crime Victims: A Social Work Response, Strengthening Skills to Strengthen Survivors project conducted in collaboration with NASW/Texas and funded by the U.S. Department of Justice, Office for Victims of Crime. She was the first social worker in Texas to receive the NASW Social Worker of the Year Award from two different communities.

Please tell me a little about yourself and your path in social work. What are some of the factors that motivated you to become a social worker? What drew you to domestic violence as an area of focus? Was it a particular issue or concern?
I got my MSW in 1976 at Stony Brook University. While there as an undergraduate, I became a feminist and participated in organizing around women's issues. After I got my MSW, I wanted to work on something related to women's issues, but it wasn't until the late 1970s that the emerging rape-crisis and domestic-violence movements became the passion for my career.

In 1980, I founded a domestic-violence and sexual-assault program in Denton, Texas, which is a town north of the Dallas/Ft. Worth Metroplex. There are two schools of higher education in Denton: Texas Woman's University and the University of North Texas. Both schools have BSW programs, and undergraduate students helped provide the support that helped me get Denton County Friends of the Family established. Today, Friends of the Family is 28 years old and has a domestic-violence shelter as well as outreach offices in several communities around the county. I was in Denton for 5 years and also had the opportunity to serve as the chair of the Texas Council on Family Violence (TCFV), a statewide coalition of domestic-violence programs. TCFV is the current home of the National Domestic Violence Hotline (1-800-799-SAFE).

The early years of the domestic-violence movement were an exciting but exhausting time. I decided to move to Austin, Texas, so that I could be closer to the policy advocacy work that I enjoyed through my association with TCFV. I worked for the Texas NASW chapter for 2 years on legislative issues, and then I had an opportunity to teach a course on social welfare policy at the University of Texas at Austin. I decided to leave NASW/Texas to coordinate a statewide research project. Soon after, I became the associate director of the Center for Social Work

Research at the University of Texas at Austin. I decided to pursue my doctorate at the Mandel School of Applied Social Sciences at Case Western Reserve University. After completing my degree, I was on the faculty at the University of Missouri for a number of years. Most recently, I was appointed associate dean at the University of Texas at Arlington School of Social Work. I am very glad to be back in the heart of the Dallas/Forth Worth Metroplex, where so much of my research and practice work has taken place!

Who are the victims of domestic violence and how widespread a problem is it in the United States?
We are all victims of domestic violence. None of us can escape the consequences, even if we are not the primary victim. Regardless of who is assaulted and abused, we all suffer collateral damage, and we all struggle with the aftermath. Perhaps the primary victim is our mother, daughter, coworker, friend, or lover. Domestic violence affects each and every one of us in one way or another. We must recognize that domestic violence is overwhelmingly violence against women, and that 85% of domestic violence is against women.

Because domestic violence is a problem that occurs beyond closed doors, we don't know exactly how big a problem it is. We know the tip of the iceberg: the police reports, the visits to emergency rooms, the hotline calls, and the shelter statistics. The data that we have suggests that that there is a lifetime prevalence that one in four women will be abused over the course of her life. For teenage girls, the data suggests that one in five teenage girls will be the victim of domestic violence. The longer a woman lives, the greater the chance that she will be a victim of domestic violence. It's a huge problem that has yet to get the kind of attention it deserves.

One of the ways society is victimized by domestic violence is the huge burden it places on taxpayers. The financial consequence of domestic violence is staggering. In 1995, estimates suggest that domestic violence cost taxpayers $6 billion per year. This figure is derived from an analysis that calculates the loss of work productivity caused by domestic violence, combined with the costs of medical and mental health care. What it doesn't include are the expenditures associated with providing domestic-violence shelters and services, and the expenses related to processing domestic-violence cases in the criminal justice system. As I said, we only know the tip of the iceberg about the extent and consequences of domestic violence, but the damage is deep, the cost is exorbitant, and the problem is pervasive and severe. However, I believe the real cost to society is the intergenerational transmission of violence: Think of domestic violence as the lowest common denominator of violent crime, think of all the people in our prisons and jails who have committed a violent crime. Factor into the calculation the costs and consequences of child abuse, since in many families, domestic violence precedes child abuse. What would our society look like without violence? How many personal, professional, and economic resources could be freed up if we were able to prevent domestic violence?

What are the risk factors associated with domestic violence?
The risk factors associated with domestic violence are somewhat different for the victim and the perpetrator. For the victim, the major risk factor is being a

woman. With regard to the perpetrators, research suggests that they have often been exposed to violence in their home at an early age, perhaps growing up in a house where one parent was abusive to the other, and/or being a victim of child abuse. Marital instability and volatile relationships may provide a context in which domestic violence is more likely to emerge. Societal factors include weak community sanctions against violence and cultural norms that support hypermasculinity and the use of aggression to solve problems. When society teaches people that it is permissible to solve or correct bad behavior by hitting people, it becomes socially acceptable for men to batter women. Substance abuse, unemployment, and low self-esteem are correlated with domestic violence, but no single factor has been proved to cause domestic violence. No single theory can predict or explain why a person will engage in domestic violence.

What is the impact of family violence on children and youth?
The impact of violence on children is mediated by numerous factors, including the age of the child, the child's temperament, and the severity and duration of the abuse. We know that there can be tremendous variation among children about how they are affected, even among children who live in the same home. Our understanding about the impact of domestic violence on children has evolved over time. We used to ignore the fact that kids were in the home at all, and then we began to think of them as "witnesses" to violence. Today we know the impact of family violence is much more complex.

One problematic unintended consequence of our growing awareness that children are negatively affected by domestic violence is that the child welfare system has begun to hold mothers accountable when their children witnessed domestic violence, and some state child welfare systems have charged mothers with failure to protect a child from witnessing abuse. Once that happens, the child welfare agency is empowered to remove the child from his or her mother. This practice has had a very negative effect, as it punishes the child as well as the mother for the behavior of another individual. Many women are terrified that they will lose their child if they report an abuser. This is particularly threatening to Native American women, because Anglo culture has a long history of taking their children away and placing them in foster care and boarding schools.

Some children who are exposed to domestic violence become aggressive, whereas others internalize the experience, becoming withdrawn, suffering from low self-esteem, and a sense of low social competence. We know that delinquent behavior can be associated with unhealthy role models, and we are very concerned that engaging in violent crime is linked to growing up in a violent home. We see children who do poorly at school because they are up all night hearing the abuse through the walls of their bedrooms. Some children clean up the messes, and live in fear that the slightest little thing will set abuser off. Some children become quite traumatized and exhibit somatic behavior. Other children focus their lives on activities outside the home, excelling in school, joining organized athletic programs, and attending church groups. It's important for social workers to tap into the strengths and resiliency of children to help them develop their own safety plans and to engage their mothers in their own safety planning.

What should social workers be aware of in order to accurately identify and assess domestic violence?

Domestic violence is an issue that cuts across practice settings. Social workers in the field of mental health, substance abuse, and school social workers will certainly have clients on their caseload who are victims of domestic violence. Social workers have to realize that domestic violence is so prevalent that one can't make assumptions about who is likely to be abused, but rather social workers should assume that anybody who walks through the door may be a victim.

Since the majority of social workers are women, there is the strong likelihood that a large number of social workers have had some personal experience with domestic violence. Social workers need to be very self-aware of how their own personal feelings and experiences with violence shape how they view clients. Do we blame ourselves for being in an abusive relationship? Were our own abusive relationships easy to end or hard to get out? Social workers must ask themselves, "How does my personal experience impact how I treat my client?"

How can social workers avoid "blaming the victim" when they are working with people in abusive relationships?

We have to understand why women stay in abusive relationships. Some of the major reasons are economic dependency, fear, desire to hold the family together, and guilt for being a "bad" wife and mother. If a woman is dependent on that relationship for a roof over her head and clothes for her and for the children, it's complicated and hard to get out. Some women are concerned about loss of their homes and their social status in the community, or they believe they are bound by a marriage vow of "for better or for worse." Many abusive relationships start out good. Men don't kick their wives or girlfriends in the beginning. When these relationships began, the men were often loving, attentive.

Maybe in retrospect, one can see that there were warning signs: the man was a little too controlling or became nasty and demeaning after a few drinks. But in the beginning, these moments were few and far between, and the plentiful romance made it easy to ignore the danger signs. Women hope and pray that the man that they fell in love with will reemerge.

It's important to understand how relationships evolve, how people grow dependent upon one another, how a woman creates an investment in a relationship. Some women are so afraid to be alone that they would rather be in a bad relationship than in no relationship at all. Women try to placate their partner, they start enduring abuse, and they blame themselves and believe somehow the abuse is their own fault. Eventually they lose their sense of self.

How do different cultural norms about relationships impact issues related to domestic violence? What can social workers do to ensure culturally competent practice?

We must understand that all cultures and individuals within specific cultures are not alike. We cannot have a one-size-fits-all model for understanding and responding to domestic violence. Behaviors that occur in the context of a relationship are mediated by culture.

As social workers, we focus on cultural strengths, and we tap into survival and resiliency. We must respect a client's cultural norms and traditions. We cannot ask a client to give up her cultural identity and community, to do what we think is right or best for her. That is not good social work. That is not effective practice.

What kinds of interventions are effective in responding to domestic violence?
We don't know what is effective in responding to domestic violence. We do know that we can't keep people locked up forever. Domestic-violence social work practice has to move beyond working with victims. It has to be focused on the perpetrator. We need an appropriate criminal justice response, but most important we need to have best-practice interventions addressed toward boys and young men who are at risk for engaging in violent relationships in later life. Primary prevention for children in homes characterized by family violence is necessary if we want to stop the cycle of violence against women.

Society needs to stop giving boys and young men the message that if you are a hypermasculine aggressive male, you are more of a man. We need to teach boys and men that it's okay for relationships to be formed by equal partnerships.

DID YOU KNOW?

- October is National Domestic Violence Awareness Month.
- Approximately 3.3–10 million children witness the abuse of a parent or adult caregiver each year (Child Welfare Information Gateway, 2008).
- The Family Violence Prevention Fund (http://endabuse.org) estimates that 1–3 million women are physically abused by husbands or boyfriends every year.

SECTION THREE: FIRST-PERSON NARRATIVE

Men Who Work in Domestic Violence: Perspectives from the Field
Rus Ervin Funk, MSW

Rus Ervin Funk, MSW, is a consultant specializing in the prevention of sexual and domestic violence, in the promotion of cultural competence, and in antioppression. He is an adjunct professor at the Kent School of Social Work, University of Louisville, kentucky and serves as president of the Board of the Indiana Coalition against Domestic Violence and is secretary of the Board of the National Resource Center on Sexual and Domestic Violence.

Mr. Funk is the cofounder and executive director of MensWork: Eliminating Violence Against Women, Inc., a Louisville-based organization that focuses on educating, engaging, and mobilizing men to respond to and prevent all forms of sexual and domestic violence. In 2006, he received the Helene

Bartlett Award from the Indiana Coalition Against Domestic Violence for outstanding service to victims of domestic violence. He is also the recipient of the 2005 PreVent Award of Excellence, for his leadership in developing violence-prevention efforts, and the 2000 Frederick Douglass Award from Men Can Stop Rape, Inc.

Mr. Funk is also an author. Some of his latest works include:

Be realistic, demand the impossible: Taking action against pornography. In *Pornography: Driving the Demand for International Sex Trafficking* (2007, Demand Dynamics)

Reaching Men: Strategies for Preventing Sexist Attitudes, Behaviors and Violence (2006, Jist Publications)

Men's work: Men's voices and actions against sexism and violence, *Journal of Prevention and Intervention in the Community*, 36, 1–2, 2008

I have been working in the areas of domestic and sexual violence for more than 25 years. I have worked with battered women and their children, with men who batter, and in community organizing and public advocacy—including contributing heavily to the initial version of the Violence Against Women Act. I began working in this movement as an undergraduate intern in a rural community in South Texas, moved to Washington, DC, and am currently in Louisville, Kentucky. Domestic violence is never boring, often challenging, and not uncommonly extremely frustrating and aggravating. It is also some of the most valuable and meaningful work I can imagine being a part of. For the purposes of this vignette, I am going to focus on my experiences of working with battered women and their children.

Domestic violence is a very complex and challenging issue, in general, and in particular for social workers. This complexity requires a different understanding of doing social work than just about any other area of social work, with the exception of rape/sexual assault. The complications of domestic violence, in my experience, have been exacerbated, depending on what aspect of domestic violence I'm working in (with women/men who have been victimized, children who have been exposed, men who batter, or on the community level). It has required some major rethinking, for me, about what it means to do social work in a number of critical aspects. Very little about what I know about doing effective work with domestic violence was learned from my formal social work training. Some of what I had been taught, in fact, I found contraindicated the reality of working in domestic violence.

One of my first initial lessons was redefining what it means to do social work. I have never had the luxury of doing one aspect of social work. While working as a therapist, I was also a case manager, a babysitter, a legal and/or medical advocate promoting policy changes (on the organizational or community level), and a community educator and organizer. I have changed diapers and cleaned up vomit in the midst of writing multithousand-dollar grant proposals and planning communitywide events in honor of Domestic Violence Awareness Month. In many ways, doing social work in the context of domestic violence harkens back to the roots of our profession—Jane Addams and Hull House.

Another learning curve for me was defining my client. In my social work education, I was taught that my client is the person, group, or community that is in front of me. I was taught that the client (i.e., the person sitting in my office or in whose home I'm visiting) is the person to whom I am most accountable. In domestic violence, on the other hand, my client (the person to whom I am most accountable) is always the person who was victimized by domestic violence (usually the wife/girlfriend and her children), regardless of whom I happen to be working with. This means that when I am working with men who batter, or with the community (as a client), or on a public advocacy effort, I must consider how my social work practice and actions are impacting my primary client—the women and children who are victimized by domestic violence. I may work with a man who batters and certainly have some responsibility and accountability to him, but my client is his partner and children.

Addressing issues of safety and confidentiality takes a higher priority in domestic violence than with other populations. Every time there is a situation of domestic violence, there is a possibility of lethality. It is enticingly easy to join my clients (battered women, their children, men who batter, the community) in minimizing this danger. Few people want to consider that their lives are in danger. In fact, there aren't many people who can function while fully cognizant of how much danger they may be in. As a social worker, I don't like thinking that a woman with whom I am working and her children may be killed. I come to care for and about them (at first professionally, and often personally), and it's terrifying, enraging, and it hurts to think that she (or her children) may be killed. So far, I have known six women who have been killed by their partners during or after the time I was working with them. (Thankfully, so far, I have never been working with a man who killed his partner, nor to my knowledge have any of the men I have ever worked with killed their wives or girlfriends.) There was nothing in my social work education or professional development that prepared me to deal with the pain, anger and rage, self-doubts, confusion, and morass of other feelings that were triggered by having a client of mine murdered. Thankfully, in general, the domestic-violence movement is a very close extended family, and the degree of support and care for each other is indescribable. It is only because of the support that I have received from these people—my colleagues, friends, and "family" (mostly women)—that have made it possible for me to continue in this work for all these years.

Working in domestic violence also challenged and solidified the importance for me of both empowering and strengths-based social work. While much of my education used this language, I realized through my work in domestic violence that what I learned was still based on a deficit-based paradigm. Women or men who are battered, and children who witness domestic violence, are incredibly strong, resilient people. Rather than asking, for example, "Why do you keep going back?" I have learned a more empowering and frankly more meaningful question: "How did you resist?" All partners who are being or have been abused resist the violence (just as critically) and the efforts of power and control that the violence tries to enforce. Women who have been battered often minimize or don't recognize their own resistance strategies (or to put it another way, like most of us, don't recognize or define their resilience), but by asking them this question, with the assumption that they did resist (and thus that they do indeed have some resilience), it forces them to begin identifying their resistance strategies, and thus begin realizing their strengths.

Professional boundaries have been another area of challenge in working with domestic violence. I've had to rethink what I mean by professional boundaries and how I maintain those boundaries. The clinical messages that I received in school and in my early experience, I found, got in the way of my ability to connect with, and be empowering of, people who had been victimized by domestic violence as well as men who had perpetrated domestic violence. What I've learned is that boundaries in domestic violence (and, I believe, in general) are defined in the context of the relationships between social workers and their clients (persons or communities). The core of social work is the expression of care. To honestly reflect my care for the women, children, and men with whom I have worked, I've learned that I have to actually care for them. This is particularly true for people who have been traumatized, and in the context of domestic violence, traumatized for long periods of time by a person they love and who claims to love them. As such, battered women and their children are often very well tuned in to people who are authentic. It is part of their amazing survival strategies. If they can tell by the way the abuser is walking up the sidewalk whether or not he is going to be abusive tonight, they can certainly tell whether or not my care for them is authentic or a professional play.

Furthermore, working in shelter contexts (which has been where most of my work has been) provides additional challenges to traditionally defined professional boundaries. I may have a professional role by working at the shelter, but I am there when women are in their bathrobes; I help change their babies' diapers; I hold their children while they are in court or are having a badly needed and well-deserved meltdown. What I've come to realize is that professional boundaries mean that I am doing my best thinking about my clients. The boundary is to stay focused on them. Whatever the behaviors are, the focus is on them and their improvement. For example, I am often challenged as to why I (as a man) am working in this movement and, in particular, at a shelter with women. One way that challenge is often expressed is asking if my mother was battered or if I was abused. Traditionally defined professional boundaries demand that we not disclose personal information. I have come to ask why it is important for her to know that information. If she can make a good argument about how it will help her in her healing, development, empowerment, etc., to know whether or not I have been affected by domestic violence, then I'll tell her. The professional boundary (like personal boundaries) is defined by the context of the relationship, not some arbitrary rules.

As a male, working in the area of domestic violence has surfaced certain additional complexities and challenges. When I meet a woman who has just been battered, interact with her children, engage a man who has been abusive, or present myself to the community, the first thing they notice is that I am a white man who is doing domestic-violence work. They all have questions and confusion: "Are you gay?" (which is somehow always expressed as a way to detract from or explain away my involvement); "Are you trying to get dates?" etc. The underlying question for all of these is why would I, a male-type person, work in domestic violence? There is usually (always?) a level of incredulousness to many people (including the women at the shelter) that I, a man, would want to do this work.

Women who come to the shelter generally start with a level of distrust. They often feel me out for a bit to see if I'm for real. Before long, because I am consistent and strive to be helpful, they begin to see me as an ally. For example, although it was never my role nor in my job description, I created the habit of being available during dinner, just to help. Dinner is often chaotic in any household. The children are running around; moms and/or dads are trying to get dinner prepared and set; mom and dad (or mom and mom or dad and dad) are trying to wind down from their days and connect; parents and children are trying to connect after being gone all day. In a domestic-violence shelter, this chaos is ramped up several degrees. Being there and available to help (carry food with a mom to her table; sit with kids while mom talks with a friend; help feed one of the kids so mom can feed herself; clear the dishes for a mom and her three kids [all under age 5], one of whom is having a fit; etc.) was a way for me to connect with the women and the children so that they began to see me as someone they could trust and talk with. Once they started to trust me a bit, they would often ask, "How can you understand?" My answer to that question was/is as authentic as I can be: Quite honestly, I can't understand. I am not a battered woman; I have never been a woman and have never been beaten on a consistent basis by the person I've shared a piece of my soul with. I can't understand. What I can do is listen. I can listen with my ears, with my heart, with my hands, and with my whole body.

An additional challenge for me, as a man, has been learning how to respond to flirting from the women in the shelter. These were women who were very badly hurt by the men that they loved. I was a man (usually the only man in those shelter settings) who was attentive, present, and supportive. In addition, I tend to be a fun-loving person and bring that into my work contexts. So in the context of being supportive and attentive, I would also tease and be teased by the women with whom I worked (both colleagues and clients). It was not uncommon for women in the shelter to respond to these behaviors by flirting with me, often overtly. My response to this flirting relates back to my understanding of professional boundaries. It would, most decidedly, not benefit the women who were flirting with me for me to respond to their flirting. I learned to use my humor and fun to divert the flirting while maintaining the boundary. For example, as I was getting ready to leave the shelter one evening, I was joking around at the front desk with several women who were staying there and a couple of colleagues. One of the women at the shelter said to me, "You need a girlfriend," meaning, it was quite clear to all of us, that she was referring to herself as the girlfriend that I needed. I responded by saying, "That's an interesting proposal; before I respond, let me ask you this. You know where we work; there are a lot of very empowered and strong women in this building.

What do you think they would do to me if I were to accept your offer?" I would say this somewhat tongue in cheek, but would do it in a way to point out how utterly inappropriate it would be.

As a man in this movement, there is also an issue of isolation. There aren't many men who do this kind of work. I was almost always the only man in the programs in which I've worked, and when I wasn't, the other men were the technical guru, the maintenance crew, and in one case, the development director. The men who did work at the shelter did not have the same relationship with the women, nor did they necessarily see themselves as part of a movement to end domestic violence. Being the only type (fill in the blank) of person in any situation is never comfortable, and there is always an increased level of self-consciousness. In some ways, it's been a great experience for me. Although women as well as men and women of color often experience this dynamic, white men don't. Through this experience, I've come to realize many layers of male privilege that I probably would continue to be ignorant of had I not chosen this movement.

I've also had to examine my own behaviors and my own understandings and expressions of masculinity. Men are not born batterers. They learn it. I've come to realize that the lessons that encourage or allow men to batter are lessons that all men get. I've had to rethink what it means to be an empowered male-type person (just like many of my female colleagues have expressed that being a part of this movement has forced them to redefine what it is to be an empowered woman). Given the lack of role models of what it is to be a man in this movement, this is a process I've largely had to do with women. It's not been easy, and the support that I've been offered has not always, at the moment, felt like support (sometimes it was challenging, confrontational, and critical), but I've found that it is often through those experiences—of being forced to examine aspects that I don't want to (really don't want to)—that I have had my greatest growth spurts. They call them "growing pains" for a reason.

Domestic violence involves a pattern of behaviors used to maintain power and control in a dating or marital relationship. This pattern of behaviors may include physical violence, but also includes isolation, economic control, verbal abuse and name calling, threats, sexual assault, intimidation, an imbalance of accountability, blame-shifting, and a variety of other tactics. One partner, almost always the male in heterosexual couples, asserts control of the relationship and therefore of the other person, and uses the tactics necessary to maintain control.

As I mentioned previously, this may include physical violence (the one tactic that most readily comes to mind for most folks when we talk about domestic violence), but very well may not. For example, one man who I worked with was extremely controlling and abusive: He and his partner lived in the country with one car, which he had the only set of keys to. He would lock her into the house when he would leave, taking the phone with him. He controlled the finances of the household, providing her with a very specific "allowance" that she was to use for all of the household maintenance (food, cleaning, upkeep, etc.,) and for which he demanded itemized receipts. He was also verbally abusive toward her. According to both of them, he never put his hands on her. He never hit her, pushed her, or assaulted her in any way. He did, however, clean his guns. He was a gun collector and periodically he would have her sit in the living room across from him while he methodically cleaned his gun.

Clearly, his gun cleaning was intended as and experienced as a very real threat of what he was willing to do if she didn't behave as he expected her to. But, because of the ways that domestic-violence laws are written, there was nothing illegal about any of his behavior. It is not illegal to own one car and have one set of car keys; it is not illegal to call your partner mean and disgusting things; it is not illegal to demand that your partner do all of the shopping for the household and bring home itemized receipts. And it is not illegal for a man to clean his guns, even if he looks menacingly at his partner while doing so.

By the time I began working with him, fortunately, I had several years of experience in working with men who batter. There was nothing provided to me in my social work education or training that prepared me to work with the men who perpetrate domestic violence. Social work teaches you, very strongly, to "take the client where they are coming from" and to be "nonjudgmental." Working with men who perpetrate domestic violence, however, requires that we, as social workers, be overtly judgmental ("It is NOT okay, under any circumstances, to treat your partner like that!"), and while it is true that we need to take men who perpetrate from where they are coming, it's with a bit of a twist to the general standards of social work. For example, one of the sacred tenets of social work direct practice is confidentiality. It is something that is drilled into us and something that I hold very dear. However, when working with a population of men who have used secrets as a weapon to perpetrate serious harm to the person(s) they claim to love, the notion of confidentiality has to be reexamined. I developed a practice of requiring every man who perpetrated domestic violence that I worked with to sign a release of confidentiality before I would admit him into the program for which I worked. In other words, the man lost his right to confidentiality. I was completely honest with these men; I would not abuse that authority, and they would know, beforehand, everyone who I was going to talk with about them and why. But as a practitioner, I was the one who would decide whom I talked with and what I would talk about— not them.

As I said, by the time I began working with this man, I fortunately had several years of experience and had become pretty clear about my role and how I was able to work with men. He expressed no real responsibility for his actions, other than to justify and explain everything that he did. He did not acknowledge any harm that he caused his partner and suggested that any "problems" that existed were hers.

Overall, my experience as a social worker in the field of domestic violence has reinforced for me the fact that we are the tools we're looking for. There is no magic to good social work practice. Good social work practice is made up of social workers bringing our best selves into the practice setting, creating a relationship with our clients (be that an individual, family, group, organization, or community), and doing the best that we can for our clients.

IS DOMESTIC VIOLENCE THE RIGHT FIELD FOR YOU?

- Rus states that his social work training did little to prepare him for the realities of the domestic-violence field, and one of his first on-the-job lessons about working in domestic violence was to throw out most of his preconceived ideas about what it means to be a social worker.
- Social workers who work with battered women have to learn how to understand why a woman returns to an abusive situation. Rus is able to reframe his clients' actions within the context of their strengths and resilience. Think about why this is so central to his work.
- A number of Rus's clients have been murdered by their partners while Rus was working with them. This is a reality of working in this field. Rus is able to cope with this because of support from the domestic-violence movement. Envision yourself in Rus's position and imagine how you would handle this situation.

SECTION FOUR: RESOURCES TO LEARN MORE

Web Sites
- Battered Mothers Resource Fund, Inc.: http://www.batteredmothers.org
- Family Violence Prevention Fund: http://endabuse.org
- National Coalition against Domestic Violence: http://www.ncadv.org
- National Domestic Violence Hotline: http://www.ndvh.org
- National Network to End Domestic Violence: http://www.nnedv.org
- National Sexual Violence Resource Center: http://www.nsvrc.org

Journals
- *Journal of Family Violence*, Springer
- *Journal of Interpersonal Violence*, Sage

Books
- *Domestic Violence: A Handbook for Health Professionals*, by Lyn Shipway (2004, Routledge)
- *Encyclopedia of Domestic Violence*, by Nicky Ali Jackson (2007, CRC Press)
- *Handbook of Domestic Violence Intervention Strategies: Policies, Programs, and Legal Remedies*, by Albert R. Roberts (2002, Oxford University Press)
- *Social Work, Domestic Violence, and Child Protection: Challenging Practice*, by Catherine Humphreys (2000, The Policy Press)

Professional Associations
- The Society for Social Work Leadership in Health Care, Domestic Violence Standard of Care: http://www.sswlhc.org/html/standards-domestic.php

Policy
- Family Violence. In *Social Work Speaks*, 7th ed. NASW Policy Statements, 2006–2009

Practice
- Domestic Violence—How Social Workers Help: http://www.helpstartshere.org
- Practice Update from the National Association of Social Workers: What Social Workers Should Know about Gender-Based Violence and the Health of Adolescent Girls: http://www.socialworkers.org
- 10 Things Every Social Worker Needs to Know about Domestic Violence, by Mark Sandel, LMSW. The New Social Worker: http://www.socialworker.com/domesticviolence.htm

Educational Programs/Centers
- Simmons School of Social Work, Domestic Violence Training Program: http://www.simmons.edu/ssw/dvtraining/
- The University of Texas at Austin, School of Social Work, Institute on Domestic Violence and Sexual Assault: http://www.utexas.edu/research/cswr/idvsa/

6

Social Work in Health Care

SECTION ONE: FIELD OVERVIEW AND FORECAST

Scope of Services

Social work in health care is one of the oldest and most prestigious practice areas of the profession. Dating back to the turn of the century, social workers have played an important role in health care, and in the early years of the social work profession, social workers firmly established themselves in hospitals.

The first hospital social work department was organized in 1905 at Massachusetts General Hospital (Ross, 1996). The early hospital social workers were primarily concerned with the health of the poor and with addressing social conditions associated with illnesses, such as tuberculosis (Whitaker, Weismiller, Clark, & Wilson, 2006e). In the 1930s, social work in health care continued to expand subsequent to federal social programs enacted in conjunction with the Social Security Act, such as the passage of the Federal Emergency Relief Act of 1933. The next 50 years continued to be a period wherein social work made a substantive contribution in health-care settings, within the context of a growing societal awareness that health and well-being are fundamentally linked to psychosocial factors (Ross, 1996; Cowles, 2008).

One of the major trends in contemporary health care is increased community-based care, as opposed to inpatient care. A number of factors, including cost-containment concerns and advances in medical technology, have led to a decrease in the patient length of stay in the hospital and an increase in medical care under the auspices of specialty outpatient clinics. Today, medical social workers, once concentrated in hospital social work departments, are likely to work in specialized treatment programs. For example, many social workers work in chronic illness treatment programs such as dialysis units, asthma prevention and treatment programs, and cardiac care units. Today, health care is the second largest social work practice area among social workers with a master's degree in social work (Whitaker et al., 2006e).

Settings

Working as a hospital social worker is very different today than it was in the past. Hospital social work departments were traditionally very strong, discipline-specific departments that provided social workers with a clear professional identity. In this organizational model, hospital social workers reported to a social work director, who had considerable authority within the hospital and provided strong social work leadership to his or her staff. During the mid-1990s, in efforts to reduce costs, hospitals began to restructure social work services while downsizing and dismantling social work departments. Instead of being part of a social work department, social workers today are increasingly likely to be assigned to specialized programs, such as cardiac care or pediatric oncology. As hospitals restructured, the tasks and functions of hospital social workers were transformed by the changing demands of new health-care models. The consequences of these changes have been viewed as both a source of considerable stress and an opportunity for professional growth (Berger, Robbins, Lewis, Mizrahi, & Fleit, 2003; Globerman, Davies, and Walsh, 1996; Mizrahi & Berger, 2001; Rizzo & Abrams, 2000). Social workers have to adapt to having less supervision and limited professional contact with other social workers. This can result in decreased opportunity for professional development, and makes it harder to earn the supervised experience required for obtaining clinical licensure.

At the same time, social workers are well positioned to assume leadership in medical settings. Social workers, by training, are attuned to understanding complex systems, know how to advocate and negotiate, and are skilled at communicating across disciplines. Social workers make a substantial contribution to the financial integrity of the hospital because social work services can reduce the patient's length of stay (Sánchez, 2003).

The Social Worker's Role

Social workers in health care spend the majority of their time engaged in direct practice, with psychosocial assessment, crisis intervention, treatment planning, individual counseling, and discharge planning identified as the primary tasks (Whitaker et al., 2006e). Hospital social workers play a central role in addressing multiple client needs and work with patients through the continuum of care from emergency room, admission, to discharge and post-discharge (Sánchez, 2003).

Interdisciplinary teamwork is an integral component of medical social work. Medical social workers work closely with other health professionals such as nurses, physicians, and physical and occupational therapists (Beder, 2006). Discharge planning is a major social work function in medical social work that has been somewhat appropriated by the nursing profession subsequent to organizational changes in hospitals. Turf battles between nurses and social workers over discharge planning have created tensions in many hospitals. Holliman,

Dziegielewski, and Teare (2003) dated increased discord between these two disciplines to the 1990s, when hospitals restructured. Ozawa and Law (1993) found that nurse discharge planners are paid higher salaries than social workers. Strategies for ways that social work can successfully position itself in the brave new world of post-1990s health care speaks to the importance of creatively adapting to change.

The cost-containment value of social workers in hospitals has been documented in studies that suggest that hospitals can cut costs when hospital social work is appropriately utilized (Auerbach, Mason, & LaPorte, 2007). Social workers have the skills and training to reduce patient length of stay with an older patient population that has increasingly difficult and complex needs. Utilization review, which involves assessing the appropriateness of patient care plans, is another professional function that is viewed as an important model for successful professional hospital social work practice (Rizzo & Abrams, 2000).

Credentialing

The National Association of Social Workers (NASW) offers one specialty credential in health care. The Certified Social Worker in Health Care (C-SWHC) requires an MSW degree; no less than 2 years (equivalent of 3,000 hours) of paid, supervised, post-MSW health-care social work experience; current state MSW-level license or a MSW-level exam passing score; an evaluation from an approved supervisor; and a reference from an MSW colleague.

Emerging Issues and Employment Trends

Health care is one of the most rapidly changing practice areas for social workers. According to the Bureau of Labor Statistics (2008), employment opportunities for medical and public-health social workers are expected to grow at a much faster rate than for other occupations. However, employment opportunities in hospitals, the largest employment setting for medical social work, are expected to slow down. As hospitals continue to seek ways to cut costs and shift patient care from inpatient settings to outpatient settings, it is predicted that the demand for social workers in hospitals will grow more slowly than in other settings. At the same time, employment for medical social work in community-based settings, particularly employment in home health-care services, is growing.

An important factor for consideration is the extent to which changes in setting will impact social work salaries. Hospital social workers earn comparatively higher salaries than community-based medical social workers, particularly those that work in aging. As health care shifts more and more to outpatient settings, salaries may be negatively affected. The social work profession will have to pay close attention to salaries and employment trends to ensure that social work salaries in health care are adequate.

ACTIVITIES TO LEARN MORE

- Log on to the National Association of Social Workers Web site at www.socialworkers.org. Go the Center for Workforce Studies and read the Specialty Practice Report on Health.
- The Society for Social Work Leadership in Health Care is a national association for social workers in health care. There are also many state-affiliated chapters, so check to see if there is one in your state. Their Web site has a wealth of information about this practice area. Learn more at http://www.sswlhc.org.
- Contact your local hospital and find out if there is a Department of Social Work. Find out what employment opportunities exist for social workers.

SECTION TWO: CRITICAL ISSUES
Terry Mizrahi, PhD, MSW

Dr. Mizrahi is a professor at the Hunter College School of Social Work of the City University of New York, where she chairs the community organization and planning concentration and teaches social policy and health and mental health policy. She is director of the Education Center for Community Organizing, which provides information, workshops, and technical assistance to community leaders and community-based professionals in New York City and beyond.

Dr. Mizrahi completed a Fulbright Fellowship in Israel in 2006 at Hebrew University, where she taught a seminar in comparative community development and organized two major national conferences. In 2004, she was a Kreitzman Fellow at Ben Gurion University in Israel. She continues to informally consult with the Ministry of Social Affairs after producing for them a report on best practices on client and citizen participation in improving policies in the United States. She also consults with the Jerusalem Intercultural Center and the Interdisciplinary Forum on Community Development.

Dr. Mizrahi is coeditor-in-chief of the *Encyclopedia of Social Work* (20th edition), which was released for publication by the NASW and Oxford University Press in March 2008. She is the author of 5 books and monographs and 70 articles, book chapters, reviews, and manuals. Her areas of research, training, and consultation include professional socialization, coalition building, community organizing practice, and health policy. She completed a study on social work leadership in hospitals and the leadership of deans of schools of social work in an effort to promote interdisciplinary collaboration.

Among her publications are: *Women, Organizing and Diversity: Struggling With the Issues* (coauthor); *Getting Rid of Patients: Contradiction in the Socialization of Physicians*; *Community Organization & Social Administration* (coeditor and author); and *Strategic Partnerships: Building Successful Coalitions and Collaborations* (coauthor).

Dr. Mizrahi was elected as the president of the National Association of Social Workers (NASW) from 2001 to 2003, the largest professional organization in the world, with 155,000 members. She has served as secretary of the Association for Community Organization and Social Administration (ACOSA) and is a founder of the *Journal of Community Practice*. She is also a recipient of the Hunter Presidential Awards for Excellence in Applied Research 2008 and Community Leadership in 1994, and she received the Lifetime Achievement Award from ACOSA in 2004.

Please tell me a little about yourself and your path in social work. What are some of the factors that motivated you to become a social worker? What drew you to health care as an area of focus? Was it a particular issue or concern?
I first discovered the joy of social work when I volunteered at a settlement house in New York City, but I had no interest in health care when I began studying for my MSW degree. I began my studies as a casework major, but I changed my concentration to community organizing when I realized that so many problems of clients had to do with policies that needed changing. I came to believe that creating more beneficial policies and programs and involving the clients in decision making would have a more positive impact on individuals and families than counseling alone. After improving the larger system, social workers could then effectively engage in clinical psychotherapeutic work with those clients whose problems were interpersonal or intrapsychic. I also began my social work career in the 1960s, which was of course in the heyday of civil rights and social activism inside and outside social work. It was an exciting and challenging era.

I got my first job at the Lower East Side Neighborhoods Association in the late 1960s as a community organizer, where my first assignment was to organize "the community" to build a new local public hospital (known as Gouverneur Hospital) to replace an old inferior one that had been closed years before. My task was to mobilize support for the new health-care facility that had been promised the community for at least 10 years. In this position, I quickly learned core community organizing skills and techniques at the grassroots and coalition levels, and as well, I developed an understanding about the power behind health policy in New York City: The private sector was strong and the public-health and hospital sector was weak. Yet, by gaining the support of political leaders, the agencies, and the organizations in the community, and by reaching the neighborhood residents, we won a partial victory to build a community hospital in spite of opposition by the private academic medical center and the organized hospital planning and development establishment.

After that, I got involved in organizing neighborhood health centers, because access to quality primary and preventive health care was part of the liberal President Johnson administration's solution to poverty. There are three health centers in the Lower East Side—in addition to the hospital's ambulatory care facility (Gouverneur)—in which I was professionally invested that still exist today, in part because of our efforts (Betances Health Center, the Ryan-NENA CHC, and the

Charles B. Wang CHC). I also helped organize the Lower East Side Neighborhood Health Council, consisting of professionals and community residents, to serve as a watchdog on local services. We recruited community activists from diverse cultural and ethnic backgrounds, building support from the older and newer ethnic groups in the community, working-class white Jewish and Italian long-term residents, a growing Latino and Chinese population, and the African American people who were mostly living in public housing. Central to our organizing success was the involvement of as many community stakeholders as possible, and we reached out to people from all walks of life.

The federal government first became involved in health planning in 1968, when it passed the Comprehensive Health Planning Act. I became part of a movement to establish a public rather than private regional health systems agency required by that legislation as a result of this radical policy change. Most of the people that I worked with were not social workers, but came from the ranks of politics and government as well as the student movement. I was very conscious of being a social worker and I tried to bring that unique perspective to the interdisciplinary and interorganizational coalitions that formed around, ultimately, "the right to health care."

Around this time (the early 1970s), I also became active with the NYC chapter of the National Association of Social Workers, and I began to organize social workers around health-care issues. In the 1970s I wrote three workbooks for community-health activists (Consumer Health Rights, The American Health Care System, and Organizing for Better Community Health) and continued my health organizing after I moved to Virginia in 1972. During the 1970s I had a chance to work in Appalachia for two summers, where I was exposed to rural poverty and the need for rural health services, and also to the wonderful and tenacious local residents struggling to improve their social conditions. Years later, back in New York City in the late 1980s, I helped found and cochaired the New York City chapter's Health Care Policy and Practice Network, and I subsequently served as the national secretary (1992–1994) and then president of NASW (2001–2003). I was the first social worker selected to the federal government's Primary Health Care Policy Fellowship (1994). A great deal of my research and publications have focused on health-care policy and practice, including my dissertation and book on physician socialization, a study of collaboration between social workers and physicians, and another study on neighborhood health centers in NYC. I have been and continue to be very active in the national health-care reform movement for universal health coverage. NASW has been a player in this issue since its inception.

What are the major societal trends that will shape the future for social work services in health care?
Social work has been involved in the health-care system at both the policy and practice levels since 1905. In particular, many social work leaders were active in promoting health-care insurance and reimbursement for social work services. The role and numbers of social workers expanded, and centralized social work departments in hospitals grew and strengthened. By the 1980s, social work was

considered an integral part of health-care teams in hospitals and along the continuum of health care. By 1980 it was also clear that the health policy agenda was shifting away from physicians to hospital-based and corporate medical institutions. In short, the AHA (American Hospital Association) became more powerful than the AMA (American Medical Association).

Social work services in health care will continue to respond to these powerful trends, some of which will be positive for the social work profession and others that will be negative. In particular, demographic trends and developments in disease management are driving a paradigm shift in health-care management from acute and episodic to chronic and long-term care. For the social work profession, this trend is quite positive, given our holistic approach to health and illness. The population is living longer, although increasingly with chronic illnesses. As a result, the social work function will be more vital than ever: to help patients and their families cope with and adapt to chronic, degenerative, and ultimately terminal illness; to help them achieve their optimal quality of life; and to focus on psychosocial and mental health along with medical needs. As the shift is moving away from inpatient care to long-term and community care, social workers will be needed in all settings along the continuum of health care.

In the future, society will be challenged to look beyond medical solutions to diseases, and to seek strategies that address the patient's social health and well-being. Social workers, trained in a biopsychosocial orientation, are well positioned to make a substantial contribution because the social work perspective is highly attuned to the environmental context of disease and wellness. We can predict, moving forward, that the need for social work services in health care will be strong.

At the same, this demand may not necessarily be matched by a mandate that social work services be provided by professionally trained and qualified social workers. The question is whether health-care financing will provide adequate funding for professional social workers. The danger for the social work profession is that social work functions will be provided by underqualified staff to fulfill social work tasks, as has happened to some degree in nursing and other professions. The deterrent to a healthy and vital role for social workers rests on the corporate and government definition of health and illness, for example, whether they include mental health and psychosocial aspects to them, and whether they will pay for those services. Do government and the corporations that control health-care funding believe that it is their role to meet the social health needs of the nation? For example, will they fund programs that treat stress; will they provide assistance to victims of violence and abuse who wind up in emergency rooms? As the corporate control of health care has increased and government control of health care has weakened, there is the potential to limit the role for social workers if those two sectors decide that it is not their job to cure social ills, or if they decide that they cannot afford to pay for professionally trained social workers to address social problems. We must ask, "How great is society's commitment to addressing social health?" When there is a societal commitment to the health and wellness of its citizens, then there will be a greater impetus to ensure a role for professionally trained social workers as part of an interdisciplinary health-care team.

How do health-care trends affect social workers?

As noted previously, health care in our society has undergone a series of paradigm shifts. The health-care system was once dominated primarily by physicians. In this model, physicians had significant control and influence over health-care delivery, financing, and organization as well as the education and training of health personnel. During the liberal era, under the Kennedy and the Johnson administrations, and continuing through the Nixon and the Carter administrations, there was a shift toward government control of health care, with the government playing a substantial and positive role, advocating for the rights of citizens to health care and for a more organized system of health-care planning as well as financing. In this paradigm, the government envisioned a strong role for government funding of the health-care system toward some form of national health insurance, which began with the transformative legislation of Medicaid and Medicare. Funding expanded exponentially in the 1960s and 1970s for HMOs; for neighborhood, migrant, Indian, rural, and urban health centers; and for health planning. However, cutbacks to government participation began during the Reagan years, and 20-plus years later, this country has moved to a model of corporate control over health care, with a number of major industrial and financial corporations, including insurance companies, controlling much of the reimbursement and priorities for health care. Medicaid and Medicare remain as the foundation of federal health-care dollars, but there are constant proposals to limit and restrict access and to increase the consumer share of payment, some of which have been successful.

Years ago, the Ehrenreichs introduced the concept of the medical–industrial complex in their seminal book, *The American Health Empire: Power, Profits, and Politics* (1971), in which they predicted the corporate domination of major medical centers and described the profit-driven function of health care. Today, the medical–industrial complex is bigger and stronger than ever, and it has expanded to include some new corporate players who have tremendous power and control.

The new titans of health care include the medical technology industries that make the increasingly sophisticated diagnostic and treatment equipment. Next, there are the insurance companies, under the rubric of managed care, and the drug companies. In addition to the major medical centers, there are for-profit health-care institutions, such as proprietary nursing homes, profit-making home-care services and specialty clinics, and for-profit hospital chains. Social workers who work in these settings may have especially tough ethical dilemmas to face, as these institutions may place profits over people.

Corporate control of health care has tremendous implications for social workers. Hospitals have downsized, merged, and reorganized extensively in the last 20 years, but this trend was expedited after the failure of President Clinton's major health-care reform initiative in 1994. Up until the mid-1980s, social workers were accepted in the health-care field as valued and integral members of the treatment team. As health-care capitalism—meaning for-profit health care—became the dominant force driving services, the hospitals began to reorganize health care in order to cut costs. In this new paradigm of corporate control, social work began to be viewed as a nonessential expense (along with other services), and a diminished role for social workers in many hospitals ensued. While many social work depart-ments were reorganized and others were merged with other functions, there is still a large cohort of valued and competent social work leaders coping and even thriv-ing in this new environment (Mizrahi & Berger, 2001). They are holding on, but for sure, they are doing more with less.

Yet there has been another paradigm pushing back and creating its own momentum. The patients' rights and consumer-health movements, and a variety of health, mental health, and disability advocacy organizations, have emerged since the 1970s. Those afflicted with disabilities—mental and physical chal-lenges—have become players in the system, using a variety of social-action and negotiation tactics to make their cases visible to the public and to policy makers. These organizations have provided patients with empowerment tools, albeit diffi-cult to enforce at times. And since the beginning, social workers have supported and promoted these rights at the micro and macro levels, including the right to a range of services and benefits. While there is still no universal right to health care in the United States, every state has consumer rights and protection laws and enforcement agencies.

How has managed care led to a fundamental shift in the social worker's role?
Managed care is a neutral concept. It is neither inherently good nor evil. Managed care is simply a model for structuring health-care financing. It is a financing model in which a predetermined dollar amount is negotiated up front and paid to the health-care provider. It is juxtaposed with the traditional "fee-for-service," "pay-as-you-go" ("retrospective") model of financing. In the managed-care model, the provider must typically be pre-authorized by a managed-care organization (MCO) to provide a treatment that will be reimbursed according to a formula. If the ser-vices cost more than the predetermined fee, then either the provider or the patient must absorb the difference in cost.

At first, managed care seemed like an attractive policy to everybody. Managed care was seen as cost effective and good for patient care because it would emphasize preventive health and early intervention; it would decrease referrals for unneces-sary and expensive medical tests and procedures; and it would hold providers more accountable. Outpatient and inpatient services would be integrated, and commu-nity-based care would improve. Many health-care policy advocacy groups, includ-ing NASW, originally supported managed care (known in the 1970s and 1980s as "prospective payment systems") because it was believed to be a better model that would contain costs and improve access to and coordination of care. However, the evolution of managed-care practice under the domination of for-profit companies has been to pay for as little as possible and to challenge physicians' (and other pro-viders') decision making. This often led to inadequate patient care and neglect and to lower reimbursement for clinical practitioners. The consequences of managed care have been particularly damaging to the most vulnerable members of soci-ety, i.e., the disabled, the elderly, children, and low-income and minority groups, who often need more complex and expensive health-care services. Social worker services, seen as an unnecessary expense by many managed-care companies, are restricted, underfunded, and scrutinized.

How do trends in health care affect social workers at the workplace?
Cost-cutting efforts impelled hospitals to form mergers, to develop integrated networks, and even to close their doors. Social workers, like other health-care workers, have lost a great deal of autonomy in this era of "deprofessionalization," privatization, and cutbacks. Social workers have to be much more sophisticated, more competent, and more strategic because the day-to-day structure in the hospitals offers less support and decreased opportunity for professional development. There is no doubt, however, that many social workers feel devalued and threatened in this environment, even though many studies (including my own research) show that, at the professional level, they are appreciated and respected. Physicians who have patients in hospitals or who treat vulnerable or medically marginalized patients in neighborhood health centers will speak to the importance of social workers on the treatment team.

The challenge in this world of corporate control and government cynicism is that nobody wants to pay for psychosocial services anymore, even when they have been demonstrated to be effective. When the government provides a budget to run a neighborhood health center, the center can, in principle, spend the money however it wants. However, even though they may have a high regard for social workers, they may decide that they can no longer afford a licensed and qualified social worker if they need more frontline nurses and technical personnel. Consequently, they may hire nonprofessionals or reassign social work functions to another health-care discipline, like a nurse or a physician assistant who can do double duty.

In the national studies that I conducted about social work leadership, the competition between nurses and social workers was often a result of hospital restructuring and divide-and-conquer strategies. Nurses are expected to do the work of a nurse and to take over social work functions, such as discharge planning and case management. In some hospitals, social work departments are run by nursing directors, and social work functions are subsumed under the larger authority of nursing.

Social workers and their allies are going to have to convince administrators and providers that social workers add value by lowering costs through better preventive care and by increasing consumer satisfaction (Mizrahi & Rizzo, 2008).

What skills do you think enable social workers to be successful in health care today?
In the 1990s, my colleague Julie Abramson and I conducted a national study that examined the relationship between social workers and physicians in hospital settings (Abramson & Mizrahi, 1996; Mizrahi & Abramson, 2001). Specifically, we looked at how social workers and physicians collaborate in decision making. At that time, physicians still retained significant autonomy and authority over patient care as compared with today. Our study examined the social worker–physician collaborative relationship in order to understand how to increase the social worker's ability to influence health-care delivery. We identified three models of social worker–physician collaboration: traditional, transitional, and transformational. We found that the transformational social worker–physician collaborative model, characterized by a collegial and egalitarian approach to decision making, recognized that

the social worker is an extremely valuable member of the treatment team. These doctors acknowledged the essential role that social workers play in addressing the stress factors associated with disease, in expanding patient access to health care, and in improving patients' ability to follow a treatment plan.

Social workers need to urge physicians and professional organizations at the institutional and policy levels to advocate for social work services inside and outside their settings. All of my studies suggest that the most successful social workers are proactive, positive, and confident, but they need additional skills, strategies, and support. Social workers must develop in three key areas: *compassion, commitment, and competence, and they need the support of the professional social work organizations.* The best social workers value themselves and convey this respect to others. They must demonstrate the efficacy of social work through effective qualitative and quantitative research, and they must also organize consumers and patients who have been helped by social workers to speak out in their own collective self-interest. Social workers must bridge the case–class divide, simultaneously focusing on the uniqueness of each individual and the collective good of the American society.

DID YOU KNOW?

- Medical social work is one of the oldest and most established fields of social work practice.
- Social work in health care is expected to grow by 24%, which is much faster than the average for all occupations (http://www.bls.gov/oco/oco20016.htm).
- Social work in health care is one of the largest fields of practice, with an estimated 124,000 medical and public-health social workers nationwide.

Source: Bureau of Labor Statistics.

SECTION THREE: FIRST-PERSON NARRATIVE

Sickle Cell Disease: The Family, Community, and Hospital Connection
Elise Rackmill, LCSW

Elise Rackmill, LCSW, is a senior social worker at St. Luke's/Roosevelt School-Based Health Clinics. She graduated from New York University and the Hunter College School of Social Work. For the past 32 years, she has worked in the field of hospital-based social work, primarily with African-American and Latino children, adolescents, and families. Throughout her career, she has been an active union delegate, initially in District Council 37 of AFSCME (American Federation of State, County, and Municipal Workers), and for the past 20 years in 1199 SEIU (Service Employees International Union) United Health Care Workers East. Currently, she is the cochair of the joint 1199/NASW Task Force on the Future of Social Work in Health Care.

For the past 30 years, I have been employed as a hospital social worker in a large New York City medical center. I began as a social work assistant at the BSW level, and then I worked as an MSW social worker, and currently I am a senior social worker (licensed clinical social worker) with supervisory responsibilities. In each of these positions, I have been a proud union member, serving as an elected union official and trade union activist.

Medical social work provides a unique set of challenges. We are "guests" in a host agency whose mission is to provide health care. Each day we interact with a multitude of hospital staff whose training, orientation to the patient, and goals may be very different from ours. Since they are "medical people," they may try to impose their views and decisions on us. Therefore, we must consistently define and redefine our unique expertise and role, not only to our patients and their families, but also to hospital administrators and our non–social work colleagues. If you ask people both inside and outside of health care what a nurse, pharmacist, or physical therapist does, you will get relatively similar responses. However, when you pose the same question about a social worker's role in health care, the answers will be all over the map. We are confused with the Medicaid expediter, child welfare worker, public assistance and food stamp caseworker, and hospital volunteer, to name only a few. Therefore, some of the vital qualities required in medical social work are patience, flexibility, a sense of humor, good interpersonal skills, and most importantly the willingness to constantly articulate who we are (our training and skills), how we fit into the health-care system, and how we can assist the patients and families that we meet.

While health care has changed dramatically since I entered the field, I still believe that we possess a unique role that cannot be performed by other disciplines. Our ability to see the patients in their totality enables us to assist them in understanding and adjusting to their diagnosis, cope with changing realities, plan for their future, and maximize their human potential.

While the hospital setting offers a broad range of practice areas, my career has been working with children and families. For 18 years, I was the pediatric social worker in a comprehensive sickle cell program, working as part of a multidisciplinary team. This is a specialty care area treating children and families impacted by sickle cell disease, an inherited blood disorder characterized by a predominance of hemoglobin S. The traditional belief about sickle cell disease is that it is solely found in people of African descent. However, the origins of sickle hemoglobin can be traced to countries where malaria was common and to the countries where those survivors migrated.

Today, sickle cell can be found in people of African, Arabian, Iranian, Southern Italian, Indian, Turkish, Greek, and Latino ancestry. In New York City, the largest group of patients is of African and Latino descent. Many are recent immigrants to New York City, unaware of their genetic ability to pass this disease on to their children. For an immigrant already combating poverty, discrimination, and the adjustment to a new country with few supports, a diagnosis of sickle cell disease can be overwhelming.

The principle manifestations of the disease are lifelong anemia, episodic and unpredictable bouts with severe pain, and variable degrees of organ damage produced by the blockage of blood flow. The course of the disease varies from one individual to another. Some may be very ill, while others may lead a relatively normal life and experience only episodic symptoms. There are no markers to indicate how this disease will affect an individual, and it may even change over the course of one's life.

As the social worker in this program, my duties were varied and were a departure from traditional social work. I helped families educate themselves about their children's condition and obtain appropriate resources. I also provided supportive counseling and developed unique relationships with our clients, who became "our families."

The daily living conditions of a family coping with a child's chronic illness are critical. Substandard housing, uninsured or underinsured patients, and the lack of child care and appropriate school programs heightened the stress level for many of our families. As the social worker in this program, I utilized my advocacy skills, and I believe that my ability to satisfy their concrete needs made families more receptive to individual counseling and family groups.

While some families had their own support networks of relatives, friends, and their fellow church members, others were in a new country, coping alone with this disease. Some felt judged by their families and couldn't openly ask for assistance. Couples often became estranged and even separated over this additional stressor in their family life. My role as the social worker was to provide ongoing support and create programs that fostered parents helping parents and patients helping patients. I ran groups for parents and teens, developed a summer camp program, and organized parties and outings.

As pain is one of the principal manifestations of the disease, I worked closely with the physicians to help patients manage the emotional and psychological distress that can exacerbate their physical symptoms. People with chronic pain experience higher levels of depression and feelings of anger, frustration, and hopelessness. Social work interventions were key to help our patients and families overcome their negative thoughts and to develop positive coping skills and behavioral changes.

The comprehensive sickle cell program provided well-child care as well as hematological follow-up and care for the complications of the disease. Since 1975, all newborns in New York State are screened for the sickle cell trait and disease prior to being discharged home from the nursery. Whenever an infant was found to test positive for the disease, I was the person contacted by the New York State Health Department, and I in turn contacted the family. I was the first person who told them that their newborn infant had tested presumptive positive for a serious chronic illness. In some cases, parents were aware that they were at risk either through prenatal genetic testing or counseling or through prior family experiences. In other cases, the parents had never heard of the disease and couldn't even imagine why we were calling them. This was probably the most difficult part of my job. I often found myself assisting the mother in telling the father and other family members that the child had a genetic disease and that they needed to be screened to find out whether or not they also carried the gene.

One case that comes to mind is a 38-year-old Central American woman of Garifuna heritage (part of the African diaspora that arrived in Central America more than 200 years ago) who had just given birth to her third child. When I, as gently as possible, informed her of the test results and the need for a repeat test to confirm the diagnosis of sickle cell anemia, she became angry. She stated that she didn't believe what I was saying, had never heard of the disease, knew that her newborn was healthy, and wondered why I was trying to bring bad luck to her baby. Before I could say anything, she hung up. As public-health law demands, a repeat test to confirm the diagnosis is required, and because early medical care is critical to decreasing morbidity and mortality, I called her back. This time, rather than discussing the disease itself, I inquired into her other children, her pregnancy, and her prior experiences with the health-care system both in New York City and in her country of origin. While somewhat guarded, she did eventually become engaged in our conversation. She had never spoken with a genetic counselor and expressed the belief that the "Yankee health-care system invents diseases." She spoke of having relatives back home in the medical profession, and she expressed her belief that if sickle cell disease existed in their family, she would have known. While not promising to come for a repeat test, she did agree to speak with me again. I called her weekly for the next 3 weeks and reached out to her daughter's assigned physician in the pediatric clinic. When she came to the hospital for her 6-week postpartum checkup, I met her in the clinic. This was our first face-to-face meeting. By now, I had already spoken to her several times, and I had sent her literature about the disease in Spanish. She actually welcomed my presence in the clinic waiting room, but was still skeptical of allowing us to draw her daughter's blood for a retest. Prior to her daughter's 2-month well-baby checkup, I networked with her pediatric provider to enlist her cooperation. At this time, the mother let the nurse draw another blood specimen. When I had to call the mother with the second positive result, I really couldn't anticipate her reaction. First she yelled at me, and then she cursed me out and hung up the phone. But 20 minutes later, she called up crying and wanting to know what it meant for her daughter's future.

We immediately arranged an evening family meeting when she and her daughter's father could meet with me and the medical team. After we tested each parent and found them to be carriers of the sickle cell trait, they stopped struggling against the diagnosis and wanted to understand what it meant. Their initial denial quickly turned to anger. Most important, they wanted to know how this disease would affect their hopes and aspirations for their beautiful baby daughter. Understanding their own roles in their daughter's illness made them feel ashamed and fearful of telling others, lest they would be "blamed" as they were already blaming themselves. They refused to tell their local relatives about the diagnosis, nor did they share their pain with their families in their country of origin, even avoiding the customary weekly phone calls.

While initially resistant, they did eventually join our "Spanish-speaking new parents group." The power of peer support, even from strangers, began to help them to express their fears and sense of disappointment, and to seek support from others in the same situation. Nevertheless, they still didn't feel prepared to expose their pain to family. They cancelled their yearly vacation to go back home, ostensibly because it wouldn't be safe to take their daughter there.

When their daughter had her first serious sickle cell crisis and was hospitalized, I spent hours with the family, initially in the emergency room and later in the inpatient pediatric unit. I provided them with emotional support and prepared them for the treatment their daughter would need. More than anything, this admission forced them to confront the reality of the diagnosis and figure out how to move ahead. Needing help with their other young children at home, they finally told their relatives in New York City. They were pleasantly surprised by the unconditional support that they received.

Probably the biggest reward for social workers in specialty areas is the ability to develop long-term relationships with their clients. This in turn affords social workers the opportunity to see the fruits of their labors. We can fast-forward the story, and today our infant girl is a 15-year-old high school sophomore. While having had multiple hospitalizations and some serious complications of the disease, she is also a great dancer, has attended a sleep-away camp, has many friends, and has celebrated her *quinceañera* (a huge party signifying a young Latina's entry into young womanhood). The family has visited their home country many times, and they eventually told the extended family about the disease. Interestingly, they have also uncovered two relatives with the disease and have brought them medications and up-to-date literature for their physicians. The mother has also extended herself to counsel other parents when they first learn about the disease.

One of my key roles was program development. When working with children with sickle cell disease, we tried to recognize our treatment environment as being broader than conventional health-care facilities. We created positive social programs outside of the medical setting. This allowed our young patients to see themselves as more than their disease. Perhaps the most successful and enjoyable program was the annual sickle cell camp session. Our camp efforts were coordinated by social workers from various hospitals that treated sickle cell patients.

Each year it was a challenge to recruit our campers. The social workers had to convince parents to allow their chronically ill and often extremely overprotected children to go with us, hours from the city, and to a place that they had never seen. In the first few years, it was extremely difficult to recruit campers. But each year our task became a little easier, and our happy returnees and their overjoyed parents became our willing assistants.

Meeting with families both individually and in groups, our staff emphasized how much this experience would foster independence, increase their child's knowledge about the disease and its management, provide friendship and peer support, and give the campers the time of their lives in a medically supervised setting. For some parents, "going to live with strangers" was outside of their cultural experience. While validating their beliefs and values, we utilized a massive education campaign to open them up to this new idea. In a few cases, parents drove behind the camp bus to see the place with their own eyes. With some families, it took a few years for them to agree. A few never relented, but most of our patients eventually participated.

During these weeklong sessions, we lived with our patients and learned things about them that would be impossible to find out in a medical setting. We ate together, swam, danced, hiked, and told ghost stories, and we comforted our patients when they were sick and in pain. We were able to watch their interactions and learn more about them as individuals. Living together helped to establish a rare level of trust that was a critical foundation for successful psychosocial treatment. The types of relationships forged in this experience allowed campers to depend on one another in times of crisis, not just at camp but throughout the year. I was able to incorporate the beautiful and tranquil setting of camp into relaxation exercises and visualization techniques when patients were undergoing painful episodes or procedures. While at camp, hopelessness and "why me" attitudes were rarely manifested; instead, they were replaced by optimism and profound respect for the staff that chose to come to camp to work with "sick kids." Just as in other summer camps, relationships were formed that have endured for many years.

Those first campers are now adult sickle cell patients. Some worked and volunteered at camp while in college. For those whose disease took a more severe course and are disabled, a big smile breaks out on their faces when they either reminisce or see young patients heading off to camp. To quote one 35-year-old adult patient who has been very sick, "It was the best time of my life, and I'll never forget those people."

I could go on forever about the role that medical social workers can play in the lives of sick children and their families. The potential for creativity and program planning is limitless. These activities can only enhance the provision of concrete services, health education, supportive one-to-one counseling, and group services that are the cornerstone of our efforts. My close relationship with these families has afforded me the opportunity to witness their courage, strength, and ability to confront difficult challenges. It has reinforced for me the tremendous worth of professional social work and reaffirmed my career choice.

IS SOCIAL WORK IN HEALTH CARE THE RIGHT FIELD FOR YOU?

- Elise identifies a number of qualities essential to being successful in this field, such as a good sense of humor, flexibility, and the ability to articulate the social worker role.
- Elise observes that medical social workers are "guests" in a host setting and must adapt to an organizational culture that can have significant differences with the social orientation.
- Working in community-based health settings may afford the social worker the opportunity to develop long-term relationships with clients, which can be very rewarding.

SECTION FOUR: RESOURCES TO LEARN MORE

Web Sites
- American Hospital Association: http://www.hospitalconnect.com
- American Public Health Association: http://www.apha.org
- The Case Management Society of America: http://www.cmsa.org
- Center for Disease Control: http://www.cdc.gov
- Gay Men's Health Crisis: http://www.gmhc.org
- Origins of Cerebral Palsy: http://www.originsofcerebralpalsy.com
- Johns Hopkins HIV Guide: http://www.hopkins-aids.edu
- U.S. Department of Health & Human Services: http://www. os.dhhs.gov

Journals
- *Health & Social Work*, NASW Press
- *Social Work in Health Care*, Taylor & Francis

Books
- *The Changing Face of Health Care Social Work: Professional Practice in Managed Behavioral Health Care*, 2nd ed., by Sophia F. Dziegielewski (2004, Springer)
- *Handbook of Health Social Work*, by Sarah Gehlert and Teri Arthur Browne (2006, Wiley)

Policy
- Adolescent Health. In *Social Work Speaks*, 7th ed. NASW Policy Statements, 2006–2009
- HIV and AIDS. In *Social Work Speaks*, 7th ed. NASW Policy Statements, 2006–2009
- Managed Care. In *Social Work Speaks*, 7th ed. NASW Policy Statements, 2006–2009

Practice
- Health and Wellness: http://www.helpstartshere.org
- Social Work in Health Care: http://www.naswnyc.org

Standards
- NASW Standards for Social Work Practice in Health-Care Settings

Credentials
- Certified Social Worker in Health Care (C-SWHC), NASW credential
- Certified Social Work Case Manager (C-SWCM), NASW credential

Professional Associations
- American Association of Spinal Cord Injury Psychologists and Social Workers: http://www.aascipsw.org

- American Case Management Association: http://www.acmaweb.org
- Association of Oncology Social Work: http://www.aosw.org
- The Society for Social Work Leadership in Health Care: http://www.sswlhc.org

Educational Programs/Centers
- American Public Health Association, Social Work Section, School of Social Work, Iowa City, IA
- University of Southern California, Nurse Social Work Practitioner

7

Social Work With Housing and Homelessness

SECTION ONE: FIELD OVERVIEW AND FORECAST

Scope of Services

Homelessness is an extremely complicated social problem. Social workers are at the forefront of attempts to eliminate homelessness, both as direct service providers and as advocates. Yet there is a significant debate about the best way to address homelessness. Efforts to prevent and reduce homelessness require clarification about why people become homeless, how long people remain homeless, and what factors are associated with being at risk for homelessness.

Generally, two major frameworks for estimating the scope of homelessness are utilized. The first, known as a point-in-time count, provides an estimate of how many people are homeless at any given point in time. According to the National Law Center on Homelessness and Poverty (2007), approximately 3.5 million people, 1.35 million of them children, experience homelessness in any given year. The second framework for counting homeless people, known as a period-prevalence count, focuses on the number of people who are chronically homeless over a prolonged period of time. The chronically homeless often suffer from serious comorbid conditions such as mental illness, addiction, and poverty (National Coalition for the Homeless, 2007).

The convergence of two major social problems—poverty and the prohibitively high cost of housing—are closely associated with homelessness. Poverty rates in the United States are calculated according to a formula that utilizes data provided by the Census Bureau. According to the National Poverty Center (2006), 12.7% of the U.S. population was defined as living in poverty in 2004. Children are disproportionately represented among the ranks of the poor, comprising 35% of the poor population. Poverty rates for Blacks and Hispanics are more than double than the rates for Whites.

While being poor certainly increases the statistical likelihood of homelessness, the current housing crisis in the United States and the lack of affordable housing have been identified as further contributing to the problem of homelessness. "From Foreclosures to Homelessness," a report released by the National Coalition for the Homeless (2008), examined the impact of the current housing crisis on homelessness. Findings indicate that the nearly 2 million foreclosures reported in 2007 have led thousands of former homeowners and families to spiral downward from sleeping on a relative's or friend's couch, to using local emergency shelters, to living on the streets (Erlenbusch, O'Connor, Downing, & Phillips, 2008).

According to the National Alliance to End Homelessness (2008), 23%–40% of homeless adults are veterans who have served in various wars, including World War II and the Vietnam War. Returning veterans from the wars in Afghanistan and Iraq are among the nation's fastest growing group of homeless adults. Disabling conditions such as posttraumatic stress disorder (PTSD), traumatic brain injury, substance abuse, and the difficulty of reintegrating into family life after serving multiple tours of duty are factors that contribute to veterans being at high risk for homelessness. Approximately 20%–25% of homeless single adults are seriously mentally ill. The homeless mentally ill tend to be isolated, without support from friends or family. Large-scale deinstitutionalization of persons with serious mental illness began in the 1960s, and this policy is widely considered to have led to a substantial increase in homelessness (Rosenberg & Rosenberg, 2006).

Settings

As this brief review illustrates, homelessness is caused by multiple and complex factors. Accordingly, social work clients who are homeless will vary tremendously in their needs and will be encountered in an array of social work settings. School social workers are likely to work with children who are living in a family shelter; medical social workers are likely to encounter homeless clients in hospital settings. Other settings in which social workers provide direct services to the homeless include shelters, soup kitchens, community-based organizations, supportive housing programs, substance abuse programs, psychiatric settings, and on the streets. Social workers also work to address homelessness at the macro level, and may work as policy makers, researchers, and advocates.

Two distinct paradigms for addressing homelessness have emerged as dominant in informing homeless services. One major approach is the Supportive Services Model, which is based on the provision of supportive housing programs and services that seek to help homeless people transition to independent living. The underlying concept informing the Supportive Services Model is that the homeless need assistance in building independent living skills, such as vocational and life skills. A wide range of services are targeted to help homeless people strengthen their skills and achieve independent living. Supportive housing and services are most appropriate for people who struggle with homelessness primarily as a consequence of a disabling condition, such as mental illness or addiction. Supportive housing services utilize a wraparound treatment approach in that they provide comprehensive supportive services.

A second major paradigm to address homelessness is the Housing First Model. The Housing First Model suggests that the major barrier to housing stability, particularly for families, is the lack of affordable housing. The Housing First Model points to the multiple and often insurmountable difficulties faced by people in poverty who are seeking housing: a bad credit history, an inability to provide landlords with references, and no money for security deposits or utilities. The most serious obstacle of all to permanent housing is the extremely limited supply of affordable rentals. The Housing First Model is distinct from the Supportive Services Model because the underlying assumption is that the major cause of homelessness is poverty, as opposed to dysfunction and impaired independent living skills. Accordingly, the Housing First Model seeks to place homeless people in permanent housing as soon as possible. Supportive services, as needed, are provided subsequently (Beyond Shelter, n.d.)

The Social Worker's Role

While multiple factors leading to homelessness have been identified, and proposed solutions have been derived from different models, the overall goal is to achieve permanent housing. In working toward this goal, social workers engage in prevention and aftercare, and advocacy to pursue progressive housing policies (Soska, 2008).

Preventive strategies target those at risk for homeless, and aftercare strategies are targeted toward transitioning people to independent living. Core generalist social work skills such as engagement, assessment, and case management are appropriate.

Working with the homeless can led to ethical dilemmas for social workers, particularly those that provide services to the street homeless and to homeless people with mental illness. The homeless mentally ill are often difficult to engage and suspicious of treatment professionals. They often refuse services and shelter. In a number of highly publicized cases, outreach workers involuntarily hospitalized homeless street people (Cohen & Marcos, 1990). At the heart of this dilemma is whether or not the homeless person's right to self-determination is violated when he or she is involuntarily removed from the streets.

Credentialing

No advanced credentials are necessary for social workers seeking to work with the homeless. Social workers who are interested in working at the macro level and getting involved with policy development will need excellent research and writing skills.

Emerging Issues and Employment Trends

There are numerous social trends that suggest that homelessness is likely to increase in the near future. The three main factors that can be readily identified are: (a) the the weak economy, (b) the housing crisis and an unprecedented number of foreclosures coupled with a very limited supply of low-cost rentals, and (c) the ongoing return of the 1.6 million veterans who have served in and survived the Iraq and Afghanistan wars. The convergence of these three factors is likely to lead to increases in the homeless population. Unfortunately, an increase in the homeless population does not automatically lead to an increase in homeless services. Therefore, while social workers will clearly be needed to work with the homeless, there may be reductions in services and social work employment in this area.

Services to the homeless are vulnerable to budget cuts, and as the economy weakens, homeless services are an area that may be hit harder than other social service areas. Homeless people, as a group, are highly stigmatized in today's society. They are often dirty and unkempt, and people don't like to see them or are afraid of them. Most homeless people have limited ability to influence public policy directly (an address is often necessary for voter registration), making them less of a priority to elected officials. For all these reasons, when politicians have to make hard choices about budget cuts, homeless services are among the most vulnerable. In order to safeguard and promote social work services to this population, it will be important that social workers continue to position themselves at the forefront of program and policy development.

ACTIVITIES TO LEARN MORE

- Read the NASW policy statement on homelessness in *Social Work Speaks*, 7th ed., NASW Policy Statements, 2006–2009.
- Find out what city or state agency is responsible for providing services for homeless people in your community and contact them. Explore what employment opportunities exist for social workers.
- Volunteer at a local food bank or shelter.

SECTION TWO: CRITICAL ISSUES
Madeleine Stoner, PhD, MSS
1938–2008

Dr. Madeleine Stoner earned her PhD and MSS from Bryn Mawr College and her BA from Sarah Lawrence College. She was the Richard M. and Ann L. Thor Professor in Urban Social Development at the University of Southern California. Dr. Stoner has published extensively about the homeless. Her first book was *Inventing a Non-Homeless Future: A Policy Agenda for Preventing Homelessness*, which was nominated for the Park Award of the American Sociological Association. Dr. Stoner's second book was *The Civil Rights of Homeless People*. Dr. Stoner provided expert testimony to the legislature about housing and homelessness, and she worked with government and community-based agencies on many initiatives to end homelessness. A long time advocate for the homeless, Dr. Stoner died July 13, 2008.

Please tell me a little about yourself and your path in social work. What are some of the factors that motivated you to become a social worker? What drew you to health care as an area of focus? Was it a particular issue or concern?

My involvement with homelessness wasn't planned, but rather evolved by chance. After I got my MSW, I was working for the Urban League in Philadelphia. My office happened to be around the corner from a Greyhound bus terminal. In those days, there was large-scale deinstitutionalization of the mentally ill. People were being discharged from psychiatric hospitals with no place to live, and with little more than a bus ticket. They would leave the bus terminal and, by happenstance, come into my office looking for help. These were mostly middle-aged women with a psychiatric disability. I tried to find them places to live and quickly found out there was nowhere for them to go. Sometimes I brought them home to stay with me for a few nights.

Around this time, I was contacted by a CBS news anchor who was interested in doing an investigative exposé on substandard housing programs for the mentally ill. In those days, a number of proprietary landlords contracted with the state to provide for-profit housing for people with serious mental illness. The reporter and I began to investigate these homes, which were terribly run-down places. We obtained a map of their locations from the state Office of Social Services. Some of these homes were in prominent Philadelphia neighborhoods with tree-lined streets and lovely brownstone row houses. After some undercover work, we eventually gained entry into one of these houses. I posed as a nurse, and the reporter had a hidden camera. Once inside, we found dreadful living conditions; the residents were terribly overmedicated, many of them lying on the floor in a drug-induced stupor. The house was filthy, and the food that we saw was old and rotten. We immediately filed a class-action lawsuit, which resulted in a grand jury investigation and a civil suit. Many of these landlords were fined, and the homes were shut down. Ultimately, most of these residents were put on the streets with nowhere to go; they were homeless once again. At that point, I realized how complicated housing and homelessness is, and that there are no easy solutions. This started my life's work as an advocate and researcher on homelessness.

Who are the homeless today in America?

The National Alliance to End Homeless (NAEH) is an excellent resource for information about homelessness. According to the NAEH, the fastest growing group of homeless people in the United States comprises families with children, with estimates of approximately 600,000 families and 1.35 million children who are homeless. Some of the factors contributing to family homelessness are domestic violence, low-wage jobs, lack of affordable housing, and welfare reform (www. beyondshelter.org).

Although homelessness is generally conceptualized as an urban problem, 9% of homelessness occurs in rural localities. Involvement in the criminal justice system is strongly correlated with risk for homelessness, and more than 10% of those released from prison are homeless. The U.S. Department of Veterans Affairs estimates that, at present, as many as 200,000 homeless people are veterans, and that 336,627 veterans experience homelessness in any given year. As troops return from Afghanistan and Iraq, the ranks of the homeless are expected to increase (www.naeh.org).

Why are there so many homeless people in this country?
Widespread homelessness emerged in the United States in the 1980s. A major factor contributing to the rise of homelessness was the Omnibus Budget Reconciliation Act (OBRA) of 1981. The OBRA, passed by the Reagan administration, radically cut back federal spending for social programs. This sweeping piece of legislation began an era of withdrawal from the welfare state, with deep cuts to public housing, school lunch programs, food stamps, and Aid to Families with Dependent Children (AFDC). In the first year following OBRA, we began to see large-scale homelessness emerge. While homelessness is clearly correlated with mental illness and drug and alcohol abuse, it is first and foremost a consequence of poverty. The retrenchment of social programs for the poor, which began under Ronald Reagan and persists to this day, is directly related to homelessness.

There is an extremely limited supply of low-income housing. Salaries are too low to pay rent, and many people who work full time simply cannot afford a place to live.

There is a lot of discussion about the need for "affordable housing," but the real problem is the lack of low-income housing. Affordable housing is generally calculated by a formula utilized by the U.S. Department of Housing and Urban Development (HUD) that links the cost of housing to the area median income. This formulation does not address the huge gap between wages and the median rental market. There used to be a larger supply of low-income housing so that people living on society's margins—the mentally ill, veterans and other trauma survivors, and the poor—could find housing, but that has dried up.

Developers are building lofts in Skid Row in L.A. County, where homeless people are living side by side with middle-income tenants. There is a building that was converted from a single-room-occupancy hotel into luxury condos, with the top two floors renovated into penthouse apartments and the lower floors utilized to provide shelter for the homeless. This building is polarized between the haves and the have-nots, with the rich entering through the front door and the poor coming through a metal door in the back of the building. As you can imagine, tensions between the residents is potent.

Looking forward to the next 5 or 10 years, do you think it's likely that homelessness will be reduced or increased, and why?
Many homeless advocates are predicting an increase in homelessness in the next few years. We are facing a perfect storm of a weak economy coupled with the lack of available low-income housing. Added to this mix is the large number of veterans returning from Iraq and Afghanistan, who are at high risk for homelessness. The social and economic conditions contributing to homelessness have not gotten better in the recent past, and they are not likely to improve in the near future. Mental illness and addictions are very important factors leading to homelessness, but even if we provide programs and housing for all the mentally ill and addicted homeless

people, there would still be a sizable homeless population because of economic factors. The predictors for the economy are dire, and it is a worrisome picture.

What kinds of pathways are needed to help people move from shelter living to independent living?
I was part of the initial movement to develop services for homeless people, realizing early that a shelter service system for homeless people that provides them with "two hots and a cot" is insufficient. We need prevention and intervention, and we need adequate welfare provisions if we want to end homelessness. The Housing First Model is a new and promising approach to ending homelessness. This model seeks to place families and individuals into housing as soon as possible and then to provide services. In the old model, we focused on emergency shelter services and provided intensive services to get people housing-ready, a process that took far too long. Research on the Housing First Model suggests that permanent housing builds self-esteem and helps people to develop the skills and ability to be independent. We get them into housing first, and then wrap services around them (www.beyondshelter.org).

What kinds of programs are important if society is to end homelessness?
The National Alliance to End Homelessness has proposed a 10-year plan to end homelessness. At the heart of this proposal is the belief that ending homelessness is possible with adequate planning and commitment. There are four key components of the 10-year plan (www.neah.org):
1. Investment in prevention services for people at risk for homelessness
2. Helping homeless people get into permanent housing quickly, using the Housing First Model
3. Engaging in planning and outcomes evaluation
4. Building an infrastructure of affordable housing

Supportive services for the homeless need to be individually tailored. A wide range of services may be indicated, depending on the assessment of the psychosocial needs of the client. These services often include case management, domestic violence programming, and educational support for children as well as health care services, including mental-health and substance-abuse treatment.

Housing vouchers are absolutely essential to end homelessness. Section 8 vouchers have been restricted, and there is often a long waiting period to get them. The crisis in the housing market and the increase in foreclosures have had the unintended consequence that fewer landlords are available for Section 8 programs. We have to examine welfare reform outcome data, because many poor people earn a paycheck so low that they cannot find housing.

What kinds of social policies have been enacted that have helped to decrease homelessness?
The McKinney-Vento Act, signed into law in 2000 by President Bill Clinton, is the first and only federal legislation to address homelessness. The McKinney-Vento Act authorizes a wide range of services to assist homeless people, with programs to provide emergency shelter, transitional housing, job training, and primary health care.

Considered to be landmark legislation, the McKinney-Vento Act was designed to be an essential first step in establishing a national agenda to end homelessness. While it is widely credited for helping hundreds of thousands of people, its primary focus is on emergency rather than preventive measures, and it does not address the underlying causes of homelessness (www.nationalhomeless.org).

How can social work education prepare students to work with the homeless?
Homelessness is the face of poverty. Helping eradicate poverty is core to our mission, yet few students have an interest in working in homeless services. There is a big disconnect between the values of the profession and the career goals and aspirations of new social workers. Nevertheless, homelessness is a problem that cuts across service delivery areas, and social workers will encounter these clients no matter where they are working. Therefore, it is essential that social work education incorporates the issues of homelessness into the curriculum, thereby providing students with some training in this area.

DID YOU KNOW?

- Each year, some 650,000 people leave state and federal prisons. One in five of them is homeless and is at high risk for returning to prison.
- An estimated 150,000–200,000 people are chronically homeless.
- Approximately one fourth of homeless people are veterans.

Source: National Alliance to End Homelessness.

SECTION THREE: FIRST-PERSON NARRATIVE

Homeless for Three Decades: Leroy Found a Home
Jenny Ross, LCSW

Jenny Ross, LCSW, was the director of Project HELP (Homeless Emergency Liaison Project) and worked extensively with the homeless mentally ill over a period of 13 years. Project HELP was an initiative of Mayor Ed Koch, a program serving the homeless mentally ill on the streets of New York City from 1987 to 2005.

Ms. Ross holds a master's degree in social work from New York University and is a graduate of NIP's four-year psychoanalytic training program (National Institute for the Psychotherapies, Inc.). She maintains a private practice in Manhattan. She is currently on the faculty of the Focusing Oriented Relational Psychotherapy Program, based both in New York City and Cape Town, South Africa.

Working with the persistently homeless mentally ill in New York City is simply one of the best social work jobs to have if—you like the city, like to talk to strangers, and want to be actively involved with the community of services, including other outreach programs and the police. I've always thought that it is the perfect job! It all happens on the streets of New York, amidst the hustle and bustle of people on the move: well-dressed business people scurrying down the block, people eating lunch on park benches or chatting with coworkers, and construction workers watching passersby. And, of course, there are homeless people sitting side by side with New Yorkers, writing furiously in notebooks or talking to themselves, organizing their bags and belongings, taking time to look up and talk with outreach workers.

Project HELP's mission is to assess homeless mentally ill clients for dangerousness to self or others. We are able to hospitalize someone from the street to a specialized unit at Bellevue Hospital that works with our clients. We see clients over many years, throughout their many transitions from one street corner to another, throughout hospital visits, and from street to shelter (and sometimes from shelter to street).

I have always considered my work with the homeless mentally ill to be clinical work—the cutting edge of clinical work. People who live at the outer boundaries of human existence cannot be reached without a special effort and a deep clinical knowing. What do we say to these people that might inspire them to consider a concrete change? The engagement may start with something as simple as their accepting a lunch, something to eat. More important, how do we talk to them so that it creates a shift somewhere inside?

As an outreach worker, I need to accomplish something in each contact, because I might not see the client again. Each moment with a client becomes a strategic opportunity to engage. There is an insistence on a meaningful interaction. It is a bit like being a Buddha, because I must be present and must engage fully with the force of the moment, but I must also let go of wanting the other person to change. The shifts are sometimes imperceptible, as is true for all of us. Workers who want to see immediate results, to be able to chart and measure a client's progress, will be very frustrated working with the homeless mentally ill.

All engagement must be on their terms; communication must be client centered if you want to truly engage them. They don't have to listen to you, unless you're the police. I would make a note here and commend many of the police officers who work with the homeless. I have observed many who are very skilled at becoming the parent for the client, hopefully the good parent, who tells the client what to do. The homeless mentally ill have a very high incidence of childhood abuse in their backgrounds. As authority figures, social workers who can be caring and firm can provide the client with an emotionally reparative relationship that soothes and gives a new experience of being cared for. Of course, unfortunately, there is also the possibility of abuse by an authority figure, something that is probably familiar in the client's experience, causing the client to become alienated and fearful.

How do you work with someone who is mentally ill and not on medication, who babbles or talks you in circles with your suggestions, or who never completes a thought or sentence? I often see clients who do not respond verbally or who barely make eye contact. They may be sitting in a noisy place, perhaps near a waterfall on the wall of an atrium where a small café is situated, or the nooks and crannies surrounding a viaduct, or even the entrance to the Holland Tunnel. It is a challenge to engage clients when they can't hear you and you can't hear them! But as any good therapist knows, it's all about being there and not giving up. Your predictable presence sustains the client's belief. As one client put it, when asked how Project HELP helped her, "You know that I'm here and you would know if I disappeared."

How can we understand another human being in a way that will forge a deep connection? These homeless mentally ill clients are not on medication, and they often speak in a schizophrenic jargon, repeating nonsensical sentences as if they were carrying on an interactive conversation. Once I was in the Staten Island ferry terminal, and one of our clients, who was schizophrenic and had a speech impediment, was carrying on an intense conversation with a young man, gesturing with his hands and listening as the young man delivered a lengthy reply. It turned out that the young man was a Jehovah's witness, proselytizing.

It is difficult to engage the logic of a client who is paranoid or psychotic. They will argue you into the ground! One homeless woman on the Upper West Side thought that all of the bus shelters were built for the homeless, so she would not move. No one could convince her that this was not the case, although a few outreach workers tried.

I am sure that our persistence is what convinces the mentally ill client that someone is indeed there for them. Out of these repeated contacts, trust is built, and eventually there is a window of opportunity when the client is able to get into the van and go to a medical appointment.

You can rarely engage homeless mentally ill clients in a discussion of the past. However, when you are able to, it can be a poignant moment, full of meaning. The social worker's response may or may not be heard, seemingly not important. Family connections, severed long ago, are rarely discussed. Ask a homeless person if he or she has a family, and mostly there is a vague response or no response. Indeed, the question may send a client back into a schizophrenic reverie. These clients are deeply estranged from their families, who have long ago given up or cut the homeless person out of their lives. For example, I worked with a client downtown at the World Trade Center who eventually was housed and is now applying to law school. She had a daughter with whom she has now reconnected, which helped turn her life around. But she never spoke of her during the years that I worked with her. Certainly, these clients have memories, perhaps in the form of old crumpled newspaper clippings of themselves or family members—papers that they have carried for years in a jacket pocket—and they offer these to you as proof of their past, of their existence in the world, of their personhood.

In the absence of family, they become strongly attached to fire stations, stores, and neighborhoods, becoming part of that New York family who New Yorkers come to rely on seeing on the street corner when they're on their way to the subway. As an outreach worker, I work with this extended family on a regular basis. One man with whom I worked had made a connection to a school teacher who used to walk through the park, and they would nod to each other. One day she said hello; the next day, she asked him how he was; the next week, she stopped and said she was tired; and eventually she learned that they were both from the South. When he was arrested and then transferred to a psychiatric unit, she called us to find out how he was doing. Then he went to stay with his sister in Virginia, which she found out from Project HELP, and this teacher was on a business trip and visited him there. She called us to let us know how he was. I spoke to his social workers in Virginia extensively as well as his sister, who didn't really want her brother living with her after all of these years. Finally one day, the school teacher called me to say that she had seen him on 125th Street. He was back in New York! Everyone went to see him.

Project HELP is able to hospitalize clients who are a danger to self or others. This is the other end of our work. We follow clients through the system, advocating for them to hospital discharge workers or visiting them in jail when they have been arrested for breaking some street law, such as urinating in the street. Through this advocacy, we act as an organizing principle; we are the glue that holds together the disjointed parts of a social service system; and we create a structure for the client by being a constant factor in his or her life.

Project HELP also has the advantage of covering the five boroughs in New York City, which allows us to remain in contact with clients who move about and also form connections across the New York City system with other programs that work with these transient clients. As well, most of the staff are long-term employees, and collectively we know most of the homeless people in the city over the last 20 years. Each staff member is a repository of knowledge about all of the homeless whom we have known over many years. Clients move about, and we will find the same client over and over again, in different parts of the city. And last but not least, we work in teams. We all work with the same clients, communicating constantly from one work shift to the next about our visits with the client, sifting through the nuances with coworkers daily.

The longevity of our staffing is an important point to make. It's the kind of work that forges a lifetime bond between the workers as well. First, there is something about riding around in a van and being on the move that only appeals to a chosen few. When we were recruiting for a psychiatrist a few years back, a candidate asked where her office would be, and we told her it would be in the van. She did not take the job. There is a type of person that is attracted to this population. We are all very strong advocate types, and there is a definite rebellious component to our personalities. I have often thought that it is a calling that is difficult to explain. We sit next to clients covered in filth, and we work with clients who are living in the most deplorable conditions, eating their own feces, covered with maggots, etc. We work with the truly disenfranchised, the shadow of society, whom society actively rejects. We encounter dangerous situations in which a homeless mentally ill person is actively psychotic and threatening, and we may be the target. We have witnessed clients being tasered by the police. We worked with a client who lived on a boat off the West Side pier. Telling a stranger at a party that you work with the homeless mentally ill is often a real conversation stopper.

I remember the first time I met Leroy. On January 16, 1994, the parks department first made a referral on a Black male in his 40s, living in a pile of debris.

We saw Leroy over a period of 9 years, with the last note dated January 20, 2005. During that time he was placed in permanent housing after having been homeless for 28 years. His diagnosis was schizophrenia, paranoid type. When we first visited him, he had an elaborate encampment near the heliport on 36th Street. The area was rat infested. He was in an isolated spot right on the water, littered with his bags and boxes, two postal carts, and large blue plastic tarps tented over all of these articles.

When we approached, we called out to him, and Leroy peered out from beneath the tarps so that we could only see his eyes. We introduced ourselves, asking if perhaps he wanted something to eat, offering him the traditional brown paper bag lunch of a cheese sandwich, juice, and a piece of cake. We tried to engage him, but he quickly disappeared beneath his tarps again with the bag of lunch. It was quite a spread. Although we continued to talk to him, he did not respond. We decided to leave and return on our way back downtown. Project HELP cannot take a client to the hospital against his or her will unless the person is mentally ill and is dangerous (to self or others). Section 9.37 of the Mental Hygiene Law outlines the specifics of involuntary transport and hospitalization.

We returned repeatedly over the week. Project HELP has two shifts, and we are active between the hours of 9 a.m. and 12 midnight, with different outreach workers having the opportunity to engage and assess a homeless client. Leroy took the lunches we handed to him, made eye contact, and would nod his head. His face was pockmarked and purplish in color. He started to talk with us. We were able to find out that he had a small sterno stove on which he cooked, and we thought that perhaps he used the sterno on his face. In fact, he was aware of some problem with the skin on his face, about which he was concerned. We discussed transporting him to a private small shelter, the Volunteers of America Reception Center (transitional shelter for the homeless mentally ill), where one of our psychiatrists worked part time. He repeatedly said that he would consider transport to the shelter, but he would not even come out from under the tarp. He told us that another team, Grand Central Partnership, had offered to take him to their shelter as well.

Then Leroy disappeared. It turned out, after a few phone calls, that the police had cleared him out, but no one knew where he was. We kept an eye out for him as we drove through the entire city, responding to referrals at the airport in Queens, a Citibank branch in Brooklyn, a subway station in the Bronx, but Leroy was nowhere to be seen. We did not see him again for 2 years.

On February 27, 1996, the Lenox Hill Neighborhood Association, an outreach team that covers the Upper East Side of Manhattan, made a referral on Leroy. He was wearing canvas overalls and dark glasses and had scabs on his chin. He was now encamped at 59th Street and First Avenue, a very noisy spot. We suggested to him once again that we could take him to a private shelter. We told him that it was going to snow. He was upset but said, "It's just a few days until it warms up. Then I'll go." He repeatedly refused transport over the next several months, which is typical with the persistently homeless mentally ill.

A few days later we found him downtown on First Avenue between 14th and 15th Streets, pushing a postal cart. He told us that the police had made him leave his spot uptown and that he was going to make his way back uptown. He smelled of perfume. Three days later, he was back uptown on 60th Street and First Avenue. He spoke very little to us over the next few days, but did accept food.

Several days later, his facial skin was inflamed, his eyelids were slightly swollen, and his chin area reddened; however, he refused to come for medical treatment, although he did agree that if his skin condition worsened he would come with us to Bellevue. We decided to monitor him closely. He did show us a double-edged razor, which he said he used to shave. He talked about how he used to swim in a pool and believed that this would be helpful for his skin condition. Then one of our doctors was able to get him to come out from under his tarps for a closer examination. We were elated and felt that Leroy was beginning to trust us. His eyelids and skin was reddened, and he had a slight discharge.

However, on the next visit, and over the next week, the patient was more delusional. He stroked his chin and said that he needed to go to the dentist for his condition. He continued to refuse further services. The following week, Leroy was gone again. There were no other homeless people in the area, and we realized that the police must have moved them all. Two weeks later we saw him back in his regular spot. He said that the police had made him move, but that he had come back to get out of the rain. One week later, Leroy was being moved by the sanitation department when we drove up. He was alert to the move but refused any services. Two days later, Leroy was back, sitting in the sunlight! He had water and camping gear beside him. We continued to visit him. One day we arrived and he was burning incense, soaking his hands in one inch of water in a basin. It was now summertime again, 1996, and Leroy was wearing goggles. He agreed to go to the Volunteers of America reception center "in the winter," when it got cold. He had poor self care, but was dressed appropriately for the weather.

During this time, staff discussed the possibility of treating Leroy's skin condition on the street. One of our psychiatrists was moonlighting at Bellevue, and she knew a resident in dermatology who was willing to assess Leroy's facial condition. He diagnosed Leroy's case as a staph infection of the eyelid and a fungal infection of the eyebrow. He recommended prescriptions for Hytone, Bactroban, and erythromycin, all of which are ointments. We did not see Leroy for the next 2 weeks. It turned out that he had been removed once again, although this time, he had accepted a transport to a nearby private shelter, which he subsequently left, and no one knew where he was. Then we saw him again, back in his regular spot, and we gave him the topical medication for his skin condition and instructions on how to use it. It was a sticky administrative issue. We put ourselves on the line, not knowing if he would eat the medication, which if ingested could cause a gastrointestinal reaction. We alerted a nearby outreach team, who agreed to help monitor Leroy's use of the medication. Then Leroy disappeared again. We did not know why and obsessed for the 6 months he was gone, concerned about his health. We searched the homeless systems of New York City but found no trace of him.

About 6 months later, we were walking down Fifth Avenue and saw a homeless man in front of us, pushing a postal cart. It was Leroy! His face was completely cleared up, he had lost weight, and he stood erect and said hello. He looked like an entirely different man. He told us that he had used the ointments, and was very pleased about his healed skin. Over the next 2 weeks, we saw him walking around the area of 5th and 6th Avenues, pulling two postal carts.

He told us that he no longer stayed at 59th Street. He did go back on June 13, 1997, but then we saw him during July back on the West Side, at Bryant Park, also at 40th Street and 5th Avenue, and at 51st Street and 6th Avenue. He told us that he was collecting and redeeming empty beverage cans for money.

Our psychiatrist, who also worked with the Volunteers of America Reception Center (small private shelter for the homeless mentally ill), told us that Leroy had come in for shelter and services. It was September 1998. They worked with Leroy over the next year. By December, he had applied for benefits, which would enable him to get permanent housing. By March 1999, Leroy was on psychiatric medication. In late June, he was housed at the Salvation Army residence. We would see Leroy occasionally, walking in the street, standing near a corner, fairly neat and clean. The last time we saw him was January 2005, and he was still living at the Salvation Army residence. He was now "permanently" housed. I was so thrilled when I heard. He had been homeless for 28 years! I participated in a life change for Leroy, and there is nothing more exciting than this part of the work with homeless clients.

IS WORKING WITH THE HOMELESS THE RIGHT FIELD FOR YOU?

- Jenny believes that people who are drawn to this field tend to be strong, passionate, and somewhat rebellious. Does this describe you?
- Many people living on the street are seriously mentally ill. Would you feel comfortable working with this population?
- Do you function well in an unstructured work environment where you cannot predict what your workday will bring? Do you like the thrill of the unknown, or do you prefer the relative comfort of having a set routine? If you prefer structure, then you would probably not be happy with this work.

SECTION FOUR: RESOURCES TO LEARN MORE

Web Sites
- Beyond Shelter: http://www.beyondshelter.org
- HHS, Homeless Home Page: http://www.hhs.gov/homeless
- HUD, Homeless Page: http://www.hud.gov/homeless/index.cfm
- Interagency Council on Homelessness (ICH): http://www.ich.gov
- National Alliance to End Homelessness: http://www.endhomelessness.org

- National Center on Family Homelessness: http://www.familyhomelessness.org
- National Coalition for Homeless Veterans: http://www.nchv.org
- National Coalition on Housing and Homelessness: http://www.povnet.org
- National Housing Conference: http://www.nhc.org
- National Low Income Housing Coalition: http://www.nlihc.org
- SAMHSA, Homelessness Services: http://www.samhsa.gov
- Social Work and Homeless Services: http://www.naswnyc.org/CSPP/Homelessv
- SSA, Service to the Homeless: http://www.socialsecurity.gov
- Urban Institute, Publications on Homelessness: http://www.urban.org/housing/homeless.cfm
- VA, Homeless Veterans: http://www1.va.gov/homeless

Journals
- *Housing Studies*, Taylor and Francis

Books
- *The Civil Rights of Homeless People: Law, Social Policy, and Social Work Practice*, by Madeleine R. Stoner (1995, Aldine Transaction)
- *Handbook of Social Work Practice With Vulnerable and Resilient Populations*, by Alex Gitterman (chapter 22: Homeless People, by Marcia B. Cohen) (2001, Columbia University Press)

Policy Statements
- Homeless. In *Social Work Speaks*, 7th ed. NASW Policy Statements, 2006–2009

Practice
- Homeless and Doing the Best We Can, by Neal A. Newfield. Social Work Today: http://www.socialworktoday.com/archive/swt_0104p6.htm
- Social Work and Homeless Services: www.naswnyc.org

8

Social Work in the International Arena

SECTION ONE: FIELD OVERVIEW AND FORECAST

Scope of Services

*I*nternational social work is an area of specialization that is attracting growing attention. The enthusiasm for international social work can be readily noted by the numerous conferences and scholarly publications that feature this topic. In recent years, many universities have developed concentrations, courses, and internships that provide international social work content and field experience. A sign of the popularity of international social work is the attendance at the 2008 Annual Social Work Day at the United Nations; demand for the event shut down registration within days, and over 900 social workers traveled from all over the world to attend this event. International social work is not a new field, but it is certainly an area that has come into its own. Social workers are enthusiastic and passionate about this field of practice.

The convergence of several factors provides the context for the evolution and recognition of international social work: First, the influence of globalization has strengthened the connections between professional communities around the world. The sheer number of professional exchange programs has led to increased cross-national collaborations. Second, the development of new technology, such as the Internet and instant messaging, creates opportunities for forging relationships between people from diverse countries and cultures with relative ease. Third, the post-9/11 world has led to an increased awareness within the social work community of the international dimensions of disaster and terrorism. For example, the Global Social Work Community, an Internet-based international social work community with Internet resources, a chat room, blogs about global social work, and a membership composed of social workers around the world, came about as a response by concerned social workers to the attacks on September 11, 2001, in the United States. Fourth, there is strong affinity between the social work profession's social justice mission and the human rights orientation that provides the ideological framework for international social work. Human rights has emerged as a major thrust of the international social work community, a focus that resonates powerfully within professional social work circles in the United States (Healy, 2008).

There is no single definition of international social work, and it is generally considered to be a complex construct that includes diverse professional activities. Lynne Healy (2008) provides a conceptual framework for international social work in which she defines the field as international professional action, and can involve both domestic and international practice. The defining attribute of international social work is not where it is practiced, but rather that it is social work practice involving two or more countries, that the practice is informed by international dimensions, and that it is directed toward international issues, either at the micro or macro level.

An example of domestic international social work practice is illustrated by a young social worker employed in a social service agency along the Texas/Mexico border. The social worker provides counseling, case management, housing assistance, and referrals to GED and English proficiency classes to a client population that is primarily composed of Mexican immigrant families, some of whom are undocumented. The social worker is bilingual, culturally skilled with regard to Mexican cultural norms and traditions, and is knowledgeable about a myriad of social policies that affect the client population. This social worker's practice is profoundly shaped by numerous international issues, including immigration policy, the North American Free Trade Agreement, and U.S./Mexican relations. Although the social worker is employed and works in the United States, the social worker's role falls under the rubric of international social work. Returning to the definition put forward by Lynne Healy, we can see that, in this case example, the practice population involves two countries, Mexico and the United States; that the presenting problems are shaped by international dimensions; and that the social worker's practice requires a bicultural and bilingual skill set. Another example of internationally based social work practice is illustrated by a social worker who is a member of a team sent by the United Nations Children's Fund (UNICEF) to Indonesia to monitor human rights abuses of women and children subsequent to a devastating earthquake. These two social workers, the first employed in a small U.S. border town and the second who traveled to Indonesia, share a core social work skill set: They are culturally competent, have excellent linguistic skills, and are knowledgeable abut the respective social, cultural, and political context that shapes their client population. Importantly, they are also curious about and open to new experiences.

Settings

The United Nations (UN) is one of largest settings for international social work. A number of member agencies of the UN have programs that are committed to international social welfare. UNICEF is the largest worldwide organization dedicated to promoting the rights and well-being of children. The mission and activities of UNICEF are particularly compatible with social work's commitment to vulnerable children and families. The World Health Organization (WHO), the leading public health organization in the world, is the UN program responsible for providing leadership on global health issues. The WHO works to monitor global health trends and to develop global health policies and standards. Among its many initiatives are projects that focus on: worldwide epidemics, such as HIV/AIDS; poverty reduction; and health promotion in poor and disadvantaged counties. The Department of Economic and Social Affairs (DESA) coordinates UN programs that are dedicated to promoting global social and economic development. Among its priority programs are gender issues and the advancement of women, and sustainable development. Social workers who work there at the UN, either as staff or interns, are likely to make important professional relationships that can promote career development. Their many programs can be easily explored through their Web site: http://www.un.org.

There are a number of nongovernmental organizations (NGOs) that provide excellent venues for social workers in the international arena. Nongovernmental organizations are organizations that are formed by private persons or groups with no formal government affiliation. Among the social issues commonly addressed by an NGO are environmental concerns, human rights, poverty, and disaster assistance. The most well-known NGOs in the international arena are the Red Cross and the American Red Cross; both organizations provide disaster-related services in the United States and abroad. After September 11, 2001, funding and employment opportunities for disaster-related social work increased substantially. A number of influential NGOs are dedicated to helping children worldwide. Save the Children is one of the leading organizations in this area, providing social service and life-saving interventions for impoverished children around the world.

In addition to NGOs, international social workers may be employed or work as an intern with the United States government. USAID is the principal U.S. governmental agency dedicated to providing worldwide assistance to countries recovering from disasters and support for poverty relief programs (http://www.usaid.gov).

The Peace Corps is a great way to build a career in international social work. Participation in the Peace Corps, an extremely prestigious organization, can open many doors. Founded in 1960 by President John F. Kennedy, the mission of the Peace Corps is to promote peace throughout the world. Since its inception, more than 190,000 Peace Corps workers have volunteered in 139 host countries on a range of issues from health care to environmental preservation (http://www. peacecorps.gov).

This partial listing contains just a few of the many settings available for international social workers. All of these organizations have a mission that is very compatible with social work. All of these organizations are also looking for employees that have skill sets very consistent with social work training: An ability to navigate within and across systems, cultural competence, and strong communication skills are all very desirable qualities that are useful in this area. However, the large majority of these organizations do not advertise their positions as "social work," and it will require no small degree of self-promotion and initiative to land one of these coveted positions. One solid entryway into these organizations is through fieldwork. Social work students interested in international social work should explore what internship opportunities are available to them.

The Social Worker's Role

International social workers engage in roles that share many similarities with all social work practice. International social workers can work at the micro and macro levels and utilize a range of skills. For example, social workers are employed by international adoption agencies, such as Holt International Children's Services (http://www.holtintl.org), to work with families and assist them through the international adoption process. Social workers in this area will have to be very knowledgeable about the complexities around international adoptions laws, which vary considerably around the world, and be skilled in data gathering and assessment.

Social workers can also find employment opportunities in programs that assist individuals who are victims of international human rights abuses and in combating sex trafficking. For example, the International Organization for Migration is a leading intergovernmental organization that monitors migration, with a strong emphasis on protecting human rights (http://www.iom.int/jahia/jsp/index.jsp). At the macro level, international social workers are engaged in advocacy and community building. This is particularly relevant to programs involved in international relief and development. Social workers may be involved in working with community-based groups on a variety of educational and health initiatives, such as literacy, women's and children's rights, HIV/AIDS awareness, and environmental issues (Healy, 2008).

International social work, irrespective of setting or function, is much more informed by a human rights orientation as compared with other social work practice areas. This orientation is evidenced by the primary focus on international human rights in the International Federation of Social Workers (IFSW) Code of Ethics (http://www.ifsw.org).

Credentialing

Specialized credentials are not necessary in developing a career in international social work. International social workers seeking to go abroad will need to have specialized knowledge of the culture, politics, and social welfare system of the particular country/region of interest. Computer skills and a public health background or expertise in an allied health profession is a strong asset (Glusker, n.d.). The single most important skill that an international social worker can acquire is fluency in as many languages as possible. International experience, perhaps in a field placement, is also an attractive plus for many employers. Opportunities to study abroad exist at most schools and provide a great way to develop international experience. Memberships in professional associations such as the International Federation of Social Workers are an excellent way to network and be conversant with the issues.

Employment Trends

International social work will continue to flourish because it is strongly supported by the growing recognition of and concern for global issues within the social work community. There is no question that the degree of professional interest and involvement in international social work has increased in the past decade, and that it will continue to grow. One need look no further than to note the increase in the number of educational programs with concentrations and courses in international social work, and the growing availability of international exchange programs and field placements with an international focus. However, social workers seeking to work abroad will find that the options for where they can work are shaped by global and political events. Countries that are politically unstable can be unsafe. That being said, there are tremendous opportunities in this area for social workers with a passion to make a difference at the international level.

ACTIVITIES TO LEARN MORE

- Visit the International Federation of Social Work at http://www.ifsw .org. This is a great source of information about social work practice around the world.
- Visit Planet Social Work at http://www.planetsocialwork .com. This Web site provides a wealth of information about global social work opportunities.
- Read the International Code of Ethics in Social Work jointly issued by the International Federation of Social Workers (IFSW) and the International Association of Schools of Social Work (IASSW). Compare and contrast the differences between the International Code and the National Code of Ethics for Social Workers.

SECTION TWO: CRITICAL ISSUES
Robin Sakina Mama, PhD, MSS

Dr. Robin Sakina Mama is professor and chair of the Department of Social Work at Monmouth University, where she teaches in the international and community concentration of the MSW program. She received her MSS and her PhD from Bryn Mawr College. Dr. Mama serves as the representative of the International Federation of Social Workers at the United Nations, is the chair of the International Committee of the National Association of Social Workers (NASW), and serves on the editorial board of *Social Work Education: The International Journal*.

Please tell me a little about yourself and your path in social work. What are some of the factors that motivated you to become a social worker? What drew you to international social work as an area of focus? Was it a particular issue or concern?
I have a BSW degree from Misericordia College in Dallas, Pennsylvania, where I focused on gerontology. I earned my MSW and PhD from Bryn Mawr College. While I was an MSW student, I worked full time at a small, nonprofit, community-based organization called The Philadelphia Area Project on Occupational Safety and Health. In that position, I organized and educated workers on workplace rights and health and safety. I worked there for 9 years while completing my PhD. At that

point, I decided to go into academia, in part because I was a mother with small children and the academic schedule is family friendly.

I became involved with international social work serendipitously while on the faculty of Monmouth University. As our program grew from a small BSW program to include an MSW program, we decided to start a concentration in international social work. I was closely involved in developing this concentration, and I began teaching courses on international social work. Through my teaching and research, I became involved with the International Federation of Social Workers, and ultimately became their representative to the United Nations. I was a member of the Council on Social Work Education's Global Commission, and I served as chair of NASW's International Committee.

What is international social work?
I define international social work as the ability to engage in international action by social workers. Within this formulation, international social work is framed as not limited to working overseas, but includes domestic social work practice as well. Domestic international social work encompasses issues related to globalization or international human rights concerns. For example, if you are a social worker working with refugees and undocumented immigrants in the United States, many of the issues that emerge in your practice are connected to international policies and human rights. International social work involves understanding the global context and making those links.

At Monmouth University, as in many schools of social work, we have professional exchange programs in which our social work students have the opportunity to go overseas for their field placements. We also bring students from overseas to study in our program. International social work is rooted in the premise that learning is reciprocal. It's not about Americans going overseas to sell a Western model; it's about working in solidarity with people on the issues that they want to work on, and sharing expertise and resources.

In designing an international social work educational program, it is extremely important that students have an overseas experience that lasts some length of time, so that they can be "in country" long enough to get to know the people, the culture, and to sink their teeth into the fabric of life. This year we have three students in Ghana, one in Hong Kong, and one in Chile.

What do international social workers do?
International social workers do many of the same things that all social workers do. At its essence, international social work is skill based. International social workers need to be well versed in core social work skills, such as engagement and consensus building.

Language fluency is extremely important. International social workers must speak at least one or two languages besides English. Language fluency promotes cultural understanding, enhances credibility, and enables the social worker to engage earlier when working overseas. Language skills give the social worker access to opportunities that would otherwise be unavailable.

Social workers seeking a career in international social work have to learn to market their skills rather than their degrees. Many settings, for example the U.S.

State Department or the World Bank, have employment opportunities that social workers have the skills and qualifications to apply for, yet these organizations don't advertise for a "social worker." Social workers have the skill set that these employers are looking for: We understand how to negotiate complex systems, are skilled in research and program development, and we can engage communities. Social workers have to learn to sell themselves. That involves focusing on the skills that we can bring to the table, rather than on the degree.

What settings do international social workers work in?
International social work occurs in many different kinds of settings. The United Nations, governmental and nongovernmental organizations, faith-based organizations, and private organizations all provide settings for international social work. Students may seek to work in AmeriCorps, the Peace Corps, the Foreign Service, or the World Bank. Getting your foot in the door in many of these organizations is not easy, but it's not impossible for an enterprising person. Networking and understanding how to market yourself is important.

What are some global trends that are likely to shape international social work?
It's getting trendier and trendier for programs that are not traditionally associated with international concerns to do something international. There are lots of organizations that want to participate in academic and medical tourism.

My husband, Saifuddin, is part of a medical program that goes yearly to Africa to operate. A significant part of his work involves reciprocal learning, such as teaching infection control in countries where there is a need to develop the capacity to prevent the spread of infectious diseases. At the same time, his orientation is to be open to learning from the practices in that hospital. He has seen so much creativity in hospitals that have very limited resources.

We have a growing awareness that we must refine our objectives and what we are seeking to accomplish "in country." We need to have clarity about how long we should be there, and about what we should and should not bring with us. The social work perspective holds reciprocity and consensus building as core principles that inform our work.

Globalization has opened up incredible opportunities, as have developments in technology. Cell phones and the Internet allow businesses and programs to communicate instantly and provide immediate and worldwide access to information.

How do recent political events in the United States, such as being at war, affect international social work?
War and politics change the perceptions that people have about Americans. Our intentions are questioned. People around the world, especially in countries affected by American foreign and military policies, are likely to view Americans with enhanced mistrust and suspicion. They may wonder, "What are you doing here?" "What are your intentions?" We have to be aware of and counter the "ugly American" syndrome, especially in the beginning. This is key, because if you can't build a trusting relationship with the people "in country," no matter what you do, it will not be well perceived.

War and civil unrest restricts movement for social workers and other humanitarian personnel. All of the Peace Corps workers are pulling out of Kenya because of violence and chaos. Afghanistan, a country that would have been the perfect place for community development, is just not safe anymore. At one point, our university had placements in Bangladesh, but subsequent to a State Department warning about riots, we discontinued those placements. It's impossible now to go to Iraq. Universities must consider liability factors, and the safety and well-being of our students is primary.

We do a tremendous amount of work preparing our students to go overseas. We seek to have them really understand that we carry the weight of how Americans are perceived in the global community. While that may, at times, be a burden, it is also a real opportunity for building bridges, establishing trust, and paving the way for the next American.

How can a social worker pursue a career in international social work?
A career in international social work can start right in your own community. Many social work internships and employment opportunities have flavors of international work. For example, in Elizabeth, New Jersey, there is a detention center where persons seeking asylum are housed, sometimes for quite a long time. Social workers in that setting address issues related to international human rights. Another option might be social work with international adoptions.

Social workers interested in international work should seek to make the links between a client's life circumstances and the politics and social policies in that person's country of origin. Social workers need to understand the client's cultural, social, and political biography, and how these factors impact their current situation. Making these connections is thinking like an international social worker.

The Peace Corps or Americorps are wonderful points of entry into international social work. Admission into these programs is competitive. Successful applicants will need letters of reference, medical clearance, and language skills, and they must pass an interview. These organizations provide incredible opportunities for networking and career advancement.

The United Nations has an excellent internship program. Although many of these internships are not necessarily in social service–related agencies and may involve some clerical work, for an enterprising person, these internships can be a fantastic way to network, make connections, and move a career forward.

What specific concerns/questions should I consider before accepting a position in international social work?
When considering a position in international social work, it is important to know how much training and support is provided by the agency. What are the opportunities for learning? Is there the opportunity to develop language skills and to learn about culture? Will there be financial support to attend conferences and workshops? What kind of orientation will be provided?

Before accepting a position in international social work, you should know what kind of experience your predecessor in that position had. If it was a positive experience, you may be walking into a great situation. However, a negative experience could mean damaged relationships with the community, and you will have a lot of mending to do. It's important to know what you're stepping into.

It's vital to know what to do in case of an emergency. How do you get in and out? If there's a disaster, what kind of assistance will you have? What kind of domestic support will be provided to social workers overseas in the case of disaster or political unrest?

What advice would you give to a social worker who wants to become an international social worker?
Language skills and cultural awareness are the most important skills to develop. Recently, one of our students returned from a social work internship abroad and was giving a presentation at the university. When asked what her best advice for students going overseas was, she suggested that when students get to the airport, they take all of their assumptions, put them in the airport locker, and leave them there. She recommended that students have to let go of all of the things that they think they know and to be open to new experiences.

How does social work education prepare social workers for international social work?
Social work education can prepare students for international social work by teaching students the necessary skills that they need to work in the international arena. Social work education needs to do more work around human rights and social justice. The concept of "human rights" sounds too lofty, and social work education needs to make this and other similarly "lofty" concepts relevant to practice. The United Nations Declaration of Human Rights provides an excellent macro framework for human rights, but clinical social workers do not readily connect this to their practice. Social work education needs to do a better job of connecting clinical issues to a human rights orientation, i.e., to link the problems confronting a victim of domestic violence to a broader understanding of human rights. If social workers are truly going to be international, then we have to become more fluent in understanding human rights issues, and make them applicable to students.

DID YOU KNOW?

- While social workers have been involved in global activities for a long time, there is increased professional recognition of international social work, and it is one of the strongest emerging fields of professional focus. According to NASW, an increasing number of social work programs are adding an international component or concentration to their curriculum, and greater numbers of social workers are expected to have a role in world affairs (www.socialworkers.org).
- *Social Work and Society* is a free online journal about international social work and includes articles from all over the world. To access the journal, visit http://www.socwork.net.

- The annual Social Work Day at the UN is an extremely popular one-day event that draws together social workers from around the world. For 25 years, students, practitioners, and educators have been convening at the UN to learn more about international social work. To find out more, visit http://bluehawk.monmouth.edu/swork/UN.

SECTION THREE: FIRST-PERSON NARRATIVE

My International Social Work Practice: A Snapshot of Darfur
Erin Jane Majesty-Aronson, MSW

Erin Jane Majesty-Aronson, MSW, is currently practicing social work disguised as a humanitarian aid worker in Darfur, Sudan, where she has lived and worked since 2007. Working alongside internally displaced person (IDP) populations, she currently focuses on economic empowerment for women through livelihood interventions.

After receiving a BSW from Azusa Pacific University in 2004, Ms. Majesty-Aronson accepted an internship with the Los Angeles County Department of Child and Family Services, which turned into a position as an emergency response children's social worker in South Central LA. Investigating child abuse in this setting was her "baptism by fire" into the reality of child protection and working with families in crisis.

Always interested in working abroad, Ms. Majesty-Aronson sought out a graduate program with an international track and found Monmouth University. While there, she interned with Youth Advocate Programs, Inc., and traveled to Guatemala, advocating on behalf of a local NGO working with street youth. After graduating with an MSW in 2007, She accepted a position in Darfur, working with vulnerable women and children in that region.

A social worker by training, profession, and personal commitment, Ms. Majesty-Aronson feels that, regardless of her job title or location, she will always be a social worker, and she is proud to represent the profession internationally.

Ms. Majesty-Aronson misses her family while away but is so thankful for their support of her endeavors. She feels privileged to live and work alongside the love of her life and partner, Scott, who encourages and inspires her daily.

How Did I Get Here?   It's 2:30 a.m. and a blast of hot Sudanese air greets me as I step off the airplane and into a new life. Having graduated just a month prior with my Masters of Social Work, I found myself in Darfur as a humanitarian aid worker, in a state of shock that my career as an international social worker had begun. Flash forward one week, and I'm sitting on the dirt floor of a rural women's center, listening to their concerns through shaky Arabic translation, and it hits me that I'm at work; this is what I *do* … unreal.

Humanitarian Aid and Social Work

This job and location, both equally foreign to me, present my first paid entrée into the realm of "international social work," although this will not be my job title. Indeed, there is some debate about what this term entails, a topic I don't feel the need to dwell on. As far as I am concerned, I am a social worker both by academic training and personal commitment, regardless of my job title. I find the tenets of social service work—including operating from a strengths perspective, viewing people in their environment, and considering situations in a broad context—not only helpful in the humanitarian aid world, but vital. Truly, these concepts translate naturally into this professional realm, and they are the lessons and truths I cling to when feeling far away, removed from anything familiar and the larger social work community.

A Day in the Life: Office Work and Field Trips

So let me walk you through my days here in Darfur as a program manager, overseeing youth and women's programs with an international nongovernmental organization (INGO). Due to the sensitive nature of this conflict, location, and work, there are many details that I can't share, but I'll do my best to paint an accurate picture.

The content of my days represents a broad spectrum of interactions and situations, often filled with some combination of complications that range from the unexpected and exciting to the downright frustrating and frightening. This can include simple computer malfunctions and lack of electricity in the office, to the dreaded phone call that my staff has been carjacked while on a road I myself traveled the week before. The nature of my work is highly dependent upon my location, as I am either working in an office or out in the field. Much of my office time is spent trying to check and respond to e-mails, attending meetings with various UN agencies and other NGOs, talking with staff, planning out programs, writing reports and proposals, playing with budgets (math not being a traditional strong point for social workers), and working through the myriad of issues that inevitably materialize.

I supervise a staff of five and enjoy this challenge. Practicing good communication and effectively delegating responsibility in a context strewn with language barriers and cultural differences can, on some days, seem downright impossible. I enjoy holding staff meetings in my office, listening to program ideas and feedback over coffee, trying to plan the week and month ahead, laughing through broken translation, and finishing by reading each other's fortune found in the dried grounds at the bottom of our cups.

When you are living and working in a foreign country, the local culture can sometimes play as large a role in your life as the work itself. The Sudanese people in general place great value on relationships, and stopping to talk with people or attending events outside the office is an important aspect of connecting with the staff. Even simple greetings can become quite an event and take a bit longer than you might think, but they are said with such sincerity that I can't help but smile and soak it up. Never have I felt so appreciated; people seem truly happy to see me in the morning, not to mention when I return from the field! It's as if I have been gone for years, and people are just so grateful I have returned!

Another week may find me in the field, and truly this is when I feel closest to my social work roots—getting to sit with people, see how they live, and listen to their thoughts and concerns. Night can find me sleeping out under the stars, squatting around a pot of food with the team and practicing my Arabic—always a crowd pleaser. This is the picture I had in my head when I realized I'd be working in Africa, and I treasure these moments, pinching myself to again remember that I'm really here, that this is my life and I'm at work.

I am currently working with youth and women's programs, which encompass two very different projects and locations. With a history of direct practice, my role as manager has been somewhat of an adjustment and has led to some moments of feeling disconnected from the people on the other end of the program designs. But really, this is not my job, and when I really think about the purpose of these projects and the context, it makes sense for me to step back and be more of a link between the programs, the organization, and the donors. I provide support and make decisions about program implementation, but this is all contingent upon a strong partnership with the national staff. They know so much more about the area, people, and context than I ever will, and at the end of the day, this is their home. Expatriate staff come and go, contracts end, and a new boss walks in the door. The national staff knows this, and I am amazed by how warm and welcoming they are, accepting us as family, all the while knowing that, if things ever got really bad, the INGOs would be evacuated, and they would be left to deal with the consequences.

Setbacks and Frustrations   Oh, the frustrations! This is where I could get myself into some political trouble by spouting off about the conflict and surrounding politics, so instead let's talk about something a bit more neutral, like clothing. For me, the first thing to go when the weather is really, really, extremely hot is modesty. Sadly this does not bode well in a desert region under Sharia Law, where the women around me are covered from head to toe. While I am incredibly thankful the locals don't expect the foreigners to cover their heads, the culturally sensitive thing is for me to be as covered as possible. This sounds like no big deal, but I'll admit to some momentary battles of will regarding this culturally sensitive wrap and the stifling ankle-length skirt that are not helping the sweat dripping down my back. Now, clearly, this is not the end of the world, and it is quite possibly the least serious dilemma I'm facing here, but it's amazing how the little things add up, and when combined with all the unmentioned difficulties, the result is my having to stop and ask: "Do I respect these people?" "Will I let go of a bit of personal comfort to show this respect?" Of course, these tend to be a million little decisions throughout the day, as opposed to one large yes-or-no question, and some days the totals are more positive than others.

I don't know if I'll ever get used to riding around in these Landcruisers, being the white girl who is constantly stared at, yelled to, and run after. One day I actually made a baby cry because she was so frightened by my light skin! Some days I feel like a huge spectacle and wonder, "What am I doing here? Am I effective? These scenes that I bear witness to, have I become used to them? Have I become another cliché jaded aid worker who has lost faith in international organizations, immune to the suffering of those around me and the horrific scenes I am witness to? What is my purpose?" Of course these thoughts are not exclusive to humanitarian aid; they are a general litany of the general social work dilemma. Can we walk that line between having a hardened heart and being so destroyed by people's suffering that we cry ourselves to sleep every night?

Checking Motivations

These are the moments I remind myself that I've chosen to practice social work in a conflict area. I signed up for this reality of war. It can sound heroic, romantic at times—the concept of whisking away to a far-off place to "work with people in need"—but let me clarify. I am not a hero, and although I'm not opposed to some romance in my life, most moments of my day would not be the subject of an adventure novel. There can be a certain "cowboy" attitude in the aid worker community, and certainly I have my moments of playing into this. A reoccurring realization in my life has been the need to check my motivations. Why do I want to work in Africa? What part of helping people gratifies my own needs? Truth be told, I love this life. I like hitting the road, traveling, meeting new people, seeing fascinating places that few will ever see. Now why don't I just work for a travel magazine, you ask? Well, good question—but, really, I do social work because of that little voice, the voice that keeps me up some nights thinking about the unjust experiences people are suffering. Not that I'm here to solve the world's problems; clearly, that won't be happening any time soon.

I think that many of us in this line of work will always struggle with the reality of injustice; it will plague our inner thoughts and urge us to try and do something. Perhaps one of the most significant things I've realized during my work is that I cannot "save the world." Indeed, wouldn't that put me in some position of power that exceeds one person's capability? I don't have a naively idealistic idea that the world will know perfect peace and justice in my lifetime. I do, however, have to believe that things can be a bit better than they are today. Of course, that can mean many things to many people, and so there is no clear definition or way to move forward. All I know is that my contribution finds me in Darfur today, and at the end of this day I hope to go to sleep knowing that at least I tried.

So here I am, sharing a bit about my version of international social work, thankful for the opportunities I've been given and mindful that some part of me comes alive when I'm out in the field. It can be uncomfortable and hot, and sometimes I don't shower for days, eat really crazy food, and puke behind huts. These are the day-to-day realities that usually seem incredibly small and insignificant to me.

I realize that this type of work is not for everyone. Indeed, if any part of you is uncomfortable with strange scenarios, bizarre locations, or going with the flow, please do not work abroad. (In fact, I would question your choice of social work in general.) If you do not truly love people, and do not believe that individuals are stronger than they appear and are the true experts in their own lives, then this is not the field for you. On the other hand, there are those of us who are desperate to see the world, ready to jump into uncomfortable and frustrating situations, prepared to be stared at and totally pushed beyond "reasonable" limits.

International social work is a field for people who love languages and are fascinated by the way we interact as humans. We are the ones consumed by the big picture, frustrated by the global battle of inequality and corruption, who burn with the conviction that people deserve to be treated with dignity and respect. To those who are starting to realize that stepping beyond things known and comfortable— hopefully equipped with the skills you have gained—may be the only way to truly live out your strengths and dreams, then welcome. Work hard, push yourself and your teachers, and ask questions. I hope to see you soon.

IS INTERNATIONAL SOCIAL WORK THE RIGHT FIELD FOR YOU?

- Erin's optimism that the world can be a better place helps her stay motivated and passionate about her work. Are these personal qualities that you can identify with?
- Erin has left behind many of the creature comforts that we take for granted as she adjusts to life as a humanitarian worker in Africa. Do you envision yourself being able to adapt to the challenges she describes?
- Erin relates what it is like for her, as a woman, to learn to live in a culture in which women cover themselves from head to toe. How willing are you to let go of your cultural norms and to embrace a world that is different from your own?

SECTION FOUR: RESOURCES TO LEARN MORE

Web Sites

- Association of South African Social Work Education Institutions (ASASWEI): http://www.asaswei.org.za
- Amnesty International: http://www.amnesty.org
- Human Rights Watch: http://www.hrw.org
- International Association of Schools of Social Work (IASSW): http://www.iassw-aiets.org
- International Committee of the Red Cross: http://www.icrc.org
- International Council on Social Welfare (ICSW): http://www.icsw.org
- International Federation of Red Cross and Red Crescent Societies: http://www.ifrc.org
- Planet Social Work: http://www.planetsocialwork.com
- Save the Children: http://www.savethechildren.net/alliance/index.html
- Sustainable Development International: http://www.sustdev.org
- United Nations Children's Fund (UNICEF): http://www.unicef.org
- United Nations: http://www.un.org
- World Health Organization (WHO): http://www.who.int/about/en

Journals
- *International Social Work*, Sage

Books
- *Human Rights and Social Justice in a Global Perspective: An Introduction to International Social Work*, by Susan C. Mapp (2007, Oxford University Press)

Policy
- International Policy on Human Rights. In *Social Work Speaks*, 7th ed. NASW Policy Statements, 2006–2009

Ethics
- Ethics in Social Work, Statement of Principles, International Federation of Social Workers (IFSW) and International Association of Schools of Social Work (IASSW)

Professional Associations
- The International Federation of Social Workers: http://www.ifsw.org
- NASW International Chapter: http://www.naswintl.org

Educational Programs/Centers
- Rutgers University School of Social Work, Center for International Social Work
- University of Connecticut School of Social Work, Center for International Social Work Studies

9

Social Work and Mental Illness

SECTION ONE: FIELD OVERVIEW AND FORECAST

Scope of Services

*M*ental illness is a serious social problem in the United States, one that affects millions of Americans. According to the National Institute of Mental Health, in any given year, approximately 26.2% of Americans ages 18 and older, about 1 in 4 adults, suffer from a diagnosable mental disorder. The number of persons believed to suffer with serious mental illness is estimated at 6% of Americans, about 1 in 17 people (National Institute of Mental Health, 2008b).

Mental illness can have profound and devastating consequences for individuals, families, and society. The large majority (about two thirds) of Americans with serious mental illness are not receiving any type of treatment. A report by the surgeon general (U.S. Department of Health and Human Services, 1999) suggests that stigma and shame are major factors that impede the access to and availability of mental health services. Although most forms of mental illness respond positively to treatment, millions of Americans are suffering unnecessarily with these potentially treatable conditions (Mental Health, 2006).

Services for people with serious mental illness have shifted from inpatient settings to community-based programs, under the auspices of community mental health. Community mental health services have evolved over the past 60 years within the context of several factors, including public policy, the development of antipsychotic medications, and public awareness of the needs of the severely mentally ill. Prior to the 1960s, persons who were diagnosed with serious mental illness could expect to spend years, and sometimes their entire lives, institutionalized in mental asylums. These large-scale institutions, many of which resembled the "snake pits" depicted in the movies, warehoused patients in substandard conditions and robbed them of their civil rights. The development of Thorazine in 1950 revolutionized the treatment of the mentally ill, and it set the stage for the following decades of deinstitutionalization from psychiatric wards. Thorazine was one of the first effective medications for people with psychotic symptoms. It produced marked improvement in the symptoms of mental illness, and helped to control hallucination and delusions. Thorazine also had severe side effects, and people frequently discontinued its use, leading psychiatric symptoms to reemerge. Nonetheless, Thorazine was considered by many to be a "miracle drug" that stabilized psychiatric symptoms and enabled many people with serious psychiatric illness to live in the community, and to function independently (Beitchman, 2005; Rosenberg & Rosenberg, 2006).

By the 1970s, through deinstitutionalization, close to 500,000 individuals were discharged from the psychiatric institutions where they had been living into the community. These individuals were not prepared for independent living, and there were meager supports available to help them adjust. Many of them became homeless. Promises by the legislature to develop community resources were not kept. Instead, people with severe mental illness found themselves on shaky ground, living in communities that were not prepared to include them and that viewed them with considerable mistrust and suspicion. For their part, many of the "newly freed" mentally ill had lived for decades in large institutions and were unprepared for the demands of daily life (Rosenberg & Rosenberg, 2006; Dulmus & Roberts, 2008).

Settings

Agency-based mental health services (as distinct from private-practice settings covered in Chapter 12) are provided in both inpatient and institutionally based settings and in outpatient settings. Inpatient care includes psychiatric emergency rooms and hospital inpatient psychiatric units. Some long-term institutional programs continue to exist, but they have been largely eliminated with the goal toward increased independent living. Adult group homes are commonly used for people who cannot live on their own.

Outpatient treatment settings include outpatient mental health clinics, community health centers, day treatment programs, vocational programs, psychosocial clubhouses, and mobile crisis units. Generally, hospitals, outpatient clinics, and mobile crisis units hire only licensed professionals. Some community centers, clubhouses, day and vocational programs, and adult group homes have positions for candidates who have a bachelor's degree in social work.

The Social Worker's Role

Social workers are the largest providers of mental health services in the United States, with more than 60% of mental health care in the nation provided by social workers (National Association of Social Workers, n.d.). An analysis of the social work workforce suggests that mental health is one of the largest practice areas in the profession; a recent survey by NASW of its membership reports that 35% of members identify mental health as their primary practice area (Whitaker, Weismiller, & Clark , 2006a). The Bureau of Labor Statistics (2008) identifies mental health and substance abuse as the second largest field of practice for social workers, with approximately 116,000 social workers who work in the mental health field.

Social workers in mental health function as clinical social workers. Within that context, the clinical social work role involves utilizing skills in engagement, assessment, diagnosis, treatment planning, counseling, referral, and working in multidisciplinary teams. Depending on the setting, and the needs of the treatment population, practice methods can include individual, group, family, and crisis intervention. Social workers may be involved in hospitalizing clients for suicidal and/or homicidal ideation, both on a voluntary and involuntary basis.

Since the 1970s, an increasingly popular method of social work practice with the seriously mentally ill is case management. Social work case managers work closely with individual clients in developing an individualized treatment plan. They coordinate and monitor and advocate for clients about client resources, such as housing needs and financial issues. The National Association of Social Workers Standards for Social Work Case Management (1992) formulates case management as a complex set of functions in which the social worker works with an individual client and arranges, coordinates, and monitors all the numerous services that the client needs. This can include utilizing multiple roles, including advocate, broker, therapist, community organizer, evaluator, and consultant. Social work case managers work clinically with clients to promote psychosocial stability. Social work case management positions may be filled by either a BSW or an MSW. The less trained staff will carry out less complex functions and work under supervision.

Credentialing

Social workers working in the mental health field need clinical training and, depending on the requirements of their employment, may need to hold a clinical license or to be working toward obtaining it. Social work licensure is regulated at the state level, and the requirements vary from state to state. There are four basic categories of social work licensing: bachelor's, master's, advanced generalist, and clinical, although not all states have licenses in all four categories. The Association of Social Work Boards (ASWB) is a national organization that works with state regulatory bodies to implement licensing. Social workers should determine what licensing laws pertain in their own state by contacting the Association of Social Work Boards (www.ASWB.org) or their local NASW chapter (NASW.org).

Mental health positions that entail more clinically complex tasks, such as diagnosis and treatment, are likely to require that social workers be licensed. If they are licensed at the master's level, they will most likely work under the supervision of a licensed clinical social worker. Clinical licensure is considered an advanced license, and requires 2 or 3 years of post-MSW, supervised clinical experience and passage of a clinical exam.

Another credential that might be useful for candidates seeking employment in social work and mental health care is case-management certification. There are a number of organizations that provide case-management certification. The National Association of Social Workers offers two case-management certifications, one at the BSW level and one at the MSW level. The Certified Social Work Case Manager (C-SWCM) requires a BSW degree, one year (equivalent to 1,500 hours) of supervised, paid post-BSW work experience, and a current BSW licensure or a passing grade on an American Social Work Boards (ASWB) exam.

The Certified Advanced Social Work Case Manager (C-ASWCM) requires an MSW degree, one year (equivalent to 1,500 hours) of supervised, paid post-MSW work experience, and a current state licensure or a passing score on the ASWB exam. In addition, current Academy of Certified Social Workers (ACSW) or Diplomate in Clinical Social Work (DCSW) certifications, which are NASW specialty credentials for master's-level social workers, fulfill the educational requirement to sit for the exam.

The American Case Management Association is a nationally recognized professional association for case managers. They offer an Accredited Case Manager (ACM) certification. The certification is based on passing an exam and paying a fee. The credential is valid for 4 years. Candidates must have earned a BSW or MSW in order to sit for the exam.

Emerging Issues and Employment Trends

It is likely that there will be significant demand in the future for social workers to provide community-based mental health care services. According to a recent workforce analysis by NASW (Whitaker, Weismiller, Clark, & Wilson, 2006c), social workers who work in the mental health area have a median age of 50 years old, which is higher than for other practice areas. This group of baby boomer social workers will be reaching retirement age, thereby creating employment opportunities for a younger workforce.

Social workers in mental health tend to have a higher level of education, since the MSW is frequently required for many mental health positions. Mental health also often pays relatively better than many other practice areas. In order to be competitive in this area, getting the MSW, becoming licensed, and getting additional certification and specialized training is important. Bilingual language skills are also increasingly in demand, making social workers who speak more than one language very desirable to employers.

One challenge facing social workers who work in mental health is personal safety. Social workers who work in the mental health field are more likely to report concerns about possible client violence than other social workers. Social workers who work in mental health are also affected by increasing paperwork demands and charting requirements. In many mental health agencies, social workers are struggling with large caseloads and clients with multiple and serious problems. However, despite these concerns, social workers who work in mental health report a high level of satisfaction with their ability to help clients.

ACTIVITIES TO LEARN MORE

- Interview a social worker who works in an outpatient mental health setting. Ask them about their biggest challenges and rewards, and assess their level of job satisfaction.
- Review the employment section of your local newspaper. Look for employment opportunities for social workers in mental health. What are the qualifications for these positions?
- Log onto your local NASW chapter Web site. Find out if there is a chapter committee about social work and mental health. If so, attend a meeting.

SECTION TWO: CRITICAL ISSUES
W. Patrick Sullivan, PhD, MSW

W. Patrick Sullivan earned a PhD at the University of Kansas and currently serves at the Indiana University School of Social Work, where he holds the rank of professor. While completing the MSW program at the University of Kansas, Dr. Sullivan was a member of a pilot project that led to the development of the strengths model of case management. It was from these experiences that the Strengths Model of Social Work was conceptualized.

Shortly after accepting a position at Indiana University, Dr. Sullivan was asked to serve as the director of the Indiana Division of Mental Health, and he held the position from 1994 to early 1998. During this time he helped refine and implement a unique public model of managed care called the Hoosier Assurance Plan. Previously, Dr. Sullivan was the first assistant professor to win Southwest Missouri State University's top award for research and scholarship, the SMS Foundation Award for Outstanding Scholarship. While working in Indiana, he was recognized as a Distinguished Hoosier by Governor Frank O'Bannon in 1997; received the IUPUI Glen Irwin Experience Excellence Award for Community Service in 1999; and earned the Sagamore of the Wabash, the highest award given to an Indiana citizen, from Governor Joseph Kernan in 2004. He has also won eight teaching awards at the Indiana University School of Social Work, and he was awarded the Outstanding Alumni Award from the University of Kansas in 2004. He has over 60 professional publications on a diverse range of topics.

Please describe how social work in community mental health is different today than 30 years ago.
Mental health services have evolved considerably in the past 30 years. In 1978, the National Institute of Mental Health initiated demonstration projects with innovative treatment models for persons with serious and persistent mental illness. Around this time, outpatient programs based on traditional counseling methods, such as

individual and family therapy, were replaced by specialized treatment programs for the mentally ill. We saw an increasing utilization of case management, a modality that grew to dominate contemporary treatment approaches with the mentally ill. During this period, entry-level employment opportunities for baccalaureate social workers in the mental health field increased.

What are the major challenges to providing community care to the mentally ill?
Although many clients with mental illness live independently in the community, they continue to confront tremendous social problems, such as poverty and stigma. Even though communities are more knowledgeable today about mental illness than in the past, they are not more accepting of it. As such, these clients face a significant degree of community rejection. It is extremely difficult for consumers to find adequate housing, and many persons with serious mental illness live in unsavory and dangerous neighborhoods that bring them into close proximity with crime and delinquency, placing them in a social environment that is likely to exacerbate their symptoms. Social workers are challenged because the clients that we serve have multiple problems and require significant attention. However, it is very difficult in this climate of restrictive funding to find the resources and adequately respond to the client's needs. Social workers generally juggle big caseloads and are on the run from one crisis to another. Trying to locate community resources for clients and to help them build a support system under these circumstances is not easy!

What is the most important policy impacting social work in mental health?
We have built our entire community-based mental health infrastructure on Medicaid. Medicaid policy dictates everything that we do: *what tasks we engage in, which clients we treat, what services are covered.* For example, case management services have flourished, in large measure, because they are Medicaid-reimbursable. If Medicaid dollars were to be restricted, the entire mental health system would collapse. Given the current weakening of the economy, we can predict that local and federal governments will make budget cuts and target mental health care. This seriously threatens the integrity of the mental health infrastructure.

What is the consumer movement?
The consumer movement affirms the dignity, rights, and self-determination of persons with serious mental illness. It is composed of a group of very well organized and active mental health consumers who seek a voice in developing mental health policy and treatment. The consumer movement asserts the civil rights of persons with mental illness, emphasizing their right to have friends, lovers, positive leisure-time activities, employment opportunities, and control over their own treatment. Some members of the consumer movement see the psychiatric community as evil, and there is a place for this viewpoint at the table. The consumer movement is an important force that combats stigma and demonstrates that persons with mental illness can function in society, given adequate community support.

How does the concept of recovery inform treatment approaches to mental illness today?

Recovery is a new model in which the antiquated perspective of mental illness as chronic is replaced by a vision of hope and optimism. The recovery model espouses a positive approach to working with people who have serious challenges. I am proud that, as the former Indiana State director of mental health, I directed mental health administrators to focus on recovery principals and to develop programs that offered more than group homes and partial hospitalization.

Mental health professionals must be cognizant that when clients seek treatment, they are generally in a period in their lives of great instability, at a time when they are in the greatest need of services. However, there are also a great many people that we do not see in treatment, individuals who struggle on their own with symptoms of mental illness. Generally, these individuals prefer to stay outside of the psychiatric community, and are making it on their own. In some cases, their life paths might differ from what we may think that they ought to be doing. Nonetheless, if one reflects on the classic definition of stability as the ability to live a hopeful and satisfying life in spite of the presence of mental illness, then this population is functioning well. We are largely unaware of these individuals, as they often choose not to make their stories public, concerned about repercussions from the societal stigma toward mental illness. Their stories are the narratives of recovery, and we must learn from their life histories and incorporate these stories into our understanding of mental illness. These narratives provide the vision of hope and inspiration that can guide the development of positive treatment approaches.

How does stigma impact treatment of the seriously mentally ill? What would be important for a social worker to understand about stigma and the treatment of the seriously mentally ill?

Stigma and negative perceptions about mental illnesses create invisible barriers for people who are working hard each and every day to be successful in their lives. It is a silent violence that denies people access to the goods of life on the basis of presumed characteristics and false assumptions about what mental illness is. Stigma propels the myth that the mentally ill are dangerous, despite the fact that the average community mental health worker spends the majority of his or her time trying to get the client moving and out of bed, as opposed to preventing the client from engaging in acts of violence. We know that clients are much more likely to internalize stigma, and to incorporate damaging social misconceptions about mental illness. This leads to a negative self-image and a pessimistic perspective about the future.

The educational community has developed great awareness and sensitivity about making the necessary accommodations to support students with physical disabilities, and subscribes to a moral imperative that we must help those with physical challenges. However, we fail to extend these same protections and rights to students with mental illness. This inequity is illogical, particularly because we know that mental illness is biologically based. Societal stigma enables discrimination against persons with mental illness to persist.

How would you describe the major challenges facing social workers today who work in mental health?

Social workers who are employed in a mental health agency work in an extremely hectic and demanding environment. They face major challenges, and they must be highly skilled in time management and excel in multitasking and juggling responsibilities if they are to be effective in their work. It is daunting to keep so many balls in the air! Social workers are under considerable pressure to fulfill productivity requirements, and frequently have performance contracts that require them to complete a set number of billable hours in any given week. The nature of the client population, with high dropout rates and no-shows for appointments, makes it extremely difficult to meet productivity standards. The increasing paperwork and reporting requirements makes it all the more challenging. Social workers who provide services to the mentally ill must learn to be advocates for clients within their own agencies as well as in the community. We know that while communities care about people with serious mental illness, they are relieved when this population is kept out of sight and out of mind. The community wants quick answers to mental illness, and community responses do not necessarily embrace the same principles of compassion toward people with mental illness as the social work profession does. The pressure on social workers, who are pushed by the competing interests of client, community, and agency, contributes to the strain of the job. Under these demanding circumstances, stress management skills are essential.

When I started training social workers in strengths-based case management 20 years ago, there were many social workers who were attracted to this work who were full of passion and were excited to be out in the community as opposed to being inside an office all day long. We need social workers for whom community mental health is not just a job. That kind of attitude hurts the quality of care. When we talk to consumers about what qualities matter most to them in their treatment team, they tell us that they want providers with hope, energy, and passion. We need social workers who are vibrant, alive, and excited.

How would you describe the major opportunities available to social workers who work in community mental health?

Social workers have a skill set that matches almost perfectly with the world of fiscal accountability in the managed-care environment. Social workers are very good at multidimensional assessments, and are well equipped to use less expensive treatments that enable clients to live independently in their own homes and in the community. Social workers can lead in the development of solid, cost-effective treatment plans that are clinically appropriate. There are many opportunities for social work to flourish; however, in order to be successful, social workers must acquire a more comprehensive understanding of fiscal management. The worlds of care and of business have collided head-on, and social workers need to learn how to successfully navigate within this complex environment.

What is a key skill that you think social workers need in order to be successful in working in mental health?

As evidence-based practice becomes dominant, the importance of the professional relationship has been given short shrift, and that is a major mistake. Regardless of what kind of treatment approach one utilizes, treatment is ultimately a relationship. It is, in essence, a conversation between two people. I often think of a comment by one of my friends who is a leader in the consumer movement. She said that the most important quality and helpful element in her treatment was when she knew that her social worker genuinely cared about her. Compassion is the essence of all social work practice. It is the necessary foundation for our skills and knowledge.

DID YOU KNOW?

- Social workers are the country's largest provider of mental health services. According to the National Association of Social Workers, 60% of mental health professionals are clinically trained social workers.
- The Surgeon General's Report on Mental Health estimates that approximately 20% of the U.S. population is affected by mental disorders during a given year.
- According to an NASW survey, social workers in this practice are the largest single group of licensed social workers (Whitaker et al., 2006d).

SECTION THREE: FIRST-PERSON NARRATIVE

Working in the Outpatient Mental Health Setting: Challenges, Obstacles, and Victories
Eileen Klein, LCSW, PhD

Eileen Klein has worked in public mental health for over 25 years as a social worker, supervisor, and administrator with mentally ill inpatients and outpatients. She has a PhD in clinical social work and a master's in public administration from NYU. Currently, she is working at South Beach Psychiatric Center as the director of operations. Dr. Klein teaches in the MSW program at LIU and NYU and has written several articles on working with seriously ill psychiatric patients. She has extensive experience with the LGBT (lesbian, gay, bisexual, transgender) mentally ill population and has been instrumental in setting up a program to meet their psychosocial needs.

As a social worker in a public community mental health center, working effectively with the patients on their identified needs has always been and remains a challenge. Currently I am employed in a New York State–operated mental health center that provides services to a very vulnerable, multiproblem, economically disadvantaged socioeconomic group in an urban environment. Many of those served live on governmental subsidies; many live in residences that are supervised by a social services provider; and clients often have limited social, educational, and financial resources.

I got my MSW in the mid-1970s. I was attracted to social work because I could help others, and I learned to do so in field internships while getting the book knowledge and theory in classrooms. This appealed to me, since I had no experience in direct services as I was applying to get my degree directly after college. My goal was to make a positive impact on those in need and to save the less fortunate. I knew I liked helping others through some volunteer jobs I had during college in a local school for autistic children and some work in a state psychiatric inpatient unit. In my very limited experience, I thought that agencies were able to provide competent services to clients and that people with challenges had extra help available to ensure that they had an equal opportunity to succeed in life.

After getting my degree, my first job was in an inpatient psychiatric unit with psychiatrically regressed female patients. I soon found out that public policy and perception drove service provision and made effective treatment and interventions quite challenging. For example, in the 1970s, the consumer rights movement picked up steam, and psychiatric patients were represented by legal counsel. They fought to have the right to be treated in the least-restrictive setting. Social workers were told to begin immediate discharge planning to return psychiatric patients to the community from inpatient settings, and to ensure their civil rights. Unfortunately, we were not trained adequately in community resources to care for the vast issues that were identified as needing intervention once the patient was no longer in institutional care. I decided my skill could be better utilized working with clients on community skills while out in the "real world," so I got a job in an outpatient mental health clinic.

To my surprise, outpatient clinical staff were not prepared for the need to provide assistance with the daily activities of living in housing supports, training in transportation, job coaching, financial benefit management, and individual support. I felt inadequately trained to serve the seriously and persistently mentally ill (SPMI) with their multiproblems, since there were so few community supports available. Not only was I not trained to handle the multitude of problems that my clients presented, but the agency did not have the resources to provide me with enough time and supervision to do an effective job. I always felt that I was playing catch-up and trying to learn how to do my job while being responsible for doing it. I would refer to my orientation to outpatient community treatment as a trial by fire.

Since SPMI individuals failed in the community because of a lack of adequate supports, they often returned to psychiatric hospitals, jails, or other institutions. A beginning social worker would not be able to adequately help his or her clients without an expansive knowledge of community resources and systems of care. I often had a sense of failure when I did not succeed at keeping a client out of the hospital and helping him or her to integrate successfully back into society. In ret-rospect, I think this happened because the client did not have adequate resources for housing, family, medical, or social service benefits to pay for food and other needs, but at the time, I thought it was because I was not a "good enough" social worker, too new, not skilled. Not only was I unaware of resources to make these referrals or connections, but I didn't even know that they were important, since the client was unable to articulate that he or she had a void in that area. This was all very demoralizing.

I often encountered "impossible" situations, and there was no real structure of supervision to help with the case management or to help me deal with personal feelings of helplessness and hopelessness or with transference issues. This was very hard as a new social worker, and continued for many years. Since I worked in an agency where supervision was part of my job requirement, I tried to make the most of this time to learn about how to work more effectively and to manage my feelings about the work. The agency provided supervision to meet quantity and regulatory requirements, but the quality and content of the supervision left a lot to be desired. After several months, I began to realize how much I did not know about diagnosis and treatment or how to effectively engage clients with serious mental illness. My frustration and dissatisfaction with the job grew as I was more and more aware of my incompetence due to lack of knowledge. I began to feel burned out and became anxious about going to work.

I realized I needed a mentor/supervisor if I was to continue at this agency. I approached a psychiatrist on my treatment team who seemed to have a good work-ing relationship with the rest of the staff and a great relationship with the clients, and I asked if he could supervise me "on the sly." He agreed to do so, and we met weekly, but I could not discuss getting this help with anyone, since it was against agency policy to do so "from another discipline." I learned a great deal from our meetings both about the work and about myself. It helped me to continue to go into work and feel good about my job as a social worker. I realized I would like to try to help clients once they were moved out of the hospital and onto a community mental health outpatient setting.

From my first experiences as a social worker, I realized that we have to try to work within or around the system to provide quality care and get clients the services they need to remain in the community. We can we make a difference in someone's life, and when our interventions work, it motivates us to keep on going. Here is an example of a case that helped me to feel that I was effective in my job.

Edwin was assigned to me as one of my first clients in the outpatient clinic. Edwin, now 32, had been diagnosed as a schizophrenic at a young age and had difficulties that resulted in his being placed in institutions by age 8. He had dif-ficulties in school, which included poor attention span, irritability, and fights with peers, and therefore he had a limited education. He had poor family support, since he came from an impoverished family that was functioning day to day to make ends meet. Spending too much time on one family member's problems was not possible, so he was on his own most of the time. Edwin was chronically delusional and marginally functioned in his self-care skills, but he did attend an outpatient program daily and was extremely personable and engaging. When Edwin was assigned to me, it was after he had been assigned to four other social workers in the agency and had been prescribed numerous psychiatric medications in an effort to stabilize him. When I saw him, I was told that "he was as good as he would be able to get" and was wished "good luck" by his transferring therapist. I decided to go back to my roots and begin where the client was at and stay with him through the process.

Edwin told me in our initial session that he wanted to go to college and get a job. Given his inability to read past a 4th grade level, I went along with his goal, but told him we had to improve his reading ability to get into college, and that the first step was improved literacy and a GED. He seemed excited that I was "the first social worker that told me that I should not pursue this because it would be too frustrating." Of course, my agency had no resources for improving reading skills, getting a GED, etc., and I knew that this would take some creative thinking on how to get this done. However, I told him it would be hard work, but that I'd go with it and we'd persevere. As time went on, Edwin joined a literacy class at the local library, did learn to read, and sometimes would read poetry to me in our sessions. He did eventually get a GED. My believing in his ability to reach his goal was what motivated both of us to go through the frustrations of agency's inability to help him through programming or funding, and to plod on to a successful conclusion.

As I gained confidence in my social work skills, I decided to get a second job working fee-for-service at an agency doing therapy with less disturbed clients. I was again reminded of Social Work Policy 101: Agencies have multiple agendas that drive their policies and standards of service provision. Many agencies have to meet a certain number of services to maintain their funding streams, and some have other objectives, either implicit or explicit, that have nothing to do with taking care of their clients. I was faced with a situation where my goals (to help others) directly conflicted with the agency's goals and the clients' goals.

The clinic was part of a large managed-care agency that served middle-class union members, mostly civil service employees. The agency had to see a certain number of clients per month, as intakes and their staffing levels and salary bonuses were based on these numbers. Because the number of clients that had an intake could not be accommodated with weekly therapy sessions once they came to the agency, the implicit goal was to see clients and, during the intake, make an assessment as to whether you could refer them out, see them infrequently, or assure them that they were fine and might not need services at all. While this served the management of the agency, it did not feel appropriate to the direct service staff, so the issue was brought to management. The result was that the policy of the agency changed so that all intakes became the responsibility of the intake social worker for further treatment; so if you were feeling the need to admit the patient, you added him or her to your caseload.

The agency set up a situation that you were actually overloaded with work if you chose to care about those that were seeking services. I felt that this was a true ethical dilemma, one of many faced by agency social work staff on a daily basis. If you give a lot to one client, you may not have the time to give adequate attention to another, since there is a quota for services delivered. We are often judged not by the thoroughness and quality of our work, but by the statistics produced for the agency.

In summary, we face many organizational, systemic, and political roadblocks in social work in outpatient mental health. Some are the result of agency funding, policy initiatives, supervision (or lack thereof), the inability of an agency to keep up with changing community needs, and inertia. These challenges can be met head on and overcome with perseverance; continuing education of staff, agency administration, and community; and hard work. In the end, it's a win-win for the social worker, the client, and the agency. We all feel good about a successful and valid result in meeting our clients' needs and helping them move on to a more meaningful and productive life. When we feel good about our ability for success in our job, we feel able to go on and not get burned out by a difficult and challenging system that has few external rewards. Our reward is seeing a client get better and move forward, and sometimes we can make changes for the greater good.

IS MENTAL HEALTH THE RIGHT FIELD FOR YOU?

- Eileen found that her social work training did not adequately prepare her for the challenges of her job, and she sought out her own system of mentorship. How comfortable would you be if placed in a similar situation?
- How do you think Eileen's belief in and support for Edwin helped him to achieve his goals?
- Eileen discusses a number of organizational roadblocks and recounts how she successfully navigated them. Envision yourself in her position and how you would cope with similar demands.

SECTION FOUR: RESOURCES TO LEARN MORE

Web Sites

- Mental Health: A Report of the Surgeon General: http://www.surgeongeneral.gov
- Mental Health America: http://www.nmha.org
- Mental Health Matters: http://www.mental-health-matters.com
- The Mental Health Social Worker: http://mhsw.org
- National Alliance on Mental Illness: http://www.nami.org
- Samhsa's National Mental Health Information Center: http://mental-health.samhsa.gov
- The National Institute of Mental Health (NIMH): http://www.nimh.nih.gov
- The Suicide Prevention Resource Center (SPRC): http://www.sprc.org

Journals

- *Best Practices in Mental Health: An International Journal*, Lyceum Books
- *Journal of Human Behavior in the Social Environment*, Haworth Press
- *Social Work in Mental Health*, Haworth Press

Books

- *Community Mental Health: Challenges for the 21st Century*, by Jessica Rosenberg and Sam Rosenberg (2006, Routledge)
- *Mental Health Social Work: Evidence-Based Practice*, by Colin Pritchard (2006, Routledge)

Policy

- Mental Health. In *Social Work Speaks*, 7th ed. NASW Policy Statements, 2006–2009
- Professional Impairment. In *Social Work Speaks*, 7th ed. NASW Policy Statements, 2006–2009
- Youth Suicide. In *Social Work Speaks*, 7th ed. NASW Policy Statements, 2006–2009

Practice

- Mind and Spirit: http://www.helpstartshere.org
- Social Work in Mental Health: http://www.naswnyc.org

Educational Programs/Centers

- California State University, Chico School of Social Work, Mental Health Stipend Program
- University of Texas at Austin, The Hogg Foundation for Mental Health
- University of Wyoming, Division of Social Work, health and mental health certificate programs

10

Social Work With the Military

SECTION ONE: FIELD OVERVIEW AND FORECAST

Scope of Services

S ocial workers have provided services to the military dating back to the Civil War, when medical social workers visited wounded soldiers in hospitals (Garber & McNelis, 1995; Rahia, 1999). The American Red Cross has played a major role in the expansion and development of military social work, employing medical and psychiatric social workers to provide social work services to the military during World Wars I and II (Harris, 1999). During the 1970s and 1980s, military social workers were used to treat substance abuse and to address family problems, such as child abuse and domestic violence (Jenkins, 1999).

The psychiatric condition known as posttraumatic stress disorder (PTSD) was originally identified in the 1970s during the Vietnam War because of the large number of Vietnam veterans who had significant difficulty adjusting to civilian life. According to the National Institute on Mental Health, PTSD occurs after a person experiences a terrifying and traumatic event or ordeal in which grave physical harm occurred or was threatened, such as military combat (National Institute of Mental Health, 2008a). PTSD is defined as a psychiatric condition characterized by several symptoms: recurrent and intrusive flashbacks of the traumatic event; nightmares; depression and anxiety; and significant distress or impairment in social, occupational, or other important areas of functioning (American Psychiatric Association, 2000).

A survey conducted by the U.S. Department of Veteran's Affairs found that the majority of Vietnam veterans appear to have successfully readjusted to postwar life, with few symptoms of psychological distress. However, the study revealed that a substantial number of Vietnam veterans have experienced multiple psychosocial problems, e.g., family and work difficulties (Price, n.d.). Given the potential for serious psychological damage associated with active combat service, significant concern exists about the long-term psychological impact of combat on the servicemen and -women who have been deployed during the current conflicts in the Middle East. Research suggests that the long-term mental health problems associated with these new wars are likely to be more severe than other post–Vietnam War operations, such as in Somalia and the 1991 Persian Gulf War (Litz, n.d.). The unique features of current military life include the unprecedented number of wounded servicemen and -women that are surviving combat with serious and disabling injuries due to advancements in medical technology; the increased use of improvised explosive devices (IEDs), which has resulted in an extremely high number of traumatic brain injuries; and military personnel who are serving multiple tours of duty, causing them to be in combat for longer periods of time than ever before.

Social work services with returning service members are an important component of the assistance that these men and women will need as they reintegrate into society. According to the National Association of Social Workers, social workers are front and center in helping military personnel and their families cope with and recover from the trauma of war. Social workers provide a wide range of services, including family-support programs and mental health care (DeAngelis, n.d.).

Settings

The major setting for social work with the military is the U.S. Department of Veteran's Affairs (VA). The VA operates one of the largest health care systems in the United States, with 157 hospitals and more than 860 community-based clinics. The VA provides a wide array of services to veterans, family members, or survivors of veterans, including health care, mental health care, education and training, disability benefits, insurance, and home loans. Employing more than 4,000 social workers, the VA is the largest social work employer in the nation. Social workers employed by the VA work in numerous capacities. A recent Internet search of vacant social work positions available throughout the country in VA centers yielded 12 job openings for the following positions: addictions counselors, vocational counselors, readjustment counseling therapists, and social science analysts. The starting annual salary for these positions ranged from $45,000 for entry-level positions to $77,000 for the more senior positions. The entry-level positions require a bachelor's degree, and the more advanced positions require a master's degree. The VA can be a challenging place to work. It is a large organization with plenty of opportunity to move up the career ladder. The salary and benefits packages are competitive, and the work is challenging and rewarding. However, the VA is extremely bureaucratic. The many rules and rigid protocols can make it a frustrating work environment for some social workers (Manske, 2008).

Social workers also work with the military as active members of the armed forces. Enlisted social workers can serve in all five branches of the armed forces: army, navy, air force, marines, and the coast guard. According to an excellent account of military social work by James G. Daley (1999), "The main function of military social work is to support the readiness of our soldiers to fight and win wars for our nation." A recent Internet search for military social work positions found several positions with the U.S. Armed Forces. The navy advertised for a licensed clinical social worker to provide counseling and crisis intervention services for military personnel and their families. The air force advertised for social workers to work with enlisted individuals, couples, and families. These positions require overseas travel. Working for the armed forces is a decision that no social worker should make impulsively. It is a commitment that, once made, cannot easily be unmade. Social workers, like all members of the armed services, can be called to active duty at any time. Being a member of the armed forces can be a lonely and dangerous life; however, some social workers express tremendous satisfaction from this unique career. This highly personal decision should be made carefully.

Social workers can also work with the military in nongovernmental settings. Many veterans receive their medical and mental health care in not-for-profit settings. There are some agencies that are dedicated to helping veterans, for example, the National Coalition for Homeless Veterans (www.nchv.org), an organization that assists homeless veterans and those at risk of becoming homeless.

The Social Worker's Role

The National Association of Social Workers (NASW) notes that social workers provide a continuum of services to the military, ranging from preventive care to ongoing treatment during active duty to aftercare following discharge from the military. Preventive services include family and parent support groups to help soldiers prepare for combat and to connect families remaining at home with supports and services. Ongoing treatment involves working with active-duty military and helping them cope with combat. This can involve treating depression and substance abuse. Working with soldiers post-deployment focuses on helping them reintegrate into civilian life. Family problems, substance abuse, and PTSD are major treatment areas. Medical social workers provide services to military that are injured and disabled. In addition to the clinical function, Cox (1999) notes that, over time, social workers have taken on important roles in administration, advocacy, mediation, program planning, and management.

Social workers working with the military are faced with a unique set of ethical dilemmas, particularly if they are enlisted in the armed forces. Military social workers have to respond to multiple and competing authorities: On the one hand, they have a professional ethical code; on the other hand, they have to follow military rules and regulations, and they are governed by the Uniform Code of Military Justice. Conflict can emerge between these two areas, leaving the social worker caught in the middle, struggling to resolve an ethical dilemma. Active-duty social workers cannot simply walk away from or quit their jobs because they disagree with a command or decision (Talent & Ryberg, 1999).

Credentialing

Clinical licensure at the state level is likely to be required for positions providing clinical mental health services to military personnel.

Emerging Issues and Employment Trends

The wars in the Middle East will continue to exert a toll on the hearts and minds of the returning soldiers and their loved ones for generations to come. The impact of these conflicts will require social work services, particularly in health and mental health care. Research estimates that more than 1.6 million American military personnel have been deployed to Operation Iraqi Freedom and Operation Enduring Freedom in Afghanistan since 2001, a significant number of whom are expected to experience serious psychological distress as a consequence of combat duty (Tanielian, 2008). Families of service members are also impacted by the war in multiple ways. A soldier's return to the family impacts every member of the family: Domestic violence and child abuse, financial problems, substance abuse, and marriage stressors are among the many problems that can impact military families. Michelle Sherman, director of the Family Mental Health program at the Oklahoma City Veterans Affairs Medical Center, emphasizes the impact of combat trauma on the family and strongly encourages social workers to include the entire family in treatment (Sherman, 2008).

ACTIVITIES TO LEARN MORE

- Contact your local veterans center or veterans affairs department and find out about employment opportunities for social workers. Many centers are actively recruiting and hold ongoing informational sessions.
- Visit the National Institute of Mental Health Web site (http://www.nimh.nih.gov/) and read the discussion about posttraumatic stress disorder.
- Learn about social work services offered in the Fisher houses. The Fisher House program provides support for families of patients receiving medical care at major military and VA medical centers. There are 40 Fisher houses throughout the United States located at 18 military installations and 10 VA medical centers. Three more are under construction. Learn more at the Fisher House Web site (www.fisherhouse.org).

SECTION TWO: CRITICAL ISSUES
Kristin Day, LCSW

Kristin Day, LCSW, is chief consultant in the Care Management and Social Work Service, Office of Patient Care Services, Department of Veterans Affairs. In this capacity, she has overall responsibility for six programs, including social work, the Caregiver Support Program, the Family Hospitality Program, the Federal Recovery Coordination Program, Operation Iraqi Freedom and Operation Enduring Freedom Case Management Program, and the VA Liaison Program. Ms. Day pioneered the development and implementation of key VA programs to serve returning wounded, ill, and injured from the wars in Iraq and Afghanistan. Ms. Day is currently enrolled in a PhD program with Catholic University of America.

Please tell me a little about yourself and your path in social work. What are some of the factors that motivated you to become a social worker? What drew you to social work with the veterans as an area of focus? Was it a particular issue or concern?

I have a BSW from the University of Kentucky and an MSW from Florida State University. While earning my MSW, I got a summer stipend with the Department of Veterans Affairs (VA) to conduct psychosocial assessments with veterans in long-term care. I completed 90 psychosocials in 90 days at the Georgia VA. I listened to the stories of these individuals, many of whom as young adults had survived the Bataan Death March in WW II or the atrocities during the Korean War. This experience changed my life. The bravery of these warriors, who served their country so well, resonated with me in the deepest part of my being. Their stories touched me deeply, and it has been a privilege for me to serve our veterans for the last 27 years.

What do social workers at the VA do?

The VA is the largest employer of social workers in the world. The VA has affiliations with over 100 schools of social work, and we train 600–800 students every year. Forty-five percent of VA social workers did student internships with us.

The wars in Afghanistan and Iraq have had a tremendous impact on social work at the VA. In 2003, the VA had a workforce of about 4,200 social workers. Today, the VA employs 6,000 social workers in order to respond to the biopsychosocial needs of returning warriors and their families.

At the VA, social workers are a core member of the clinical team and have a wide range of roles. Social workers serve in primary- and specialty-care clinics as well as in mental health and long-term care programs. They provide community-based care, work in posttraumatic stress disorder clinics, and provide case management in spinal cord injury and transplant clinics.

What are some of the major trends impacting social work practice with the Department of Veterans Affairs?

The adjustment challenges facing the soldier and his or her family are enormous, and it's normal to experience challenges while adapting to postdeployment. The term *battlemind* is now used to describe the challenges that soldiers face in the transition home. Soldiers live in survival mode for months, and develop hypervigilant and guarded behaviors. Suddenly they return home and their combat-coping skills don't apply to civilian life. For example, on the Baghdad roads, soldiers have to drive fast and furiously to avoid attacks and explosive devices. However, while this kind of driving keeps you alive in combat, it can get you killed at home on I-95.

There is the initial joy of reuniting with family upon returning home, but life can quickly become extremely stressful. The warrior who has been gone for an extended period is returning to a family that has changed significantly. The spouse who stayed at home has grown accustomed to doing things on his or her own; the children have grown older and have different needs. All of these changes require flexibility and lots of negotiation, and that can be very challenging when you are 21 years old and haven't been married very long. It's frightening how fast a life can unravel. The warriors may start to self-medicate, and their primary relationships may start falling apart. We owe it to our troops to be there for them when they come home. If services are provided early, the odds of a successful transition home increase. At the VA, adjustment challenges are normal, and warriors should not be stigmatized upon return from war. VA has social workers in our primary-care clinics to increase our ability to connect with those in need as quickly as possible and provide support.

What are some of the most prevalent practice issues that social workers who work with the military address?
The quality of medical care being provided on the ground in Iraq is unprecedented. Sophisticated medical teams are able to provide a level of care never imagined before. Today, 9 out of 10 wounded soldiers survive. This is a much higher rate compared with the Vietnam War. For example, when a soldier in Iraq suffers a spinal cord injury or brain trauma from an IED, the soldier receives immediate medical care at the site; is flown to Germany, where he or she is stabilized, perhaps even placed into a medical coma; and is then flown to Walter Reed Hospital in Washington, D.C., all within 72 hours.

There are six main categories of catastrophic injury: spinal cord injury, amputation, visual impairment, traumatic brain injury, burns, and posttraumatic stress disorder. Soldiers survive these injuries because of very sophisticated medical technology and expertise. Another challenge for VA social workers is responding to the differing developmental and social needs related to the demographics of the veteran population. Services are provided to 20-year-olds, who volunteered for the war, as well as older veterans who are members of the national guard. The national guard members are, on average, in their mid-40s. Typically, they joined the national guard with the intent of protecting the country in times of a national disaster. Many of these soldiers never imagined that they would become active-duty military, yet tens of thousands of them have been called for active duty and are deployed in Iraq and Afghanistan. These warriors face a different set of challenges than the younger recruits. In many cases, these warriors are deployed in the middle of their careers, disrupting both their personal, professional, and financial affairs.

In this war, unlike previous wars, military personnel serve on multiple tours. In WW II, soldiers served together and may have been deployed for up to 6 or 7 years. During the Vietnam War, the marines went for 13 months, and all other soldiers went for 12 months. They would mark the days off the calendar and survive. Today, warriors may serve multiple tours of duty, with the average tour lasting over a year. This may have a multigenerational impact on families, as the children are profoundly affected by the absence of a parent and by how well the parent who stayed home was able to cope and adapt.

What is it like for social workers to work for the VA?
At the VA, social workers are perceived as mission-critical. We are highly valued and respected. The salaries and benefits are competitive. We have excellent health care benefits.

What are some of biggest challenges confronting social workers who work in the VA?
We have a hard time finding qualified social workers to fill our management positions. We have many seasoned clinical social workers, but the pool of social workers with the appropriate leadership experience and training is very small. About 15 years ago, the VA reorganized, and as part of that restructuring, social work departments were dismantled, and opportunities for mentorship and leadership training were reduced. As a result, we are struggling with a lack of qualified and experienced social work leadership. We are working on strategies to nurture and groom social workers for leadership opportunities.

What skills do you think enable social workers to be successful in working with the VA
Social workers at the VA need to have a burning commitment to the mission. To be successful at the VA, one must have to have a tolerance for a highly structured organization governed by many rules and protocols. Social workers have to learn to adapt and be able to maneuver on behalf of the patient within the structure. But again, the mission is extremely compelling, and it is an honor to serve America's finest sons and daughters.

What advice would you give to a social worker who wants to work with the VA?
Talk to our warriors whenever you can. I make it a point, when I see a warrior in uniform at the local McDonalds or somewhere in the community, to go up to them and say hello and thank them for their service. They have a story to tell and they will often share it with you.

I believe that students and new social workers should follow their passion, and if this is not your passion, then you owe it to yourself and your clients to keep looking. If you want a career at the VA, there are extensive opportunities. Employment opportunities are listed on the Web site USAJOBS.gov. I encourage social workers to contact their local VA and speak to the chief social worker and take advantage of informational interviews.

What do you think social work practice with the VA will be like in 5 years? Do you predict career growth and opportunities? Why?
I believe that social work practice with the VA will change in ways that will be wonderful for the patients and for the social workers. Our new generation of "20-somethings" is a well-informed group of health care consumers. The old paradigm of the doctor as the supreme authority and the patient as the passive recipient is over. Today's veterans are informed consumers; they've been on the Internet, done their research, and know exactly what they want. This generation of health

care consumers is in the driver's seat, and that's great. Social workers will partner with patients in ways that are most meaningful to the patient.

DID YOU KNOW?

- A 2007 report issued by the American Psychological Association's Presidential Task Force on Military Deployment Services for Youth, Families, and Service Members found a severe workforce shortage of behavioral mental health professionals with the training and skills needed to provide treatment to military personnel. Those who work in this area are at high risk for burnout due to work-related stress.
- At present, 700,000 children in America have at least one parent deployed in the military.
- The composition of the military has changed considerably since the nation was last at war. Today, the military comprises 16% women, and women are assigned to 90% of all military job categories.

Source: The Psychological Needs of U.S. Military Service Members and Their Families: A Preliminary Report. American Psychological Association.

SECTION THREE: FIRST-PERSON NARRATIVE

Serving Those Who Have Born the Battle: Social Work With the Military
James Shepard, LICSW

James Shepard is a licensed independent clinical social worker (LICSW) in the state of Washington. He received his master's degree in social work from the University of Washington in Seattle, Washington. He is also a member of the National Association of Social Workers (NASW) in the state of Washington.

Mr. Shepard served as a clinical social worker at Evergreen Medical Center in Kirkland, Washington, in the Care Management Department, where he covered multiple units including surgery, rehabilitation, and emergency services. He then began his career with the federal government in Seattle, Washington, at the Department of Veterans Affairs, serving as a clinical social worker in the Assisted Living Pilot Program, and subsequently was recognized as an honoree at the 2005 Federal Executive Board's Celebration of Public Service.

Having found a passion in medical social work, Mr. Shepard continues to practice at the Department of Veterans Affairs in Seattle, in the Rehabilitation Medicine Department, where he serves the inpatient rehabilitation unit and the outpatient rehabilitation clinics. He is grateful to be practicing with patients who have complex medical diagnoses such as multiple sclerosis and amyotrophic lateral sclerosis. He feels honored to work with so many people who have such incredible strength and integrity.

Mr. Shepard lives in Seattle with his wonderful wife and is the proud father of Cole James Shepard who was born April 25, 2009. He feels blessed to have the utmost support from his family and does not let a day go by without recognizing them as the foundation of his life.

The U.S. Department of Veterans Affairs, the largest integrated health care network in the country, is not where I envisioned my social work interests and skills to be utilized. With approximately 155 medical centers and over 1,400 sites of care across the country, including Puerto Rico and the District of Columbia, the Veterans Health Administration is responsible for the care of almost 5.5 million patients, and the number continues to rise. In social work school, the field of social work often felt limited to very specialized locales and small community organizations, not large political institutions that are overseen by the U.S. government. When I would hear the words *grassroots* and *community activism*, a picture was painted in my psyche of protesters with signs and community centers for low-income populations. Upon entering the workforce after school, it was very apparent that social work existed in every single fabric of our culture, no matter the location, population, or size of the institution or agency.

My journey in social work began at a young age. I was emotionally impacted by a group of counselors that I adored very much. Their kindness and compassion affected me in such a positive way that I made the decision to dedicate myself to those in vulnerable situations. Later in life, I was fortunate enough to be given the opportunity to attend college. After I had received my BA in sociology from the University of Washington in Seattle, I realized that my career path was still not clear to me. It was at this time that a friend of mine mentioned that her father was a social worker at the Seattle VA Medical Center. I eagerly handed over my short and limited resume, hoping to hear something about possible employment opportunities. A couple of days later I was nervously sitting in the social work department waiting area at the VA Medical Center with an 11:00 a.m. interview. I was hired as a social work associate, acting as a liaison between the VA hospital and the Department of Social and Health Services. My career path in the field of social work began to take form.

After one year of this work, I was encouraged by my supervisor to further my education. I entered the Master of Social Work Program at the University of Washington. I completed my first-year internship at Seattle Mental Health, treating individuals with serious and chronic mental health issues, an eye-opening experience to say the least. For my second-year internship, I was fortunate enough to come back to the VA Medical Center to work in the primary-care clinic with veterans on an inpatient and outpatient basis.

After I had received my MSW, I returned once again to the VA and worked in an assisted-living pilot program, mainly focusing on placement issues and community visits and reintegration. When this program's funding was not extended, the harsh reality of budget constraints in a large organization hit home. For the time being, anyway, I was in limbo, working at the VA on a month-to-month basis, not knowing if I would have a job the next day. A hiring freeze was established, and the possibility of steady permanent employment seemed to be slipping away as fast as the budget. Then, when I thought hope was almost lost, a clinical social worker position became available in the rehabilitation care service department, and I was selected to work on this specialty inpatient unit.

Prior to this new job, I had experience working with geriatric populations; substance abuse, mental health, and low-income populations; acute medical issues; and different disabilities of many kinds. As a rehabilitation social worker, I would now learn the complex social work case-management needs of veterans with severe strokes, multiple sclerosis, and amyotrophic lateral sclerosis. Not only that, but like any other patients, these primary diagnoses often coexist with cognitive impairments, mental health issues, and substance abuse. A key difference regarding these patients is their experience in the military. During times of war, military personnel suffer the effects of physical and psychological trauma; it takes a special skill set to honor these people and work with their issues. Specifically, wartime veterans suffer higher rates of substance abuse and mental health problems, with most of these problems stemming from their time in service. Add posttraumatic stress disorder to this complex mix of medical diagnoses, and the task of developing a treatment plan is both challenging and inspiring.

Rehabilitation medicine requires a unique interdisciplinary team approach. Every morning, the entire team meets for daily rounds. A brief dialogue is held with all the team members to discuss short- and long-term goals for each patient on the unit. Team members may include but are not limited to physicians, nurses, physical therapists, occupational therapists, psychologists, social workers, recreational therapists, and speech pathologists. Individual team members share their goals and updates pertaining to each area of specialty. Using this interdisciplinary model creates a highly functional holistic approach to care that encompasses the specific needs of the patient, thus creating a strengths-based, goal-oriented plan for rehabilitation. Social work case management is an important function in this interdisciplinary team approach.

I began the rehabilitation-medicine, social work, case-management model with an open mind and an open heart. Despite whatever degree of openness I thought I possessed, I struggled with many internal and external issues, especially personal feelings about war and its effects on people. The first time I met with a veteran who was a quadriplegic, I felt an overwhelming sense of empathy and, to be quite honest, extreme sadness. This gentleman was completely wheelchair-bound and bed-bound. He had already been to war and was now facing a different kind of war, a war with his body and mind. His power wheelchair was equipped with a sip-and-puff device to allow his mouth to drive his wheelchair. His speech was almost unintelligible, and it could take an hour to complete an average 10-minute conversation. His primary support was his care-giving agency, and it was difficult for his family to be consistently present for him. He reported on several occasions that he wanted to die at home, not in a nursing facility or hospital. I thought to myself, as a social worker, what was my role going to be in this veteran's life? It was a complex situation, and I found it difficult to separate my emotions and my job. I knew this was an area I would need to work on if I were to be a successful VA social worker in the world of rehabilitation medicine.

Over time, I became familiar working with these disabilities and learned how to channel my personal emotions into positive social work experiences for the patients. After all, it is about the veterans, not about me. Self-care is definitely an essential part of being a social worker, but I always remind myself to remain client-centered and focus on their needs. However, there are other issues that contribute to this unique work environment that may not appear to be directly related to patient care.

Workplace politics are challenging, and if you are a fairly new social worker, it can be downright discouraging. In an institution that is overseen by the U.S. government, there are endless checks and balances. We are taught to be responsible for the well-being of our patients. We must tirelessly advocate for them in their ongoing pursuit of self-determination. However, it can be difficult to distinguish our ethical obligations from our bureaucratic mandates within these large organizations.

Take the aforementioned case example of the patient who was determined to die at home. This patient required 24-hour-a-day care, but his benefits only allowed a certain number of in-home care hours. His wishes to stay in the home until death appeared to be unattainable. If his condition deteriorated to the point that he required a higher level of medical care, he had to be taken to the hospital's intensive-care unit. I wanted to fight to get this patient home on a hospice program if he was indeed close to dying. This man was a distinguished war veteran who deserved to live out his every wish and die with his dignity, just as he served our country. But how could I make the argument that we should send him home when his family had a durable power of attorney and felt differently about his plan for care? The simple fact was that I couldn't. This was hard to accept.

He was not coherent at the time the family made the decision to keep him in the hospital to die. From my work with the veteran, I knew this choice was not what he wanted. At the same time, I was honored to respect the family's decision, and I completely understand why they made that decision. Even so, it was hard to see this patient unable to express his true wishes and even more difficult to see him restricted by laws and organizational policies. The most important thing to me as a social worker was that I did what I could within the particular system to preserve his self-determination. I was there for him when he needed me. With that said, I have great respect for all families that must make these difficult decisions, for the laws that are designed to protect the well-being of the patients, and for the organizations like the VA that serve some of the most vulnerable of populations.

When assisting the veteran population, dignity, self-determination, quality of life, and service to this country contribute to the fabric of social work. As social workers dealing with veterans, we must advocate no matter what obstacles, laws, or policies may dictate. The vulnerability of the human experience regarding war and trauma in a large or small organization is very important. As a civilian social worker in a large governmental system, my focus shall remain consistent with the official VA mission statement. In the words of Abraham Lincoln, the official VA mission is "to care for him who shall have borne the battle and for his widow and his orphan."

IS MILITARY SOCIAL WORK THE RIGHT FIELD FOR YOU?

- Working for the federal government involves being able to operate within a highly bureaucratized system. James describes how difficult this can be. How do you see yourself handling this challenge?
- James's work gives him the opportunity to treat clients who present with a complex mix of psychosocial challenges, including mental health, substance abuse, physical impairment, and family problems. Would you enjoy having so much variety in your work?
- James is the social worker on an interdisciplinary treatment team. This requires excellent communication skills and the ability to clearly articulate the social worker's role and contribution.

SECTION FOUR: RESOURCES TO LEARN MORE

Web Sites
- American Red Cross: http://www.redcross.org
- Family Advocacy Program, U.S. Air Force: http://www.af.mil
- Family Advocacy Program, U.S. Marine Corps: http://www.usmc-mccs.org
- National Center for Posttraumatic Stress Disorder: http://www.ncptsd.va.gov
- Today's Military, Social Workers: http://www.todaysmilitary.com/careers/job-listings/social-workers
- U.S. Department of Veterans Affairs (VA): www.va.gov

Journal Articles
- Bunch, S. G., Eastman, B. J., & Moore, R. R. (2007). A profile of grandparents raising grandchildren as a result of parental military deployment. *Journal of Human Behavior in the Social Environment, 15* (4), 1–12.
- Wheeler, D. P., & Bragin, M. (2007). Bringing it all back home: Social work and the challenge of returning veterans. *Health and Social Work, 32*, 297–300.

Books
- *Social Work Practice in the Military*, by James G. Daley (1999, Haworth Press)
- *The War Comes Home: Washington's Battle Against America's Veterans*, by Aaron Glantz (2009, University of California Press)

Professional Associations
- Department of Veterans Affairs of VA Social Workers, 1 Freedom Way, Augusta, GA 30904-6258
- The International Society for Traumatic Stress Studies: http://www.istss.org

Practice
- Military Service-Related PTSD: www.socialworkers.org
- Social Workers Help Military Families: http://www.socialworkers.org
- Trauma and the Military Family: Responses, Resources, and Opportunities for Growth, by Michelle D. Sherman, Social Work Today: http://www.socialworktoday.com
- Veterans Affairs: About Post Traumatic Stress Disorder (PTSD) and Brain Injury in Iraq's War Veterans by Katherine van Wormer: http://www.helpstartshere.org

Educational Programs/Centers
- Smith College School for Social Work Scholarship for Military Personnel
- University of Southern California, specialization in military social work and veteran services

11

Social Work With Palliative
and End-of-Life Care

SECTION ONE: FIELD OVERVIEW AND FORECAST

Scope of Services

Social work with palliative and end-of-life care is emerging as a vital and expanding field for social workers. Several factors support growth in this area:

1. The baby boomers have come of age, leading to a marked increase in the number of older adults.
2. Advances in medical care have extended the life span for many older adults, who now survive what once would have been a life-threatening acute medical episode, such as a heart attack or stroke.
3. Chronic pain is often a fact of life for many people.
4. There is growing awareness and utilization of techniques and medicines to ease pain and reduce suffering.
5. There is greater societal recognition of and support for the self-determination of people with terminal illness and of their right to die with dignity.

The National Association of Social Workers defines end-of-life care as a spectrum of services that attends to multiple dimension of illness, including spiritual, emotional, physical, and practical concerns. Services are provided to individuals and families along the continuum of the dying process. Grief and bereavement counseling for survivors is an important component of the work (End-of-Life Care, 2006)

Several laws and regulatory polices protect the rights of the terminally ill. The 1990 Patient Self Determination Act (Colleen, 1998) mandates that patients have:

- The right to participate in and direct their own health-care decisions
- The right to accept or refuse medical or surgical treatment

- The right to prepare an advance directive
- Information on the provider's policies that govern the utilization of these rights

Important health-care practices developed from this legislation, including advance-care planning. Advance-care planning encompasses activities directed toward establishing and implementing an individual's wishes for his or her end-of-life care, such as funeral planning, financial planning, designating a health-care proxy, and drafting advanced directives. Advance directives are legal documents that provide instructions about individual preferences in the event that a person is unable to communicate. These documents include a living will and medical power of attorney (National Hospice and Palliative Care Organization, 2008; End-of-Life Care, 2006).

Hospice care is a system of coordinated care and supportive services that provide assistance to dying patents and their loved ones. As such, hospice is not a designated place, but rather a philosophy of care and an integrated network of service delivery that occurs at home, in institutions, or in a combination of settings. The essence of hospice care is that it is a family-centered team approach that provides a holistic focus on the dying person's physical, emotional, and spiritual needs. Social workers are a core member of the hospice team. The close philosophical fit between hospice care and social work makes this a practice area that is extremely well suited to social workers (Kaplan, 1995).

Palliative care is designed to bring relief from the pain and stressors of serious illness. It differs from hospice care in that palliative care can be provided to all patients in need, including those who are expected to recover from their illness, whereas hospice care is designed for the terminally ill. The Center to Advance Palliative Care, a leading organization on palliative care, identifies social workers as crucial members of the palliative-care team, noting that social work education provides excellent training in assessing family dynamics, understanding the social context of illness, and engaging with and intervening for the client (www.capc-mssm.org). Social work and end-of-life care share core values: They both uphold the client's right to self-determination, and they are both strongly informed by a systems orientation that views the patient within the context of the family and the social environment. Social workers are extremely well prepared for practice and for leadership roles in this growing field.

Settings

Social workers in the field of end-of-life care work with clients in a variety of settings. Often these services are institutionally based, such as a hospital, nursing home, or assisted-living facility. Services are also frequently provided in the home or in a combination of settings.

The Social Worker's Role

A key feature of end-of-life care is that services are provided by an interdisciplinary team. Social workers will need to be skilled in effectively working as team members. Excellent communication skills, the ability to listen and to compromise, and skills in articulating and working toward a common goal are some of the essential qualities of being a good team player. The other team members may include a physician; a nurse; a religious counselor; speech, physical, and occupational therapists; and home health aides (National Hospice and Palliative Care Organization).

Social workers play a central role on these teams. The Standards for Social Work Practice in Palliative and End of Life Care (National Association of Social Workers, 2008) identifies a core set of 11 essential functions performed by social workers in this area:

1. Individual counseling and psychotherapy (including addressing the cognitive behavioral interventions)
2. Family counseling
3. Family–team conferencing
4. Crisis counseling
5. Information and education
6. Multidimensional interventions regarding symptom management
7. Support groups, bereavement groups
8. Case management and discharge planning
9. Decision making and the implications of various treatment alternatives
10. Resource counseling (including caregiving resources; alternative levels of care options, such as long-term care or hospice care; financial and legal needs; advance directives; and permanency planning for dependents)
11. Client advocacy/navigation of systems

Social work practice with clients who are dying is likely to engender a host of personal responses, leading social workers to reflect upon their personal religious beliefs and values as well as their own fears about death and dying. It is absolutely essential that social workers refrain from imposing their own values and personal feelings on their clients and client systems. To do so is bad practice, insensitive, and a violation of practice standards. Social workers are advised to seek ongoing supervision and continuing education to ensure that they do not allow their personal feelings to influence treatment. Furthermore, it is essential that social workers display compassion and sensitivity to clients who are suffering (NASW Standards for Social Work Practice in Palliative and End of Life Care, 2008; Cisikai, 2008).

Credentialing

A new specialty credential, the Advanced Certified Hospice and Palliative Social Worker (ACHP-SW), is now available. Developed jointly by the National Hospice and Palliative Care Organization (NHPCO) and the National Association of Social Workers (NASW), this credential is designed for social workers who meet national standards of excellence in hospice and palliative care. The qualifications include a master's degree in social work from an accredited university and at least two years of supervised social work experience in hospice and palliative care.

Emerging Issues and Employment Trends

End-of-life and palliative care are among the most important emerging fields of practice in social work, garnering significant attention from private foundations, think tanks, academics, practitioners, and social work leaders. The Soros Foundation Open Society Institute's Project on Death in America (PDIA) provides support to social work and end-of-life care. Through leadership awards and grants, the PDIA imparts prestige and support to this expanding practice area. This foundation helped make possible the first National Social Work Summit on End-of-Life and Palliative Care, which was convened in 2002. Among its many accomplishments, the summit helped bridge the gap between practice and education by promoting the integration of end-of-life care as a specialization of study in social work academic programs. The second Summit was held in June 2005. One of the outcomes was the formation of the Social Work in Hospice and Palliative Care Network (SWHPCN). This is a growing and dynamic network that comprises social work leaders and organizations committed to improving end-of-life care. It serves as an excellent resource for social workers who want to learn more about this field.

There is no question that the field of health care is rapidly changing. In the past, medical social workers might have found their niche in a social work–led hospital department. While this model still exists, it is on the decline. Other health-care specialties are becoming more dominant, reflecting the changing demographics and developments in medical technology. Perhaps no field in health care is as likely to expand as much as end-of-life care. There will be many employment opportunities in this area, as well as opportunities for leadership in a field that is still in a state of flux and growth. Essential qualities for the interested social worker are compassion, ability to respond to the needs of the dying and of their families, good teamwork skills, and the ability to work in multiple settings.

ACTIVITIES TO LEARN MORE

- Read the NASW Standards of Practice for Social Workers in Palliative and End-of-Life Care online at the NASW Web site (http://www.socialworkers.org/practice/bereavement/standards/default.asp).
- Contact your local hospital and find out what social work services are available to end-of-life-care patients.
- If you are a member of Facebook or LinkedIn, consider joining the American Academy of Hospice and Palliative Medicine (AAHPM) group. This is an interesting and easy way to network with hospice and palliative-care professionals. Find out how at the AAHPM Web site (http://www.aahpm.org/index.html).

SECTION TWO: CRITICAL ISSUES
Terry Altilio, LCSW

Terry Altilio, LCSW, is coordinator of social work for the Department of Pain Medicine and Palliative Care at Beth Israel Medical Center in New York City. She is a recipient of a Mayday Pain and Society Fellowship Award 2006 and a Social Work Leadership Award from the Open Society Institute's Project on Death in America, which supported a social work postgraduate fellowship and a social work listserv, both of which are continuing programs within the Department of Pain Medicine and Palliative Care. In 2003, she received the Social Worker of the Year award from the Association of Oncology Social Work as well as a Professional Volunteer Recognition Award from the American Cancer Society. She is also on the Advisory Council of the Alliance of State Pain Initiatives. Prior experience includes 14 years in oncology social work: 7 years with the Pain and Palliative Care Service at Memorial Sloan Kettering Cancer Center and 7 years in a community hospital. In addition to direct work with patients and families, she has lectured nationally and internationally on topics such as pain management, palliative caregiving, and psychosocial issues in end-of-life care. She lectures in the post-master's Palliative and End of Life Care Program at the New York University School of Social Work and Smith College School of Social Work, teaching Pain and Symptom Management and Ethics. She has coauthored publications on symptom management, psychosocial issues at the end of life, and caregiver advocacy issues.

Please tell me a little about yourself and your path in social work. What are some of the factors that motivated you to become a social worker? What drew you to pain and palliative care as an area of focus? Was it a particular issue or concern?
Ever since I was a young child, I have always wanted to be a social worker. I was a psychology major in college, and after I graduated, I worked for the New Jersey Bureau of Children's Services. That job was an amazing experience, and I did everything from adoption to foster care to preventive services. Following that position, I worked for a number of years at a residential program, taking advantage of a program that paid for its employees to get their MSW. I went to Hunter College School of Social Work and graduated in 1971, after which I returned to the residential program and worked in foster care until 1975, when my son was born. By 1977, I had taken a part-time position in a day center and begun a small private practice until 1983, when the need for increased income intruded, and I took a full-time position in a local hospital in an oncology unit. It was a new program, and getting into it from the ground floor appealed to me, even though I knew nothing about cancer treatment. During this time, I took courses in the psychosocial aspects of oncology at Memorial Sloan-Kettering Cancer Center, which is one of New York City's foremost oncology treatment institutions. After 7 years, I took a position at Memorial, which began a period of tremendous professional growth and learning. I was fortunate to work with some of the most skilled and talented people in the field of pain and palliative care. I began to realize that there are many common aspects that converge in the assessment of patients, whether they

are being treated for pain or in oncology or palliative-care settings. I continued to enhance my skills and to integrate the use of cognitive behavioral techniques, and I developed an appreciation for the infinite ways that social work skills are transferable to palliative care. In those days, social work was underrepresented in the field of pain and palliative care, yet I was fortunate to work with Matthew Loscalzo, one of the social work pioneers in this field.

What is palliative care? What kinds of clients and presenting problems do you generally work with?
Palliative care is the multidimensional, holistic care of patients and families who are living with a life-threatening or chronic illness. This perspective, which is congruent with social work's person-in-environment orientation, provides care to the person who happens to have an illness, as opposed to the medical model, which focuses solely on the illness itself. Palliative care involves understanding and responding to the whole person in context of his or her unique life story, and addresses all the aspects of life that are impacted when a person faces illness, such as socioeconomic concerns, spiritual beliefs, pain and symptom management, and family issues.

One thing that I really enjoy about this work is that we provide treatment to patients along the health continuum: Some of them are facing terminal diseases; others are living with chronic conditions; some may be facing an acute episode; and others are at the end of their life. We often facilitate the decision-making process for patients and families around significant life choices as well as treatment options. For example, what are the considerations in a young family who may want to have a child when a member of the family has a life-threatening illness? What are the pros and cons of taking a family leave of absence? What kinds of treatment might a patient select or not, given his or her goals, values, and beliefs? Families are often forced to make decisions, such as whom one appoints as a health-care proxy, under moments of tremendous pressure, and these decisions can impact survivors for the rest of their lives and affect how families work together. In the hospital, the pace is often quick and frantic. When possible, we work to slow things down so that families have a better opportunity to make the best choices for themselves, so that patients and families have an opportunity to process these very significant life choices.

What is it like to work with people who are suffering so much?
This work is challenging and incredibly exciting. At times it can be extremely sad. I've learned that if one is to engage in this work day after day, over a period of years, it is necessary to partialize and break things down into small pieces. This enables one to clearly see how one's work has a meaningful impact on a patient's life, even when we may not be able to change the outcome of a terminal illness. Being aware of how the seemingly little things that one does can profoundly affect the end-of-life experiences of patients and families makes this work meaningful and rewarding. Naturally, there are situations that I find difficult. When I find myself avoiding a specific patient or situation, it is a signal to me that there is something going on that is bothering me. I have to be self-aware to work through my

own feelings and reactions in order to engage in the work. What makes this work endlessly challenging and interesting is that it affords the opportunity to appreciate the uniqueness of the individual. The way that people choose to manage this chapter of their life differs for each individual, and it is a process that unfolds and evolves over time. It is essential that social workers in this field have the ability to be awed by the human spirit.

Do you believe there is there such a thing as a "good death?"
I am very cautious about having defined outcomes about what a good death is supposed to look like. There are multiple ways of dying and personal choices vary tremendously. Some people want to die alone; others prefer to be surrounded by loved ones. There is no one model of a "good death." One of the problems with defined outcomes is that they do not necessarily reflect good practice. For example, just because a patient has been assisted in identifying a health-care proxy does not mean that the work was of high quality and was respectful of the uniqueness of the individual. We have to develop better ways of understanding how to measure outcomes that reflect good practice.

What kinds of societal trends are likely to shape the future demand for social workers in palliative and end-of-life care?
We know that the field is responsive to changing demographics that include an increase among older adults and among those living with chronic illness. Social workers are well positioned to make a contribution, particularly since we are the only discipline that is trained to see the whole person within the context of his or her environment. However, I find that there is an increasing disconnect between the classroom and the world of work. When it's been several years since a professor walked the halls of a hospital or agency, that person's ability to train practitioners is diminished. Too often, I find that professors are more comfortable with concepts and models, but they are not preparing social work students for real work. The demands on new social workers are stronger than ever because of the accelerated and frantic pace in hospitals and agencies. Social workers have to be prepared to work effectively on interdisciplinary teams, and that means having the skills and knowledge to jump right in and clearly demonstrate one's expertise and what one can contribute to the team. Perhaps in the past there was greater opportunity for new social workers to get up to speed, but that is no longer the case. If social workers wants to earn the respect of their colleagues and they want to be relevant to the treatment process, they must be prepared to clearly articulate and demonstrate their value.

What kinds of social work services are important when someone is dying?
Social work is the only discipline that involves training to conduct an assessment of the patient within the context of his or her social environment. Our training provides us with the lens through which we view the dynamics during family meetings. We apply these skills when we make an analysis of the organizational dynamics that exist during interdisciplinary team meetings, of the formal and informal power structures, of the alliances and antagonisms.

It is imperative that the social worker have the ability to present himself or herself effectively and in a manner that is respected and listened to. We must have the skills to chart effectively. Sometimes when I look at the social work notes, I read "provided support." In today's economic climate, no managed-care insurance company is going to reimburse for a service that simply provides support, when a volunteer can sit and hold a person's hand. Social workers need the skills to write chart notes that are precise and to have command over a vocabulary that makes people believe that they are making a skillful and vital contribution to patient care. If you are sitting in silence with the patient, holding his or her hand, make sure that you can describe the clinical judgment that drives your work, that you are silent for a reason and not because you have nothing to say. Unfortunately, when social work faculty have limited practice experience, when they have not spent much time working in an agency-based setting or a hospital, they do not really know what skills they should be teaching. The practice recommendations that came out of the second social work Summit on End-of-Life and Palliative Care in 2005 recommended that social work faculty who teach practice skills have practice-based social work experience (Altilio, Gardia, & Otis-Green, 2007).

How much of your work is with families and with survivors?
Approximately half of my clinical work is with family members. We work closely with families on the hospital units, as long as this is an acceptable arrangement with the patient. We seek to reflect the real experience of a patient who is part of a family system and facilitate necessary input into decision-making processes. I follow very few survivors, because many patients who are at the end of life are cared for in hospice, which provides formal bereavement services. Social workers employed on a hospital unit would quickly get burned out if they continued to follow family members once the patient has been discharged or has died. There is a continuing stream of new patients and families to be cared for, and there is generally no protected time to follow those who have left in a comprehensive and ongoing treatment relationship.

Do you think there is a resistance in our society to treat pain? If so, why is that?
I think that there is a very strong societal prohibition to some pain management medications based on fears and concerns about addiction and diversion. There are many barriers to treating pain. For example, a "good patient" may not complain about pain, as he or she does not want to distract the physician from trying to cure the illness. On a macro level, the media attention to opiates and addictions creates a climate where it is more and more difficult to provide pain medications because some classes of medications have become so politicized. Health professionals in this country encounter societal and legislative barriers and, in addition, many are not well trained in the management of pain or the appropriate use of these medicines. At the same time, it's an ethical breach when we allow someone to suffer because we are uninformed about pain and symptom management.

Our resistance to treating pain is a tragedy that has gotten much worse. Our social policies designed to contain substance abuse and addiction are a dismal failure. It seems that we would rather go after physicians than face the reality that the "war on drugs" has not solved the problem of addiction and diversion. As a consequence, many medical professionals fear using opioids, and many patients suffer needlessly—and that, to me, is the real crime. Pain is necessary and provides a life-preserving function: Without pain signals, we would be unable to protect ourselves. Pain signals help keep us safe from harm and danger. It is what helps us to know that we have broken a bone or are burning ourselves. However, while on the one hand pain is universal, it is also experienced subjectively, and one has to rely on patient self-report for beginning assessment. The medical profession is much more comfortable with symptoms that can be objectively measured. As well, they are at much greater risk of regulatory scrutiny and potential professional risk than are social workers. We are much more comfortable with subjective reporting and, if skilled in the multidimensional aspects of pain, can assist our prescribing colleagues to create a treatment plan that provides safe, responsible, and competent care that may or may not include opioid medications.

What are some of the ethical dilemmas that you have encountered in your work?
The undertreatment of pain presents ethical questions. We have a mandate to do no harm, yet when we allow someone to be in pain because of professional ignorance or not having the appropriate skill set, we are ethically culpable. To behave ethically means having the courage to respectfully challenge work that is being done for expedience, to have the courage to stand up for clients, and to speak up and take a risk.

What is the most rewarding aspect of your work?
Working with patients and families is to be part of a narrative that evolves. When we work well together as a team, there is something about the shared work that is profoundly rewarding. It is amazing to recognize that one can make a difference, even if it's something that seems so small. Sometimes it's the seemingly minor things that count, like making sure to move the overhead tray table back so that the patient can reach it before one leaves the room. When we see the difference we can make in the lives of others, it inspires our continued work and informs our own lives.

What is the most important quality that social workers need in this field of practice?
The most important quality is to have an ability to tolerate and to live with uncertainty. Working in this field, one can become a bit superior and begin to think, as individuals and as a team, that we know better. For me, what I find very steadying is the recognition that uncertainty exists and that we do not always have to be in control. We can assert what we know and how we can help and still recognize that mutual learning and growth are never ending.

DID YOU KNOW?

- The provision of hospice care has expanded to include patients with a disease trajectory of longer than six months. These patients may be referred to as "chronically dying," or the "chronically terminally ill."
- Health disparities based on race have been identified in palliative and end-of-life practices. In the year 2000, 82% of all hospice patients in the United States were white.
- Minority racial groups receive comparatively limited pain treatment. Research shows that African American nursing home residents with cancer had a 64% greater chance of getting no pain medication than non-Hispanic whites.

Source: National Association of Social Workers.

SECTION THREE: FIRST-PERSON NARRATIVE

*Caring and Compassion: A Day in the Life
of a Hospice Social Worker*
Krystal Ashling, MSW, ACSW

Krystal Ashling, MSW, ACSW, is director of social services at Signature Hospice. She has worked in hospice for 14 years. She has been on the ethics committee at Southwest Washington Medical Center for 10 years. She has been chair and cochair of Oregon NASW's Ethics Committee since 1993.

Ms. Ashling has been a social worker for 20 years and is a certified ethics consultant and certified gerontologist. She was Oregon NASW Social Worker of the year in 2004. She has been a toastmaster for 4 years. She is a Usui and Karuna Reiki master. She enjoys speaking about ethics, Reiki, gerontology, and end-of-life issues.

For the past 14 of my 20 years in social work, I have worked in hospice. Hospice is "comfort care" for a terminally ill patient and his/her family. Comfort care, a commonly used term in hospice, is one of the clearest examples of Carl Rogers's concept of unconditional positive in regard to his philosophy of client-centered therapy. It asks us to listen to what the patient says about his or her comfort without our agenda. By demonstrating unconditional positive regard, the social worker provides the best possible condition for personal growth of patient and family. We assist them in achieving comfort, however they may define it. This could include pain control, or arranging for care in another hospice so that the patient may take that important last vacation, or contacting family members who have been estranged and facilitating reconciliation. A hospice social worker needs to be trained in mediation, negotiation, and bereavement as well as systems access and ethics.

In order for a patient to qualify for hospice care, a doctor has to state he/she has 6 months or less to live. Hospice care can happen in any environment, from personal homes to foster care, assisted living, or nursing homes. However, patients and families come to us with varied amounts of information about their disease process. A doctor may be very disclosing or may simply refer the patient to hospice without explanations. A nurse and a social worker will arrive at the home not knowing what emotional environment they may encounter. I personally have been met with friendliness, tears, anger, outrage, and in one instance, a gun.

Patients may be in hospice from a few hours up to years, since patients can get recertified every few months. The hospice social worker must be emotionally healthy enough to do what one can as a social worker, knowing that the patient *will* die and that holding a patient's hand can be as important as any other skill.

To offer a fuller picture of hospice social work, I will describe how my day may pattern. I start my day with prayer or meditation. Usually, I say a short prayer that I be guided in all my efforts during the day. I believe that I could not do the work that I do without spiritual assistance. It helps me remain positive, responsive, and kind for myself and for all those that I encounter during my day.

Hospice social work can be emotionally exhausting. Since I work in an environment where all of our patients are dying, I must deal with sadness, depression, and emotional and physical pain of patients and families on a daily basis. If I have any losses in my life that I have not processed, I may find myself getting too involved or crossing boundaries in a way not healthy for the patient or myself. It is important for me to be continually aware of my emotional needs and take care of them.

I also usually walk or run in the morning. I have found that physical activity is essential in coping with the many emotions that my work brings to the forefront. It gives me time to sort things out in my head. Physical activity balances the emotional activity.

Working in a hospice environment means accepting a certain amount of chaos during the day. I listen to my messages before getting to work so that I will know who died during the night and who has potential care-giving and bereavement issues. When I get to work, my immediate concern is if anyone is in crisis or dying at the moment. If so, I grab my paperwork and fly out the door. If someone is in the dying process, I assess how much of my presence is needed so that the patient and family are as comfortable as possible. This could be as little as a phone call or staying in the home for a few minutes, or it could mean that I spend the entire day with this family. Each patient/family unit comes with unique needs.

Many days include a team meeting. Hospice workers commit to being part of an interdisciplinary team. A hospice team usually consists of a doctor, a nurse, a social worker, a bath aide, a chaplain, and several other on-call or as-needed team members such as a pharmacist, a dietitian, a volunteer, and bereavement counselors. We discuss our clients' and families' current concerns and how we can best assist with them. All members of the team are involved. Being able to work as part of a team is challenging, mandatory, and rewarding. It demands that we value each professional's expertise in his/her field of knowledge, melding it all together for the best outcome for the patient. For example, a patient may be in bed and in pain. It might be important for the nurse to get the patient's pain under control, while the social worker assists the family in finding care-giving resources and enlisting the assistance of a bath aide and a volunteer. All of these activities would become part of the patient's care plan.

Another part of any day in our hospice involves social workers doing admissions. We look at caseloads, family conference schedules, and stress levels of other social workers to decide who does what during the day. We have to be willing and able to balance our individual needs with those of others; we must each advocate for ourselves if we are in need. This can create a certain amount of tension, but if everyone is willing to work at it and discuss it, it can work.

Being involved in admissions allows social workers to be involved at the onset of hospice care. Being present while the nurse does the physical assessment gives the social worker important knowledge about how the patient and family are adjusting to the care-giving situation and in the bereavement process. Seeing the home environment provides information about how well the family is functioning and what help they may want or need.

After crises are managed and admission duties assigned, I assess which patients and families need attention that day. Do I have a family conference? Does some patient need social worker involvement with community agencies? Does a family member need bereavement assistance after a patient's death? Are there some situations that might best be handled by a phone call? Because of crises, admissions, paperwork, and travel time, I can only plan for four or five visits during the day.

Ethical questions and concerns are involved in every aspect of hospice care, and it is vitally important for hospice social workers to be trained in ethics. For example, how much does the patient know about her/his illness and how much does the family want the patient to know? What is the meaning of pain in the patient's life, and how does she or he want it treated? Is the patient competent to make his or her own decisions? Autonomy is valued very highly in our mainstream culture, but may or may not be in other subcultures, for instance, in some Asian or Russian families. When I asked one Russian patriarch what he wanted in hospice, he kept saying, "Ask the family."

An example of ethical boundaries would be gift giving. Patients and families often want to give us gifts for our work. They may become angry or disillusioned if we refuse their offer of kindness. Knowing when, how, and why it is important to limit acceptance of gifts is a learned skill and one that the hospice social worker must constantly monitor.

Travel is a large aspect of our daily lives as hospice workers. We often travel up to 100 miles a day. One must know how to use a map and what to do if lost. We often go on unimproved roads for miles. I remember in the first few years getting lost in areas where my cell phone was out of range. It was frustrating and somewhat scary. We also eat in our cars and carry paperwork, equipment, and supplies as needed. We literally "live" in our cars.

Family conferences are a common part of hospice care. Families, especially those members who are not involved in primary care for the patient, may not understand what constitutes hospice care. They may think that we are "killing the patient." They may incorrectly assume that we are involved in physician-assisted suicide. Hospice is often seen as the harbinger of the death sentence. In a family conference, I explain that I am there to help the patient and family. I discuss what we can and cannot do in hospice, what physical changes the patient may experience, and what we expect the family to do. I typically do this many times for a particular patient or family, as the ideas need reinforcing or the situation changes. Family conferences can help alleviate many other problems that may arise, such as which family members will be care providers or relieve the stress of the primary family care providers or how to contact social service agencies.

The cultural background is important in family conferences. Although as hospice social workers we are current with training in cultural competencies, nothing is as educational as doing the work! For instance, in our area, many families are of Russian heritage. They are not all the same; they have many different religions and life experiences. Cultural concepts are helpful as basics, but they are insufficient to describe the variety of individuals and situation. We use translators when the patient doesn't speak English, even though other family members do. This can be hard to explain to family members, as it can seem that I don't trust them to translate correctly. I explain that hospice has many medical aspects, and even experienced English speakers may not have the knowledge to translate medical terminology.

Active and accurate listening skills are essential for a hospice social worker. I usually have a family member or patient during the day that I go to see to listen to what is happening for them. My response may also involve tasks such as contacting social service agencies, but my first job is to listen. I thank Carl Rogers for his teaching about unconditional positive regard. This is a place where my opinion doesn't matter. It is absolutely important that I am there with them at the moment and that I validate what they are experiencing. I may end up calling another patient or family and cancelling an appointment in order to be with this patient and family. Patients and families tend to be fine with this if they understand that when I am with them they will get the same attention.

At our hospice, social workers are paid a salary. I am expected to work however many hours it takes to get the job done. That may mean coming in early or staying late. I have to be at peace that my family never knows when to expect me to be at home.

Extracurricular activities are opportunities for growth and support, which keep me on the cutting edge of professional social work issues. I belong to Toastmasters because I give a number of social work workshops and I want to be able to improve my presentation skills. I also use presentation skills when discussing hospice care with patients and families. I am cochair of the ethics committee of our local chapter of the National Association of Social Workers, in which we often discuss questions that come from hospice social workers. I also supervise for licensure new MSWs practicing as hospice social workers. Each of these activities trains me more broadly or deeply in skills needed for hospice social work.

People often say, "I don't know how you do the work you do each day." Hospice social work involves presentation, negotiation, listening, advocating, mediation, bereavement assistance, diligence, persistence, and hopefulness in the midst of the direst of circumstances. It can be the hardest job you will ever love.

If you think you might be interested in hospice social work, think about volunteering at your local hospice. Call the volunteer coordinator to get started. Hospice care is hard emotionally, spiritually, and physically. It can also be an extremely rewarding and satisfying career.

IS PALLIATIVE AND END-OF-LIFE CARE THE RIGHT FIELD FOR YOU?

- To cope with working with terminally ill clients, Krystal makes sure to pay close attention to her own emotional needs. What strategies would you employ to protect yourself from getting emotionally exhausted by the work?
- Krystal describes her work as involving a fair amount of chaos. Are you comfortable with that?
- Krystal is a member of an interdisciplinary team and notes that tensions can arise when working on a team. Are you a team player who enjoys the give and take and compromise that is required to work effectively with others?

SECTION FOUR: RESOURCES TO LEARN MORE

Web Sites
- Americans for Better Care of the Dying: http://www.abcd-caring.org
- Association of Oncology Social Work: http://www.aosw.org
- Center to Advance Palliative Care: http://www.capc.org
- Duke Institute on Care at the End of Life: http://www.iceol.duke.edu
- International Association for Hospice & Palliative Care: http://www.hospicecare.com
- Kidney End of Life Coalition: http://www.kidneyeol.org
- National Hospice and Palliative Care Organization: http://www.nhpco.org
- National Palliative Care Research Center: http://www.npcrc.org
- The Social Work in Hospice and Palliative Care Network: http://swhpn.org/lhp

Journals
- *Journal of Social Work in End-of-Life Care*, Haworth Press

Books
- *Living With Dying: A Handbook for End-of-Life Healthcare Practitioners*, by Joan Berzoff and Phyllis R. Silverman (2004, Columbia University Press)

Policy
- End-of-Life Care. In *Social Work Speaks*, 7th ed. NASW Policy Statements, 2006–2009
- Hospice Care. In *Social Work Speaks*, 7th ed. NASW Policy Statements, 2006–2009

Practice
- Death and Dying: http://www.helpstartshere.org

Professional Associations
- American Academy of Hospice and Palliative Medicine: http://www.aahpm.org
- Association of Pediatric Oncology Social Workers: http://www.aposw.org

Credentials
- Advanced Certified Hospice and Palliative Social Worker (ACHP-SW): developed jointly by the National Hospice and Palliative Care Organization (NHPCO) and the National Association of Social Workers (NASW)

Standards
- NASW Standards for Social Work Practice in Palliative and End-of-Life Care

Educational Programs/Centers
- New York University School of Social Work, post-master's certificate in palliative and end-of-life care
- The Smith College School for Social Work, End-of-Life Care Certificate Program

12

Social Work and Private Practice

SECTION ONE: FIELD OVERVIEW AND FORECAST

Scope of Services

Social workers provide over 60% of the mental health care in the United States, making them the single largest provider of mental health care in the nation. Within the social work profession itself, more social workers work in mental health than in any other area. Overall, mental health is the highest paid field in social work, with strong earning potential, particularly in private practice (Center for Workforce Studies, 2007). Private practice is a very popular career choice among social work students. A recent study designed to assess the private practice career intentions of MSW graduate students found that two thirds of the respondents planned to go into private practice at some point in their career (Green, Baskind, Mustian, Reed, & Taylor, 2007).

Social workers in private practice provide clinical services such as psychotherapy, couples counseling, and family therapy. Private practice is sometimes referred to as independent, solo, or autonomous practice because private practitioners are self-employed and work on their own. Many private practice social workers develop a specialized practice niche. This might be with a specific population, for example, working with children and adolescents or lesbian and gay couples. A niche could also be developed around a particular treatment approach, such as cognitive-behavioral health or hypnotherapy. Another method is to develop a specialization treating a specific problem, such as substance abuse or eating disorders, or anxiety and depression. Having expertise in a specialized area is a good way to distinguish oneself and build a professional reputation within a crowded field.

Private practice is an appealing career choice for multiple reasons: It affords social workers the freedom of working for themselves without having a boss; there are no office politics; it has a flexible schedule; it has professional status; and it can be very lucrative. However, private practice is financially risky. There is no safety net, and there is no job security or benefits package. Private practice can be lonely and isolating. There are no coworkers to have lunch with. Private practitioners are on their own, with all the freedom and responsibility on their shoulders. For all of these reasons, private practice can be a wonderful career choice or a lonely path that places one in financial jeopardy. To be successful requires planning, discipline, initiative, and effort. One solution for minimizing the financial risks and isolation, especially in the early stages of building a practice, is to keep a part-time job. This will provide daily contact with professional peers, some measure of a stable income, and (hopefully) health insurance.

Settings

Private practitioners work independently in their private offices, which are often rented. Some social workers jointly rent a suite of offices and share expenses. Others choose to work out of a home office. These can be good ways to defray the overhead expenses of a private practice. Safety issues are especially important for private practitioners, as they typically work alone in isolated settings. While attacks or threats to personal safety are not a common, everyday occurrence, they do happen. According to a survey conducted by the National Association of Social Workers (Whitaker, Weismiller, Clark, & Wilson, 2006d), 57% of social workers in the field of behavioral health relate concerns about personal safety. While the sample for this study was drawn from mental health practitioners who work in a variety of settings, including hospitals and agencies, it does underscore the potential danger that exists when treating people who have emotional problems. Private practitioners have to be mindful that they are working without the infrastructure provided by an agency setting. Most recently in New York City, a psychologist was tragically murdered in her waiting room. In this case, the attacker did not know the psychologist and was waiting for a psychiatrist who shared the office suite. This tragic event illustrates the random and unpredictable nature of danger in this field. Nonetheless, there are steps that one can take to promote personal safety, and it is essential to be knowledgeable about safety precautions. Certain clients, for example those who are severely psychotic, are not appropriate for private practice settings.

The Social Worker's Role

Social workers in private practice are first and foremost clinicians. While the method utilized can be informed by differing orientations, such as interpersonal psychotherapy or a cognitive-behavioral approach, and clients are individuals, couples, families, or groups, the overall function is clinical, and involves diagnosis, assessment, and treatment. The New York State Education Law (2004) defines clinical social work as "the use of verbal methods in interpersonal relationships with the intent of assisting a person or persons to modify attitudes and behavior which are intellectually, socially, or emotionally maladaptive."

One of the major challenges for private practitioners is that private practice is a business, and social workers are not taught business skills in social work education. Few social workers are conversant with the multiple aspects involved in running a business: how to write a business plan, develop a budget, maintain records, and conduct billing. There are many details to be attended to: getting a phone and fax line, printing business cards and letterhead, getting and furnishing an office in a good location, working with managed-care panels (or deciding not to), and getting proper liability insurance. Building a private practice is time consuming and requires being well organized. Many social workers are uncomfortable discussing financial issues with clients, yet private practitioners have to be able to set and collect fees.

One of the most important elements of building a successful private practice is marketing. One has to develop a solid and credible reputation in order to get referrals. None of these skills are taught in social work education. A study that examined the extent to which social work education prepares students for private practice found that graduate schools do not provide content relevant to building a private practice, and that many faculty actively discourage the discussion of private practice career aspirations (Green et al., 2007). The reason that schools of social work do not provide encouragement or teach the skills necessary to build a private practice is because controversy continues within the profession as to whether or not private practice is consistent with the profession's core values (Barker, 1995). The Clinical Social Work Association (http://www.clinicalsocialworkassociation.org) can be an excellent source of information and provide a supportive network for private practitioners. As the largest national professional membership organization dedicated to the concerns of social workers in private practice, it is an excellent resource to learn the ins and outs of building a practice.

Credentialing

In order to engage in private practice, one must be licensed by the state in which one is practicing. At present, every state in the United States has a law that regulates private practice. The Association of Social Work Boards (ASWB) is a national association that assists states in the regulation of social work practice and helps to develop and implement licensing laws. ASWB states that the minimal standard to obtain the clinical social work license is an MSW from an accredited university and two years post-master direct clinical social work experience. Many states require three years post-MSW clinical practice and documented clinical supervision. Social workers should find out the specific licensure requirement of the state in which they want to practice. Once a social worker earns the necessary educational and experiential requirements to qualify for clinical licensure, they must pass a clinical-level social work licensing exam. These exams are developed by ASWB, and information about the exam as well as the particulars about specific state requirements can be obtained from its Web site (www.ASWB.org).

There is no advanced credential beyond state licensure needed to practice privately. Although the National Association of Social Workers (NASW) has a specialty credential, known as the Academy of Certified Social Workers (ACSW), its relevance has become somewhat diminished subsequent to the passage of clinical licensure in all 50 states.

Many states require continuing education as a condition of license renewal. Social workers can check with their local NASW chapter for information regarding continuing-education requirements. If continuing-education credits are required, it is important to make sure that any conferences or training attended are acceptable by the state licensing board. One must make sure to keep a copy of proof of attendance or completion of training, as documentation will be required by the state to renew one's license.

Emerging Issues and Employment Trends

There is considerable debate within the field about whether or not to participate in managed-care plans. Many social workers are unhappy with managed-care plans, which are run by private insurance companies and control many aspects of treatment. Managed-care companies set reimbursement rates, can insist on specific treatment interventions, and decide the duration of treatment. There is an increasing demand for accountability, and private practitioners are challenged by managed-care companies to prove the efficacy of their services, and to measure and document treatment progress.

Some social workers, therefore, have decided to forgo participating in managed-care panels and will only accept self-paying clients. The downside to this strategy is that it is difficult to find self-paying clients. Some social workers wouldn't survive financially if they did not accept managed care.

Social work in private practice is likely to continue to be a very popular career choice because it affords so much autonomy and flexibility. However, it is increasingly competitive. There are currently six licensed mental health professions: social work, psychology, psychiatry, psychiatric nurses, mental health counselors, and marriage and family therapists. With a field this crowded, social workers have to work hard to build a stable practice. Building a strong private practice takes ongoing work, time, and energy. One has to stay on top of the field and be up to date with the latest research and practice skills. Marketing oneself is an ongoing necessity. Few private practitioners are so well known and professionally recognized that they can afford to kick back and relax, because clients do not just walk through the door. A strong client pool has to be nurtured. It's important to maintain professional networks and to stay connected to a good referral source. However, for the enterprising social worker who wants to put in the time and energy and who is organized and has good business skills, the financial rewards and professional freedom of having a private practice are tremendous.

ACTIVITIES TO LEARN MORE

- Visit the Web site for the Clinical Social Work Association at http://www.clinicalsocialworkassociation.org. The Clinical Social Work Association is the national professional membership organization for Clinical Social Workers. There are many affiliated state chapters throughout the country as well, so check and see if your state has one to get more information that is specific to your state.
- The Association of Social Work Boards (ASWB) is the national association of boards that regulate social work. ASWB develops and maintains the social work licensing examinations used across the country and in several Canadian provinces. You can find state-specific licensing laws that govern your state on this site and also learn about the licensing exams. Go to http://www.aswb.org to learn more.
- *Psychotherapy Finances* is a newsletter written expressly for mental health practitioners in private practice. It is extremely informative about a range of issues from managed care to billing practices to legislative issues. At $79 for an annual subscription, it is worth it if you are seriously interested in this field. Approximately 10% of the newspaper can be accessed for free online at http://www.psyfin.com/newsletter.htm

SECTION TWO: CRITICAL ISSUES
Laura W. Groshong, LICSW

Laura W. Groshong, LICSW, received her master's degree in social work in 1974 from the School of Social Service Administration at the University of Chicago. She also received advanced training in adult psychotherapy at the Seattle Psychoanalytic Institute and received her certificate in 1979. She has been in private practice with individuals, couples, and families for 32 years.

Since 1996 Ms. Groshong has also worked as a registered lobbyist in Washington State for eight mental health groups, helping to pass several bills promoting access to mental health treatment. Since 2006 she has served as the director of government relations for the Clinical Social Work Association, a national organization that advocates on behalf of clinical social workers.

Ms. Groshong was inducted into the National Social Work Academy of Practice in November 2004, the national group that promotes cross-disciplinary collaboration at the national level, for her clinical, legislative, and organizational work.

Ms. Groshong has also written several articles on legislative activity as well as coauthored social work licensure laws in 10 states. She has a book in press (to be published by University Press in the fall of 2009) called *Clinical Social Work Regulation and Practice*, which compares clinical social work licensure laws and scopes of practice across all states and jurisdictions in the United States.

Ms. Groshong has been married to an attorney for 40 years and has two children, 27 and 31, and a daughter-in-law, 31.

Please tell me a little about yourself and your path in social work. What are some of the factors that motivated you to become a social worker? What drew you to school social work as an area of focus? Was it a particular issue or concern?
I never intended to be a lobbyist. I went to graduate school at the University of Chicago with the intention of becoming a clinical social worker. Although I was not necessarily planning to go into private practice, I was fascinated in learning about how people view their inner worlds. I wanted to help people discover how their internal images and constructs get in the way of how they want their lives to unfold, and how to achieve the life changes that they want to make. In graduate school, I was trained as an advocate as well as a clinician, and it was always in the back of my head that I would work in both capacities at some point in my career. After I had been a clinician for about 20 years, I had an opportunity to engage in some advocacy work, and I eventually began to work as an advocate for what was then called the National Organization Membership Committee for Clinical Social Work in Psychoanalysis, now the American Association for Psychoanalysis in Clinical Social Work. I found the work extremely rewarding, so much so that I made it a major part of my career. Today I have a private practice, seeing patients approximately 10–15 hours a week, and I work on legislative issues on behalf of eight different state and national mental health groups for about 40–50 hours a week. It's a busy professional life, but I wouldn't want to give up any aspect of my work.

What kinds of activities would be useful to engage for a social worker seeking to build a private practice?
Building a private practice requires developing excellent connections with other professionals and colleagues. The mental health field is so broad that, in order to stand out, one does better by defining oneself with a specialization, for example, psychodynamic psychotherapy, family therapy, cognitive-behavioral treatment, or child and adolescent treatment. A niche can also be defined by specific expertise, i.e., depression, forensic social work, eating disorders, etc. Becoming an expert in a given area of mental health practice is a great way to build a professional identity and to distinguish oneself in a somewhat crowded field. Private practice is a business, and as with any business, marketing is essential. Activities that are helpful in building a professional and credible reputation are attending and presenting in conferences, publishing in journals and newsletters, participating in membership associations, contributing to professional listservs, building a Web site or a blog, and developing professional contacts.

What kinds of systems should private practitioners be aware of?
Since private practitioners engage in independent and autonomous practice, it is necessary to take responsibility for understanding the numerous systems that impact our work. As responsible professionals, we need to be proactive about making sure that we are knowledgeable about the code of ethics, federal laws,

and the state-specific laws that govern private practice. The private practice world is also shaped by the court system; clinical social workers should know how to respond to legal events and the basic cases that have affected clinical social work practice. Major issues such as confidentiality, mandatory reporting laws, continuing-education requirements, licensing, and scope of practice are determined by the political and legal processes. Understanding those systems is part of the job. Getting active in one's local and national professional associations is a great avenue for being informed. Private practitioners will want to become skilled navigators of the often confusing maze of health insurance systems: *how to get on the panels, how to get reimbursed, and how to troubleshoot an insurance complaint.* Being an active learner will engage one in the kinds of professional activities that are useful to building a strong practice, and to developing a strong referral network.

What is important to know from a business perspective in order to develop a successful private practice?
Working as an independent clinical social worker represents a professional evolution. Most private practitioners began their careers working in agencies. In the agency, the external structure provides the clients, the supervision, the office space, and so forth. Independent clinical social workers have the potential to earn more money and to enjoy greater professional freedom, but with that comes the burden of being responsible for the additional work of running a business. Clinical social work training is quite weak when it comes to teaching good business practices, and most of us have to learn on the job how to be in business. We need to learn how to keep accounts, how to keep records that comply with federal and state laws, and how to have access to good legal counsel and an accountant. Independent clinical social workers have certain fixed costs, including rent, utilities, taxes, supervision, consultation, accountant, attorney, continuing education, etc., and we need to be able to cover these costs, which can range from $1,000 to $2,500 per month. I have talked to colleagues in all six of the licensed mental health disciplines—clinical social work, psychology, mental health counseling, marriage and family therapy, psychiatric nursing, and psychiatry—and none of these professions, in my view, do a good job of including business practices in their training.

Business is seen as irrelevant to the social work curriculum; unfortunately clinical understanding of the inner worlds of clients, the heart of clinical social work, is also often minimized in social work curricula. In some social work circles, a bias exists that it is somehow not quite respectable to engage in independent clinical social work, that independent clinical social workers are less committed to social work principles and ethics. Many independent clinical social workers have turned to the Clinical Social Work Association (CSWA) as their professional association of choice, an organization that tries to balance the clinical, business, ethical, networking, and practice needs of clinical social workers. There has been a bit of a split in the social work profession between those that see themselves as helping only disadvantaged clients and those in private or independent practice. To me, this division is unfounded; almost all independent clinical social workers strongly identify with the profession's ideals, but at the same time, don't think the ways clinical social workers can help individuals, couples, and families should be limited to only those with lower incomes.

How important is supervision for licensure and beyond? What other criteria are required for licensure?
Decisions regarding supervision will depend somewhat on whether or not one is working toward licensure; supervision in this context is a requirement. However, many clinical social workers continue peer supervision after becoming licensed, as a best practice. While every state in the United States has some form of clinical social work licensure, the supervision standards to become licensed vary widely from state to state, from an undefined amount over 2 years to 150 hours over 3 years. Of course, other criteria regarding the qualifications for the supervision must also be met. Many states require post-MSW clinical experience in order to sit for the licensing exam, and have continuing-education requirements. State standards are subject to change, with the trend toward standards being raised. If licensure is a goal, then make sure to keep on top of the licensing laws in the state where you seek licensure. It is up to the candidate to make sure that he or she knows what the requirements are so that there will be no surprises as they go through the licensing process. In general, the Association of Social Work Boards (www.aswb.org) Web site provides up-to-date information about state laws and standards, but it is best to consult with the state oversight agency or board for licensed social workers in a given state to be clear about licensure standards. Approved supervision from a licensed clinical social worker is a requirement in most states for at least some of the required individual supervision. Finding a qualified supervisor in an agency can be a struggle, and some social workers must pay for private supervision to meet licensure supervision requirements.

How can clinical social workers best protect themselves against malpractice litigation?
There are many pitfalls to avoid. Become familiar with the codes of ethics of the Clinical Social Work Association or the National Association of Social Workers, and let them guide you. Complaints regarding sexual misconduct are the most common ethical violation, and account for 70%–80% of all complaints. The CSWA and NASW codes of ethics prohibit sexual contact under almost any circumstances; by way of comparison, standards for psychologists are more lenient and permit sexual relations between psychologists and former clients 2 years following termination. Otherwise, dual relationships of other kinds, i.e., business, social, family, etc., are to be avoided whenever possible when seeing a patient for clinical social work treatment. Clinical social workers who work in the area of divorce and child custody are most at risk in terms of having malpractice complaints filed against them. All clinical social workers should consult with an attorney before responding to a malpractice complaint or to any other legal process, such as a subpoena.

Do you think that there is a trend toward increased regulation of private practice? How has this affected social workers?
There is a clear trend toward the increased regulation of private practice. Regulation includes the general laws and rules that govern the practice of clinical social work.

All states have licensure laws, but the rules that support them are in a constant state of flux, generally becoming more specific and restrictive. For example, in the past 10 years, nine states licensed clinical social workers for the first time. It takes about 10 to 15 rules to implement a licensing law and 1½ years to implement each rule. It is a very long, slow process! The states with recent licensure laws are still working on their rules, whereas other states that passed clinical social work licensure in the 1980s and 1990s may have outdated rules on the books and are now reviewing and revising them. It is important to know that every state has a different agency responsible for oversight of clinical social work licensure laws and the rule-making process. In New York, it is the Department of Education, but in most states it is the department of health or departments of professions. These regulatory bodies have the authority to create rules to implement the law, but cannot change the licensing law itself. Only the legislature has that power. Legislative change is slow, usually 2–3 years to pass a bill, but if you do your homework and invest time in getting an issue on the legislative agenda, one can accomplish a lot, even within a year. For example, in Washington State, the clinical social work licensure law, RCW 18.225, required that the criterion to become an approved supervisor was 5 years postlicensure clinical experience. We found that this standard was too restrictive and that social workers needing a clinical supervisor were having a very hard time finding a qualified person. We went back to the legislature and passed a bill to change the requirement to 2 years.

What are the benefits of combining a private practice with another job?
The primary benefit of having part-time employment is that it provides a stable salary, often with health insurance. Agency-based employment can also be an avenue to build one's professional network and make important contacts and relationships. Being in private practice can be isolating, and having a part-time job is a great way to have ongoing contact with other people. Those who like the combination of clinical practice and advocacy can have the satisfaction of being able to use their skills in both areas, if they go that route.

What do you think about the impact of managed care on private practice?
Fifteen years ago, managed care was seen as the devil that lowered reimbursement fees for psychotherapy, family and couples therapy, and other clinical social work services. However, managed care has also helped clinical social workers become more established in the mental health practitioner network. Almost all health insurance plans now reimburse social workers. However, some plans pay very little, potentially causing financial hardship for the clinical social worker. There is a fair amount of variation in fees across the country, both in managed care and fee-for-service treatment. Every few years, the newsletter *Psychotherapy Finances* conducts a study of the reimbursement rates for each area of the country. Fees are generally lower in the South and the Northeast than they are in the Midwest and on the West Coast. One major problem with managed care is that it impacts the confidentiality of client records, because one cannot guarantee that records kept by insurers are as confidential as records kept only by the independent clinical social worker. When insurers pay for services, they require that some information

about the treatment be provided. These records are then available to many more people and systems, increasing the risk that confidentiality will be violated. This is an increasing concern as we move toward consolidated electronic health records.

What kinds of specialized training or certifications would you recommend for a social worker who is interested in private practice?
The primary goal for independent clinical social workers who wish to be in private practice is the license to practice, i.e., the LCSW (Licensed Clinical Social Worker) or LICSW (Licensed Independent Clinical Social Worker), depending on the state. Education in human development, diagnosis, psychotherapy treatment, ethics, research, best practices, and business practices is an important precedent to becoming an independent clinical social worker. This can be obtained in graduate school, in postgraduate programs, or in continuing-education courses. To become licensed, clinical social workers must also pass a national examination, and a preparation course for this test can be very helpful. Specialty credentials were valuable before licensure because they provided credibility or recognition, but that is no longer necessary. Being licensed as a clinical social worker is sufficient.

What do you think are the greatest challenges facing private practitioners?
Building and maintaining a private practice is a challenge. Clinical social workers need to keep connections fresh and to maintain strong referral networks. Many clinical social workers become isolated without realizing it. One cannot just sit in one's office and wait for people to come knocking. While it is also challenging to develop marketing skills and to learn how to sell oneself, these are the business practices in which we must engage to be successful. In addition, clinical social workers need to advocate at the state and national levels for better reimbursement rates, equal pay for equal codes, good licensure laws, etc. We have to tolerate the frustration of interfacing with the legislative, legal, and insurance systems, to name a few, and work toward changing what is unfair or problematic for our profession. Finally, the passage of mental health parity does not guarantee coverage of an optimal mental health benefit, i.e., 40–50 sessions a year. This is an area where clinical social workers need to advocate to make sure treatment is covered long enough to produce benefits when it is needed.

DID YOU KNOW?

- Social workers are the largest providers of mental health care in the nation.
- According to a national study by NASW, private practice has been shown to be the highest paying field of practice.
- One study found that, on average, social workers in private practice work approximately 21 hours per week.

Source: The National Association of Social Workers.

SECTION THREE: FIRST-PERSON NARRATIVE

Thriving in Private Practice
Lynne Spevack, LCSW

Lynne Spevack, LCSW, maintains a full-time private practice offering psychotherapy and individual and group practice-building consultations in her offices in Manhattan's Financial District and in the mid-Brooklyn neighborhood of Flatbush. Ms. Spevack conducts professional workshops on various topics, including practice building and combating anxiety and depression. A social work psychotherapist for 25 years, she has been in private practice—free from the intrusion of managed care—for 18 years. Since 2002, she has been the founder and chairperson of the Private Practitioners Group, a committee of the New York City chapter of the National Association of Social Workers that focuses on the pragmatic business considerations of establishing and maintaining a social work private practice. She received her bachelor of arts degree from Vassar College, and her master's of social work degree from Hunter College School of Social Work. She completed a post-master's intensive training program in family and couples therapy. Prior to entering full-time private practice, She was a supervisor at the Jewish Board of Family and Children's Services. A veteran volunteer tour guide at the Brooklyn Botanic Gardens, her annual "Chase Away the Winter Blues" tour series has been featured in the *New York Times* and on ABC's World News Webcast.

Coming from a family who were, a few generations ago, poor immigrants who, from time to time, relied on the charity of the butcher and the grocer to feed 10 young brothers and sisters, I consider myself fortunate that just a few generations later I can earn a good living doing work that I love. For the past 18 years I've practiced clinical social work in private practice in the largest city in the United States, New York City.

I first recognized my passion for counseling as a teenager while volunteering as a telephone hotline peer counselor. Some years later, as I embarked on a master's of social work degree, I eagerly enrolled in the clinical track. After seven years working long hours in agency practice, I felt thrilled and scared to meet with my first private practice clients. My first clients found me mostly by word of mouth. We met in the evenings and weekends, working around the schedule of my full-time agency job, a situation that led to working even longer hours, while only marginally increasing my income. However, despite these demands, I felt very lucky to be earning a living doing the work that I loved.

Like most part-time private practitioners, I had no conception of myself as a businesswoman. Whether working in an agency or in my private practice, I saw myself as a clinician—only the setting had changed, just as it had before when I moved from one job to the next. It wasn't until I left my agency job and ventured into full-time private practice that I stumbled onto the rocky road that led me to see myself as a professional entrepreneur.

I quickly recognized that I needed some guidance and support in navigating this role transition. I also realized that many of my colleagues were grappling with similar doubts and fears. In response, I decided to form a group for myself and other social workers in private practice, and, under the auspices of the New York City chapter of the National Association of Social Workers, I started the Private Practitioners Group. In just a few years the Private Practitioners Group has swiftly grown from our first meetings with a handful of colleagues to an online virtual community of hundreds, a testament to how powerful the need for support is. Initially, I invited established private practice clinicians to speak with the group about how they developed and maintained their practices. The question on everyone's mind was, "How do you get clients?" The group also addressed other topics, such as setting and implementing fee policies, preparing taxes, making decisions about recordkeeping, and navigating and surviving the onerous managed-care system. Many of the members who attended these meetings were, like me, skilled and seasoned clinicians, but we were novices when it came to business. For this reason, I focused our meetings on the nonclinical, business aspects of running a private practice. After hosting meetings for a couple of years, I found that I myself had learned enough about practice building to facilitate a bimonthly fee and marketing support group and to conduct practice-building workshops and consultations.

I have come to see that, like me, most clinical social workers struggle mightily with the transition into private practice, and that many of us do not think of ourselves as being in business until confronted with the necessity to generate referrals and earn a real income. Only then do we recognize how conflicted we feel about being in business. Early in our careers as clinicians, we identify ourselves as "helping professionals," guides and counselors, mentors and advisers. Once in private practice, we often feel uncomfortable about collecting money in exchange for our help. We ask ourselves, "If I collect a fee, can I still consider myself to be a caring, helpful professional?" "Can I be helpful to my client and also 'help myself' to her money?" "If I attend to my own need to earn a living, can I also attend to my client's need for a compassionate ear?" "Can I strive to earn not just enough to get by, but more—a good living, with money for vacations and savings and retirement, and still be a dedicated, caring social work professional?" What I've learned over time is that we can—and, in fact, we must—find a way to comfortably integrate the professional, the altruistic, and the entrepreneurial aspects of our identities in order to earn a good living while doing good work. And as financially successful professionals, we can be positive role models for our clients, encouraging them to strive and achieve in their own lives.

Paradoxically, while many of us have misgivings about accepting payment from our private clients, we are also eager to earn a good income. We want to have greater control over our income potential than we have while working in agency settings. Like many senior clinicians in agency practice, I found that my salary had stagnated, and I realized that if I wanted to increase my income, I had to accept supervisory or administrative positions that drew me away from working with clients. Private practice, on the other hand, offers the opportunity to continue to work directly with clients without hitting a low-income ceiling.

In my practice-building workshops, I encourage the social work attendees to recognize that they have the potential to earn a good income working in private practice. In a 2006 national survey of its readers, the newsletter *Psychotherapy Finances* found that almost 14% of social workers in full-time private practice earned more than $100,000 a year, and a few (0.5%) earned over $180,000 a year. In this same survey, more of our colleagues from other disciplines earned high incomes: Almost 7% of psychologists, 1.3% of professional counselors, and 1.5% of marriage and family therapists earned over $190,000 a year. There is no reason that clinical social workers cannot be equally prosperous. We should keep in mind that social workers earning a six-figure income are the exception. This same poll found that the median annual salary for full-time clinical social workers in private practice was $58,000. In interpreting these numbers, it is important to remember that these figures represent the clinicians' gross salaries, and as such, they are not truly comparable to agency salaries because private practitioners incur expenses (e.g., marketing, office rent, health insurance, etc.) that agency-based clinicians do not have. Business-related expenses can be estimated to consume roughly one third of a private practitioner's gross income.

So private practice has provided me with the opportunity to earn a good living doing the work I love. Beyond that, it has also enabled me to have greater control over my working conditions and circumstances. In private practice, I am my own boss; I decide on the hours of my workday, the length of my commute, my days and hours off, my holidays and vacations, and the type of clients that I choose to treat. For me, one of the most glorious aspects of being in private practice is the freedom to design and pursue the kind of practice that I am most passionate about.

A couple of years out of graduate school, I arrived at my second professional job with some experience working with children; I felt bored and frustrated working with young children individually in play therapy, although I enjoyed working with families, teenagers, and adults of all ages. When I shared this preference with my supervisor, I was informed that regardless of my interests, I would be assigned several child cases and was expected to engage them in play therapy. Seeking to make this news more palatable, my supervisor proposed that we work together to overcome my disinterest in play therapy. Now, in my private practice, I can turn down play therapy cases or choose to see children in family therapy. In private practice, clinicians have the autonomy to design the type of caseload that we prefer, whereas in agency practice our preferences take a back seat to the agency's needs.

In private practice we can often follow our passions, whether it is the treatment modality (e.g., group work or family therapy), or the age group (e.g., seniors, children, college students), or the focus of the work (e.g., relationships, shyness, parenting). And, as our passions and interests change over the course of our career, our practice can evolve in tandem. Private practitioners have the opportunity to craft a practice that complements the rest of their lives. For example, a night owl might see his or her day's first clients in the afternoon. In my work as a practice-building consultant, I advised a social worker with school-age children to focus her practice on retirees, stay-at-home parents, and college students, all of whom are likely to be available for sessions early in the day, thus leaving her free to spend time with her children after school and on the weekends.

However, to be successful, savvy private practitioners know that they must be responsive to the realities of the market, considering which clients can afford to pay for services, what types of problems can be treated in an outpatient setting, and when clients are available and want to be seen. One colleague had to set aside her goal of focusing a practice on poor, formerly homeless adults in recovery from mental illness and addiction when she learned that New York State's Medicaid program does not reimburse services provided in a private practice setting.

Thus far, my account has focused on the advantages conferred by the autonomy inherent in private practice, autonomy that allows each practitioner to determine his or her own earnings and working conditions. However, this autonomy also brings responsibilities. One such responsibility is marketing, one of the greatest challenges that private practitioners encounter. Successful private practitioners need to learn marketing skills, to become comfortable with promoting themselves, and to devote time and effort to marketing their services. Many private practice social workers feel uninformed, intimidated, and frightened about marketing and, seeking to avoid it, instead enter into contracts with managed-care companies in which they agree to accept a reduced rate in exchange for the promise of a steady flow of referrals.

While some managed-care providers do get referrals, others are disappointed, and find that even with participation in managed care they must still conquer their marketing demons. And those who rely heavily on managed-care work find that participating in managed care causes them to lose much of the autonomy and freedom from bureaucracy that they had hoped to enjoy in private practice. Managed-care companies often seek to dictate how treatment is done: mandating short-term treatment, emphasizing medications, and disregarding the clinician's judgment and the client's needs and preferences. Furthermore, the billing, paperwork, and audits imposed by the managed-care bureaucracy erode the already paltry managed-care fees and steal time away from doing clinical work. At a professional meeting, one harried senior clinician complained that she was seeing 40 managed-care clients a week in a futile effort to maintain a reasonable income. And, just like with agency work, managed-care work restricts a private practitioner's earnings. What many clinicians don't realize is that it's not necessary to participate in managed care to have a successful private practice; I myself, and many of my colleagues, are thriving without any managed-care income while maintaining a reasonable caseload of 20–30 sessions a week.

When I first ventured into private practice, I imagined that I was leaving behind the humdrum, nonclinical responsibilities of agency work. I soon found that I was mistaken. I came to learn that, in fact, being in private practice is in some ways like creating your own agency of one in which you're responsible for everything the agency you once worked for had taken care of behind the scenes. In addition to marketing, there are billing, bookkeeping, supervision, policy setting, janitorial and clerical duties, among other things. Like many of my colleagues in agency practice, I bemoaned and resented the documentation requirements that I felt stole precious time from working with my clients. In private practice, I've come to understand that, while I have the authority to decide how to document my work, I also have the responsibility to ensure that I'm fulfilling my obligations—legal, ethical, and professional—to maintain complete and accurate case records.

There are many other double-edged aspects to the autonomy of private practice work. One of the gravest responsibilities is that of caring for clients in crisis. I daresay that every private practice clinician encounters critical circumstances that necessitate decisive action, often at a moment's notice: child abuse, suicidality, homicidality, impulsivity, substance abuse, and addiction are some of the potentially life-threatening crises social work clinicians frequently encounter. One summer, a colleague called me from her vacation; distraught and in tears, she confided that a depressed client had failed to show up for her session a few days earlier and subsequently hadn't returned her calls. The social worker now feared that the client might be suicidal, and wasn't sure how aggressive to be in ensuring this client's safety. Should she call the client's sister? Her emergency contact? Or should she leave it be? Despite conferring with her supervisor and other colleagues, this social worker continued to agonize about her client's safety.

Although the details will vary, you can be certain that every private practitioner will encounter many situations in which she grapples with what to do and how far to go. Should a suicidal client be hospitalized, or treated from home? Should parents be told of a child's drug use, or will that harm the therapeutic alliance? What should be done about a dangerously underweight anorexic client who refuses medical treatment? Is a parent's slap child abuse or corporal punishment, and should it be reported? Although we all receive training about these various situations, in reality there are many gray areas and many judgment calls, often followed by many agonizing days, if not weeks, before the situation is resolved.

Although clinicians in various settings encounter such situations, when working in an agency we have the comfort of knowing that we're part of a team of clinicians participating together in making such staggering, life-altering decisions. In private practice, the responsibility rests with us alone. I myself encountered such a situation with a longtime client, a police detective and eldest son who had been the voice of reason in his family. Distraught over the imminent breakup of his marriage, I was shocked when he revealed to me that he had thought about murdering his wife. Over the next few hours and days, we traveled together to turn in his firearm and badge, and to enroll him in an intensive outpatient treatment program. Clinicians practicing privately must have sufficient clinical training, experience, and skill to handle such unexpected situations at the moment they arise, often without any opportunity to consult with supervisors and colleagues.

A related issue is that of arranging for emergency coverage for clients. It's my policy to inform my clients that they can contact me any time of the day or night if the need arises (for example, if they are having thoughts of suicide). In such situations, I may have a distressed client call me on a daily basis until the crisis has subsided. But when the topic of emergency coverage arose in a professional meeting, one colleague was appalled at the idea of being "on call" every day and night for the rest of her career, and instead instructed her clients in need to contact a suicide hotline or hospital emergency room. With this, as with many of the decisions you will make in your private practice, there is no standard policy or procedure to follow; you will have the freedom, and the responsibility, to decide for yourself, and you will then bear the consequences of your decisions.

Some of the things I find most objectionable about being in a full-time private practice are also some of the most mundane: the work is largely sedentary, and it takes place almost exclusively indoors. Many of my private practice colleagues complain about feeling isolated from their peers; readily available collegial contact is another gift of agency work that we often take for granted. Some private practitioners round out their workdays by teaching, supervising, or consulting. It takes some thought and effort to carve out time from a busy schedule to take care of your own needs, whether it's getting together with colleagues or going out for a walk. Similarly, a full-time private practitioner must set aside time and money for supervision, continuing education, vacation, and sick days. When one is not salaried, it's tempting to scrimp on self-care and to devote every hour to income-producing activities, but this would be a serious mistake.

Some social workers contemplating private practice mistakenly believe that their practice will have to be restricted to working with privileged white, wealthy, and well-educated clients, often referred to as "the worried well." One bilingual Asian-born colleague was surprised when I encouraged her to follow her interest in working with an Asian clientele in her private practice, as she had summarily dismissed this as unfeasible. I've found that my offices in Brooklyn and Manhattan draw clients of various races, religions, ethnicities, and socioeconomic status, as well as émigrés from other countries. For me, this is one of the pleasures of having a private practice in a cosmopolitan city like New York. Of course, having a diverse caseload carries with it the responsibility to strive to be culturally sensitive and as knowledgeable as possible, a challenge in a city where 170 different languages are spoken by people who have come from all over the world.

While it may seem contradictory, many social workers in private practice are interested in earning a good income and also committed to working with poor and working-class clients. Many of us resolve this matter by offering a sliding fee scale or reserving a portion of our caseload for low-fee or pro bono cases. It's my experience that one can have a viable private practice with a good income if this is done judiciously. However, it's important to be aware of the challenges that can accompany working with low-income clients in private practice.

I began working with W when she was a graduate art student at the city university. I've found that offering a reduced fee to college students has been a good way to build my practice, as some have either continued to work with me after graduation or returned again later, when employed and able to pay a reasonable fee. However, when W graduated, she lost her medical insurance, and working as a freelance artist she had no benefits, and she earned too little to be able to afford to purchase insurance for herself. W's medical coverage was crucial in that she required psychiatric medication. One alternative would have been to refer her, at graduation, to continue her therapy at a local clinic where she could obtain psychiatric and counseling services at a reduced fee, but only if both services were provided by the clinic. Feeling an ethical duty to provide continuity of care for my clients, I instead continued to see W at a reduced fee, and I located a teaching hospital and a free medical clinic where she could obtain the psychiatric and medical treatments she needed. Without these services, our work would have been hopelessly stalled.

When a private practice social worker accepts poor and working-class clients, she may find herself doing case management and advocacy work in locating affordable resources. I'm fortunate that in a large, urban area like New York City, with its many teaching hospitals and training institutes, such services are available, but in more remote areas, locating ancillary services may be more challenging, if not outright impossible.

For me, one of the greatest satisfactions of private practice is the ability to be available to my clients over the course of many years of our lives. Many of my clients begin therapy doing one piece of work and later return for help in tackling a new challenge. One such client, E, was stuck in a low-paying career and a dead-end relationship when he began therapy. When we concluded our work, he was happily involved in a new relationship and earning a good living in a new career. A few years later, E briefly resumed therapy when he found he had "cold feet" about his wedding plans. Since the wedding, E has continued to stay in touch, sending me birth announcements and photos of his two sons. It's unfortunate for the clients that agency-based work generally doesn't afford them the opportunity to work with the same clinician over a long period of time. And because much agency-based work is managed-care driven, clients are pressed to focus on behavioral goals within a brief time frame. While working in an agency, I was sometimes fortunate enough to work with a family over the course of a couple of years, but if the family returned at a later time, they generally were assigned to work with a different therapist because I'd been promoted and reassigned to work in a different program. In contrast, my private practice clients can continue our work as long as we agree that it's worthwhile; at termination, I encourage them to stay in touch, which many of them do. It's satisfying for me and, I believe, a better arrangement for them, perhaps like having the same, trusted family doctor just a phone call away.

Eager for better working conditions and a better income, some newly minted MSW social workers have asked me how they can get started in private practice. I counsel them to do what I did: be patient, and wait. It takes many years of agency-based work, post-master's degree training, and supervised clinical experience before one is ready to practice autonomously. I myself worked for 7 years in full-time agency positions and had 5 years of intensive post-master's education before venturing to see my first private client. I do recall how difficult it can sometimes be. I remember earning a salary so low that, although I earned 5 weeks of vacation every year, I couldn't afford to travel and spent most of my "vacations" touring around my own hometown, New York. I've endured controlling, cold, and arrogant supervisors (as well as being blessed with some memorably wise and supportive ones!). And I've suffered lousy hours (late evenings followed, perversely, by early mornings) and putrid, flooded, and moldy offices.

Perhaps we might think of our professional career path as similar to that of physicians; having completed medical school, the recently graduated doctor works, generally for low wages, as an intern or resident in a hospital or clinic setting, completing an apprenticeship in which her work is supervised and her education continues. While in the social work profession our post-degree career is not so precisely prescribed, we nonetheless have an ethical obligation to ensure that we have honed our skills for several more years by working in agencies and learning in institutes prior to practicing independently. This also holds true for those older students who come to social work as a second career (often having worked and studied in a related field), who also should devote several years to agency-based work before venturing into private practice.

So what can an eager, would-be private practitioner do right now? Plenty!

- *Take stock*: Being a professional entrepreneur requires certain qualities of character: confidence, assertiveness, energy, flexibility, organization, attention to detail, an ability to see the big picture, and a willingness to take calculated risks. Identify those characteristics you lack, and work to cultivate them.
- *Learn*: Begin now to educate yourself about the business of being in private practice. Read up on risk management, professional insurance, ethics, marketing, niches, bookkeeping, tax preparation, and fees. Determine which post-master's degree credentials you may need to obtain, and which others may be advantageous. Public speaking and writing are valuable marketing tools, so think about developing your comfort and facility with one or both of these skills. Consider learning and practicing group work in addition to other treatment modalities; group work is a fabulously powerful and lucrative treatment modality that is woefully underutilized in private practice.
- *Plan*: Think about, and write down, your goals for your private practice, complete with time frames and action steps to take toward those goals. This document will be a work in progress that you should revise periodically as your ideas about your future practice grow and change.
- *Strategize*: Think about the type of work you believe you might enjoy doing in your private practice and what types of future job settings could best support that type of work. Consider positions that can provide: the opportunity to work with a particular clientele or problem focus that interests you, superior supervision and education, or valuable networking opportunities.
- *Network*: As you move from one field placement to the next and later on to your first professional jobs, remember to stay in touch with your favorite classmates, colleagues, and supervisors, all of whom may later become future referral sources for your private practice.
- *Reflect*: As with any clinical work, you will need to know yourself, and be willing to reflect on yourself honestly. But this is particularly important in private practice, because there's no one else to watch over you and your clients, and because your decisions about your own best interests (for example, about fees) could potentially be in conflict with your client's best interests. So get in the habit now of being brutally honest with yourself, with your supervisor, with a few trusted colleagues, and with your therapist.
- *Grow*: As clinicians, we are the tools of our work, and for this reason it's important that we attend to improving ourselves while, paradoxically, accepting that we are and will always be (as our clients are) a work in progress. For me, as for most other clinicians, this has meant engaging

as a client in my own therapy, initially just before entering social work school, and then again from time to time over the subsequent years. I've found that being a perennial client-therapist also serves to remind me of the great courage demanded of our clients, who struggle to reveal themselves and to change despite their fears and doubts. Being a client-therapist renews my admiration for my clients who, despite the challenges, choose to do the work. Becoming your best self, personally and professionally, will ultimately help to attract more business to your practice.

- *Take care of yourself*: Make time to play, to laugh with friends, to relax, and to enjoy life. Even if you love your work, your life requires balance.

Freud famously said, "Love and work.... Work and love, that's all there is." I'm very lucky: I do, indeed, love my work.

IS PRIVATE PRACTICE THE RIGHT FIELD FOR YOU?

- Lynne had to learn to be a businesswoman. Do you want to take on the responsibility of running your own business?
- Private practitioners are on their own. Do you work well independently?
- Are you willing to invest time and energy in marketing yourself?

SECTION FOUR: RESOURCES TO LEARN MORE

Web Sites
- American Association of Social Work Boards: http://www.aswb.org
- American Board of Examiners in Clinical Social Work: http://www.abecsw.org
- Managed Care Directory of Resources for Clinical Social Workers in Private Practice: www.socialworkers.org
- Psychotherapy Finances: http://www.psyfin.com/index.htm

Journals
- *Clinical Social Work Journal*, Springer

Books
- *Clinical Social Work: Beyond Generalist Practice With Individuals, Groups, and Families*, by Lambert Maguire (2002, Brooks/Cole)

Practice
- Clinical Social Work: www.socialworkers.org

Standards
- NASW Standards for Clinical Social Work in Social Work Practice: http://www.socialworkers.org/practice

Credentials
- Diplomate in clinical social work (DCSW) (NASW credential)

Professional Associations
- California Clinical Social Work Society: http://www.clinicalsocial-worksociety.org/
- Clinical Social Work Association: http://associationsites.com/main-pub.cfm?usr=CSWA
- Clinical Social Work Society of Delaware: www.cswsdelaware.org
- Connecticut Society for Clinical Social Work, Inc.: www.cscsw.org
- Greater Washington Society for Clinical Social Work: http://www.gwscsw.org
- Kentucky Society for Clinical Social Work: http://home.insightbb.com/~kscsw/wsb/html/view.cgi-home.html-.html
- Louisiana Association of Clinical Social Workers: http://www.lacsw.org
- Maryland Society for Clinical Social Work, Inc.: http://mscsw.org
- Minnesota Society for Clinical Social Work: www.mnclinicalsocialwork.org
- Missouri Society for Clinical Social Work: www.mscsw.com
- National Membership Committee on Psychoanalysis in Clinical Social Work: http://www.nmcop.org
- New York State Clinical Social Work Society: http://www.clinicalsw.org
- North Carolina Society for Clinical Social Work: www.ncscsw.org
- Pat McClendon's Clinical Social Work: http://www.clinicalsocialwork.com/socialwork.html
- Pennsylvania Society for Clinical Social Work: http://www.pscsw.org
- South Carolina Society for Clinical Social Work: http://www.scclinicalsocialwork.org
- Texas Society for Clinical Social Work: http://www.txscsw.org
- Washington State Society for Clinical Social Work: http://wsscsw.org

13

Social Work in School

SECTION ONE: FIELD OVERVIEW AND FORECAST

Scope of Services

Approximately 25,000 of the nation's 500,000 social workers are employed in school settings. Their primary function is to promote and support the academic achievement of the students. School social workers provide individual counseling, run groups with students and families, work with communities and organizations, and engage in advocacy and research. School social workers work in teams with other school personnel such as teachers, guidance counselors, and psychologists. School social workers work across systems and often refer students for specialized services such as health care or mental health services. School social workers make home visits, particularly in rural areas. School social workers work with mainstream and special-needs students, defined as children and youth with an identified developmental or physical disability or a cognitive, emotional, or behavioral disorder. Among the wide gamut of presenting problems addressed by school social workers are bullying, gang violence, substance abuse, academic difficulty, school phobia, family problems, and issues related to sexual orientation and gender development (National Association of Social Workers, n.d.).

School social work is one of the oldest and most established areas of social work practice, dating back to 1906, when the first school social work services were provided in New York, Boston, and Hartford. The subsequent development of school social work was greatly advanced by the passage of compulsory school attendance laws.

During the 1940s and 1950s, school social work consolidated a clinical orientation, providing counseling services to children and families. This shift in role from "truant officer" to caseworker increased the status and prestige of school social workers (Freeman, 1995). In the 1970s, school social work became increasingly directed toward special-needs students subsequent to the passage of two major federal laws that make provisions for children that are identified as disabled (Allen-Meares, 2008).

Several pieces of federal legislation recognize the vital role of school social work. In 1975, Congress passed Public Law 94-142 (Education of All Handicapped

Children Act), reauthorized and expanded in 1990 as IDEA (Individuals with Disabilities Education Act). These laws provide protection to disabled students and require educational institutions to make accommodations so that disabled students may participate in educational settings. Among its provisions is that schools must provide social work services to children identified as disabled. The law requires that "children and youth receiving special education have the right to receive the related services [including social work] necessary to benefit from special education instruction (IDEA, C.F.R.: Title 34; Education; Part 300.16, 1993). The federal No Child Left Behind Act of 2001 (Public Law 107-110), passed in 2002, defines a school social worker as an individual who has a master's degree in social work and state licensure. The law notes that in "the absence of such State licensure or certification, [the candidate] possesses a national credential or certification as a school social work specialist granted by an independent professional organization" (U.S. Department of Education, n.d.).

These laws are extremely important to the development and expansion of school social work because they emphasize the critical role of school social work and set federal standards for the utilization of school social workers around the country. School social work practice, perhaps more than in most other areas of social work practice, is largely determined by state and federal funding and legislation.

The School Social Work Association of America (SSWAA) is the largest professional association for school social workers in the United States. Their mission statement conceptualizes school social workers as "instrumental in furthering the purpose of the schools. School social workers are hired by school districts to enhance the district's ability to meet its academic mission, especially where home, school and community collaboration is the key to achieving that mission." (www. SSWAA.org). Within this framework, the primary purposes of school social work services are to help students reach their highest level of academic functioning. This can (and often does) involve significant time spent on outreach to families, organizations, and communities, as well as counseling individual students. Rural school social work confronts a specific set of challenges. Safety issues must be given special consideration because the rural school social worker often works in isolated settings and drives long distances in order to make home visits.

Settings

Most school social workers work in public schools, although some school social workers work in private schools. One of the challenges of being a school social worker is related to working in a host setting, meaning that a school is not a social work agency or department. There is usually only one, or at the most two, social workers employed in any given school. As a result, school social workers generally do not have a reference group with a shared professional identity or ethical code. For this reason, some school social workers, most often those who are relatively new to the field, find themselves feeling professionally isolated. To compound this problem, "turf wars" between related helping professionals, such as psychologists and guidance counselors, have been documented (Gibelman, 2001).

The social work licensing laws have created some specific challenges for school social workers. In most states, in order to be licensed at the clinical level, a social worker will need a number of documented hours of client contact and a documented number of hours of supervision by an approved supervisor. There is significant variation among the states about who is an approved supervisor and how many hours of supervision and client contact are required, but the general standard is 3 years. Many, if not most, schools do not have any social worker on staff who meets the standards for qualified supervisor, and the nature of the work itself does not fall within the guidelines of what is considered clinical practice by state regulatory bodies. For this reason, school social work is a career path that may not provide the requisite experience or supervision that will enable a social worker to qualify for clinical licensure.

This is an unfortunate consequence of the licensing laws, because some new social workers who would be excellent school social workers may choose not to go into this area of practice if they cannot utilize their experience toward earning the clinical license. The best way to be certain about whether school social work can position one toward the clinical license later down the road is to check first with the state regulatory body that governs social work licensing. In most states, this will be the department of health; however, some states, for example New York, are regulated by the state education department.

The Social Worker's Role

Federal funding for special education services has expanded opportunities for school social workers to provide special education services. Under the IDEA law, once a child has been designated as in need of special education services, "related services," such as social work, must be provided to the child and his or her family. Social workers often get involved prior to a referral to special education being made because, under law, parental consent is required for a child to be evaluated for and receive special education services. Social workers are the members of the team who are trained to work with families and generally take on the role of engaging families (Suppes & Wells, 2008). Working with families requires a great deal of skill and sensitivity, because families are naturally often mistrustful and reluctant to have their child participate in special-needs services. Social workers must be culturally competent when engaging families from diverse cultural and ethnic backgrounds. When family members do not speak English, language fluency becomes essential.

School social workers generally work in teams often known as a "school-based support team." Other members of the team typically include a psychologist, a guidance counselor, and a speech therapist. A large part of the social worker's function is to conduct assessments. Students are generally referred to the school-based team by a teacher who observes problems in the classroom. Social workers conduct psychosocial assessments that examine the student within the context of his or her psychosocial environment. This assessment includes a social and developmental history and the child's current behavior at home, with peers, and in the community.

Social workers generally interview the parents to acquire this information and to obtain parental consent.

One of the challenges facing school social workers is maintaining confidentiality. Schools have long been recognized within the profession as one of the most complex arenas to negotiate proper protection of confidentiality. School social workers typically navigate numerous systems and often receive information about clients from multiple sources: students, families, and school personnel. To complicate matters, the National Association of Social Workers (NASW) Code of Ethics does not provide guidance about the confidentiality of minors. The School Social Work Association of America (SSWAA) recognizes that school social workers often encounter ethical dilemmas relating to confidentiality and has issued a position statement to provide greater clarity. It notes that "social workers must follow guidelines established by the state and school district in which they work." Furthermore, recognizing that situations arise that supersede client–social worker confidentiality, school social workers are cautioned that "information should be shared with other school personnel only on a need-to-know basis and only for compelling professional reasons." School social workers should familiarize themselves with the respective statute about client confidentiality that governs the state in which they work.

Credentialing

The National Association of Social Workers (NASW) offers a nationally recognized school certification: the Certified School Social Work Specialist (C-SSWS). Qualifications for this certification include current NASW membership, an MSW degree, and documented 2 academic years of paid, supervised, post-MSW experience as a school social worker in a school setting.

The requirements and credentialing process to become a school social worker vary by state. Some states have regulations that mandate a social worker in the schools, while others do not. Some states require an MSW; a few states will accept a BSW. Some states require a license, while other states require school social workers to be certified by the state education department. A few states require both the license and certification (for example, New York, and Indiana). A recent national study conducted by the Pennsylvania chapter of the National Association of Social Workers found that 27 of the 40 states surveyed require a social work degree (BSW or MSW) to function as a school social worker, and that 21 of these states require school social workers to have a master's degree in social work. The study found that 18 out of the 40 states surveyed require school social workers to be licensed and that an additional 6 states require school social workers to be certified as well. In total, of the 40 states surveyed, 24 states follow the federal guidelines that school social workers be licensed or certified. States that adhere to accepted best-practice standards for school social workers include, but are not limited to, Maryland, Massachusetts, Michigan, New Mexico, New York, Ohio, Rhode Island, and Vermont (personal communication with Jenna Mehnert, MSW, executive director, NASW-PA).

Social workers seeking to become employed in the schools are advised to familiarize themselves with the requirements of their respective states. There are a few ways to find this information, but be warned: It can be a frustrating process! The local school district may have this information on its Web site. It is also possible to access this information from the state education human resource department. One friendlier and easier way to find out the requirements of a specific state is to call the local NASW state chapter.

Emerging Issues and Employment Trends

The demand for school workers is closely tied to federal, state, and local funding. In order for funding to be consistent, federal laws that mandate social work services in the schools are critical. While a federal law such as IDEA does specifically reference social work services, a great deal of discretion and interpretation is left up to the local school districts regarding implementation, and there is an inconsistent application of this law across the country. The Bureau of Labor Statistics (2008) projects an increase in the demand for school social workers, citing the trend on integrating disabled children into the general population. The demand for culturally competent bilingual school social workers will also be strong, reflecting the growing diversity in our nation.

School social work can be an excellent career choice. Depending on where one lives, it can be one of the highest paying areas of social work practice. If one lives in a state that is unionized, public school social work is a union position that will have excellent salary and benefits packages. In other states, it may be very difficult to find a decent paying job, if one exists at all. Working with children is generally rewarding and fast paced. For an energetic social worker with a good sense of humor, few practice areas will be as good a fit.

ACTIVITIES TO LEARN MORE

- Visit the Web site for the School Social Work Association of America at www.sswaa.org. SSWAA is the only professional association in the United States that is dedicated exclusively to school social work, and the Web site contains a wealth of information. A student membership is $60 per year and well worth the money if this is an area that you want to specialize in.
- Contact your local department of education and find out what employment opportunities exist for social work.
- Public school social workers are generally extremely accessible to the communities that they serve. Call your local public school and ask to speak to the school social worker. Explain to the social worker that you are interested in learning about school social work. They are often more than happy to make the time to talk to you.

SECTION TWO: CRITICAL ISSUES
Lynn Bye, MSW, PhD

Lynn Bye is associate professor of social work in the Department of Social Work at the University of Minnesota, Duluth, where in 2006 she received the Outstanding Faculty Award for the College of Education and Human Service Professions. Dr. Bye has a PhD in social work from Rutgers University and an MSW from the University of Minnesota. She was employed as a school social worker for 18 years, during which time she was honored as the Minnesota School Social Worker of the Year. More recently, in 2004, she was chosen by the Minnesota School Social Worker's Association to receive the Friend of School Social Work Award. She coedited the book *School Social Work: Theory to Practice*, published in 2007 by Brooks/Cole/Thomson, and was also part of the team that developed an online state reference manual for school social workers in Minnesota. She currently serves on the National Association of Social Workers School Social Work Practice Section Committee, the Eleventh District Minnesota Bar Association Ethics Committee, and the Educational Testing Service Test Development Standing Committee for the Praxis School Social Worker.

Please tell me a little about yourself and your path in social work. What are some of the factors that motivated you to become a social worker? What drew you to school social work as an area of focus? Was it a particular issue or concern?

I began thinking seriously about my career goals when I was a sophomore in college. At that time I met with staff in the university's career services department who suggested that I was a "good fit" with a human services career. Based upon their recommendation, I interviewed a number of social workers to learn more about the social work profession. I was tremendously impressed with their work and their passion, and I decided to pursue a social work degree. Part of my motivation to become a school social worker was also shaped during my experience in elementary, junior high, and high school. As a student, I witnessed emotional and physical violence perpetrated on school classmates by other students as well as by teachers. I realized how important it was for schools to be academically nurturing places that foster positive social and emotional development. I passionately believe that all children have the right to attend a safe school. I wanted to become a school social worker in order to support and encourage a school environment that provides optimal conditions for *all* children to learn and to grow.

What do school social workers do?

School social workers facilitate students' academic success by addressing the social, emotional, and behavioral issues that interfere with learning. School social workers help students succeed by building bridges between schools, communities, and families, and work to bring these groups together on behalf of the students. The functions that a school social worker engages in vary somewhat based on several factors, including the social worker's unique skill set and the specific vision of the school's administrator. Assessment, consultation, counseling (both individual and group), crisis intervention, coordinating with community resources, and working with families are common school social work tasks.

What are the major educational policy trends that shape school social work practice?
Federal legislation has had a major impact on school social work services. Prior to 1975, when Congress passed Public Law 94-142 (Education of All Handicapped Children Act), school social workers were hired primarily with local and/or state funds. After the passage of this legislation requiring that all children receive a free and appropriate education, federal funds became available for special education services that included school social work. While this legislation provided a funding stream for social work services, it also placed restrictions on what school social workers could do, since fundable services were targeted toward children who were diagnosed with special education needs. School districts could only be reimbursed for social work services related to special education for students with handicaps. Prevention and work with students who were not handicapped were not funded.

Fortunately, the 2004 reauthorization of the IDEA opened the door to using federal funds for preventive social work services with students. This change in legislation enables school social workers and other support staff to utilize evidence-based interventions with at-risk children and youth prior to their classification as needing special education services.

Another piece of legislation that assists school social workers in advocating for the rights of students is a civil rights law, Section 504 of the Rehabilitation Act of 1973. This law prohibits discrimination due to a handicap by any agency that accepts federal funds. To comply with this law, public schools must make reasonable and appropriate adaptations and modifications for children with disabilities.

In what ways do you think demographic trends, for example the increase in the number of people from diverse cultural backgrounds, impact school social work?
Racism and homophobia persist in schools, and school social workers need to be aware of the impact these attitudes and behaviors have on students. Recently, a Minnesota high school student committed suicide after enduring homophobic harassment by his peers. Research shows that many schools do not have a harassment policy that addresses sexual orientation (Olsen, 2008). We have to do a better job of implementing and enforcing harassment policies and addressing all forms of school violence in the halls, in the classrooms, and in the curriculum. School social workers must work hard to gain the trust of the communities they serve, which includes an increasingly diverse population. This is particularly true when the school social worker and school administration are mostly white and the local communities are comprised of people from diverse backgrounds. Our country has a history of oppression by a dominant white population. Based upon this history, communities of color may be mistrustful of interactions with school personnel. For example, in the United States, the Native American population experienced years of cultural genocide at the hands of white Americans. Many of their children were forced into boarding schools, where their cultural practices were strictly forbidden. School social workers have to be aware of the history as well as the cultural norms of the populations they serve and earn their trust as they seek to build bridges with the school.

What kinds of social policies are important to support social work in the schools?
There is considerable variance in the requirements to be a school social worker, as each state has its own regulations. Many states require a master's degree, and some states also require state licensure as well as certification by the state board of education. Often states require continuing-education credits and completion of specialized training in school social work.

A master's degree in social work is required in most states to be employed as a school social worker. In Minnesota, school social workers have to be certified by the state board of education and licensed by the state board of social work. In order to be certified by the Minnesota Board of Education, one has to pass a background check. State licensure requires a bachelor's or master's degree in social work as well as passing the licensing exam.

Many public school social workers are not licensed at the clinical level; however, there is a trend toward schools preferring licensed clinical social workers because school districts can bill government and private insurance for third-party reimbursement for social work services related to mental health. Many of the services provided by school social workers are not considered within the scope of clinical practice because they are not based on making a diagnosis and engaging in psychotherapy. This can make it difficult for school social workers to obtain the requisite experience in order to be eligible to sit for state clinical social work licensing exams.

At the local level, the school board generally has the discretionary authority regarding whether or not to employ social workers. Federal law mandates specific services be provided in the schools, but stops short of legislating that these services be provided by social workers. In some locations, school social workers are employed by cooperatives that serve several school districts. In these cases, each district contributes to the funding of the services.

It is essential that we have strong policies that ensure clean, safe, properly staffed, and not overcrowded schools. We know that student engagement in academic pursuits is strongly correlated with having adults available that they connect with. We must have appropriate staffing in our schools if we want students to succeed.

How can school social workers effectively engage families?
A core social work value is to treat each person with dignity and respect. School social workers exemplify this value by reaching out to families in a respectful and honoring way. To engage families, they must feel valued. This entails working with families at times and locations that are convenient for them. Most school social workers make home visits as a routine part of their job and schedule home visits according to what is best for families. School administrations need to allow flextime for social workers in order to support this type of family engagement.

What skills do you think enable school social workers to be successful?
Relationship building and communication skills, especially the ability to listen, are essential. School social workers have to be skilled problem solvers, mediators, and

advocates. In addition, they need to be organizationally savvy and be good team members. Professional self-care skills are also essential. School social work is very rewarding, and there is a lot of positive momentum on the job because sometimes seemingly small interventions can have a major positive impact. This makes it easy to work long hours. However, working too many long hours can have negative consequences on health and well-being. School social workers need to be able to seek out good supervision and professional support. At times they will hear and see events that are gut-wrenching and will benefit from professional venues to process these feelings.

How would you describe the major challenges facing school social workers today?
Inadequate funding and resources are major challenges in public education. Across the nation, many programs have been cut. With the current emphasis on testing, the focus is often on making adequate yearly progress in academic areas. As a result of this narrow focus, art, music, and physical education programs have frequently been reduced or eliminated. For example, at the 2008 School Social Work Association of America Conference, the keynote speaker asked a large audience of a few hundred people, "How many schools still have recess?" Sadly, the response was nearly unanimously negative. As the pressure for students to pass standardized tests increases due to the fact that test scores are linked to school funding, many school districts have eliminated recess.

The general public is often unclear about the role of the school social workers. Improving public understanding about what school social workers do is a priority for the National Association of Social Workers and for the School Social Work Association of America. Individual school social workers can also help educate the public about their role in the schools. More specifically, they can give presentations so that the teachers and staff understand what school social workers do. It is very important in the current climate of accountability and evidence-based practice that school social workers document their interventions and demonstrate their success. We need data to show that social workers make a difference and that, because of school social work, school attendance improved, and parental involvement increased, and students are doing better behaviorally, emotionally, and academically.

What advice would you give to a social worker who wants to become a school social worker?
Social workers interested in this area of practice should get some specialized training in school social work. An internship in a school is a great way get a foot in the door. Joining the local NASW chapter and getting to know other social workers in the state will help with networking. Obtaining a school social work position is often very competitive, so it is important to sharpen your interview skills. You must be able to articulate your knowledge base and your skills and your ability to work with students to assist them in overcoming social and emotional barriers to academic achievement.

DID YOU KNOW?

- School social work is one of the oldest and most established fields of practice, and school social workers are often better paid than in many other fields of social work.
- The Bureau of Labor Statistics reports that almost half of all social workers self-identify as working with children, families, or in schools.
- According to the Bureau of Labor Statistics, the demand for school social workers is expected to increase because of rising student enrollment as well as the continued emphasis on integrating disabled children into the general school population.

SECTION THREE: FIRST-PERSON NARRATIVE

Boundary Dilemmas and the Privilege of Knowing Heroes: Rural School Social Work

Julie Richards, LICSW

Julie Richards received her MSW from McGill University in Canada. She is a licensed clinical social worker, having practiced school social work in Vermont since 1990. Since 1997, she has been a full-time faculty member, initially providing coordination, consultation, and technical assistance to school districts throughout Vermont regarding best practices for inclusion of students with emotional and behavioral challenges in the regular educational system. Since 1999, Ms. Richards's responsibilities have been to coordinate the Undergraduates Social Work Program. Her teaching areas include introductory social work courses as well as practice and field experiences courses. Recently, she has also expanded her practice arena to develop and foster service-learning partnerships with nongovernmental organizations (NGOs) in Mumbai, India, including working extensively with a school that serves children with developmental disabilities and their families. Moreover, Ms. Richards has extensive experience providing supervision to graduate social work and counseling students working in schools throughout northern Vermont.

For the past 10 years, I have been providing school social work services and consultation to my local middle school. While I am hired directly by the school, most school social workers in our state are contracted through the local community mental health agency to work in the school. Because I work just a few hours per week, and most of my work is done during home visits often outside of school hours, I rely tremendously on the school/guidance counselors and building administrators to update me, and vice versa, in order to keep the lines of communication between the home and school open. My school is the most rural school district in our county. I live and practice in my local community, where my husband is a teacher and my children go to school. I have had to navigate boundaries and ethical dilemmas every day in my practice. And I love it!

While I find the navigation of boundaries particularly fascinating in my practice, I also find the clinical content intriguing. Recently, some families were referred to me because some of their children were truant from school due to mental health issues. Yet because these children were so bright, none of them were identified as in need of special education. So they were left adrift, without adequate educational services to meet their needs. Moreover, at the time, few of them were accessing any sort of consistent mental health services. As I began working with these families, it was clearly evident that some of these children were dealing with extremely pervasive mental health issues. Some symptoms included hallucinations, suicidal ideation, extreme social isolation, and some obsessive-compulsive behaviors. Clearly psychiatric and additional mental health care were needed.

However, one of the challenges that each of these families faced involved health insurance access. None of these families received any public assistance benefits, yet their health care insurance policies did not provide adequate coverage for psychiatric assessment. Medication and therapy copayments made accessing services an extreme financial hardship. Families were rapidly depleting their life savings in order to access mental health services for their children. Many of these families' parents were struggling in their partner relationships (marriages and other long-term relationships), as the strain was exhaustive and too much for the relationship to bear. In these situations, the school asked me to consult with the families, assess the child and family system, make recommendations for services, as well as assist with accessing services or raising concerns to the next (political) level when needed services were nonexistent.

As I see it, comprehensive health insurance coverage for a child with serious mental health needs is critical. Without Medicaid, most of the children with whom I work are unable to access inpatient psychiatric assessment or respite services, and, occasionally, the cost of therapy is prohibitive. When I assist families with completing the necessary paperwork to apply for Medicaid due to their child's mental health condition (as opposed to income need), I need to tell them to anticipate the application possibly being rejected initially and to be prepared to appeal the decision. For a family who is trying to keep their child from spiraling down further, trying to salvage a marriage, and trying to pay attention to some of the other children in the home (always difficult to do when the child with the mental health issues consumes so much of the parents' energy), and somehow manage to grocery shop, work, and get some laundry done, just completing the initial paperwork is daunting. Families don't have the energy to fight for benefits. It takes all one can muster to keep track of all the different players who have tried to help—from the school, from the community, and so forth. These parents need to be extremely organized and in a place of humility in order to complete the necessary application forms and tell their painful story to the strangers who will determine eligibility. Some of my job responsibilities include helping these families organize their materials, complete the applications, add supportive documentation to their applications, and follow up with the various service providers/school personnel to ensure that all the materials have been submitted and are being considered.

I truly love practicing social work in my community because I do feel that I can make a difference. I believe that it takes an entire community to wrap its arms around its members in order for us all to grow, develop, and thrive. To be able to practice in your own community requires quite a bit of reflection and skill. You have to be prepared to face all sorts of boundary dilemmas, confidentiality challenges, and so forth. When you least expect it, you run into your clients (whether it be at a neighbor's party or out jogging). You need to know how to engage both personally as well as professionally simultaneously. Sometimes, you even need to know how to address the general derogatory comments that your friends make about "the kinds of people social workers work with" right in front of your clients, all while these detractors are completely unaware that your clients are present. While this can be really difficult, it's also one of the things that I feel the most proud of as a rural social worker. I know that I can both say and model behavior that changes how my community perceives human needs and injustices. I can educate my community of peers to be more empathetic toward one another. I can raise awareness about social issues from a very real perspective and say it in a way that others can grasp and understand why things need to be different. I can do all of this right alongside my clients. I am privileged to be able to have such a window into my community and put a voice to the needs that have yet to be addressed.

A novel and very complex experience that I found particularly interesting recently involved one of the students with whom I work and my family. I was working with a student whose family was referred to me because the student had some disturbing behaviors and thoughts. The child was struggling academically and socially in school. One of the concerns that the parent had was that the student was hanging out with older youth, including teenager drivers, and was engaging in some risky behavior. The student shared with me that her parent's concerns were justified. While addressing these areas and connecting this student to services in the community, the student began to befriend one of my children.

Because of our code of ethics and our confidentiality mandate, I do not talk about my work at home (even in the most nondescript ways, for fear that it will be easy for my family to figure out with whom I work). One day, my daughter told me that she was talking with my client, and my client told her, "You sound just like your mother." My daughter asked my client how she knows me, and my client responded, "Your mother's my counselor." My daughter was struck with how I could "keep a secret" (her term for *confidentiality*).

Some time after that interaction, my client invited my daughter out on a Friday night with some other kids as well. My daughter had something already scheduled and declined, so I didn't need to address that boundary immediately. But to be honest, I was very concerned about how I would handle it had my daughter asked my permission. I knew that these kids would be several years older and involved in activities to which I did not want my daughter exposed. Yet, on the other hand, I wondered if this was the way my client was reaching out to try to build a different set of friends, ones that may make safer choices.

The next week, when I saw my client at school, before I had a chance to bring it up, my client asked me if I had forbidden my daughter to go out with her. The student said that she figured I wouldn't let my daughter go because I wouldn't want my daughter "hanging out" with her, knowing the kinds of things that my client has done. I spoke with her about this being the first time that a client of mine has befriended my child and that, while I did not say "no" to my daughter about going out, I was struggling with the boundary issue that would have occurred had my daughter been available to go out. I spoke with my client about my concerns of ensuring that our boundaries as client and social worker do not become blurred. I was transparent about how I was trying to navigate my personal life with my professional life here in our community. The student and I continued to work together throughout the school year. However, she decided not to continue to try to befriend my daughter outside of school.

These families are my heroes. They model for me what it means to love one another and put everything aside in order to meet basic needs. They model what true family commitment is. Yes, sometimes they can get frustrated, feel depleted, divorce, and "lose their cool," yet they do this because they are human. They are trying their best and keep trying to do whatever it takes to survive. And as a fellow community member, I want to help them not only to survive, but to thrive. It is because of who they are that they make me who I am. And to me, I feel privileged to bear witness to my fellow community members' stories and to be able to be a page in their story, to help them access what they need to grow. This is why I choose to practice rural social work and to practice in my home community.

IS SCHOOL SOCIAL WORK THE RIGHT FIELD FOR YOU?

- School social work is described as an area of practice in which maintaining client confidentiality is particularly complex. Julie describes how these challenges play out in rural social work. Envision yourself in a similar situation.
- School social workers have an excellent opportunity to intervene in the lives of children and families. Julie finds her work very rewarding because she is able to help families resolve multiple problems.
- Julie, like most school social workers, makes home visits and is available to meet with families after school hours. Is this something you would be open to doing?

SECTION FOUR: RESOURCES TO LEARN MORE

Web Sites
- Attention Deficit Disorder Association: http://www.add.org
- Autism National Committee (AUTCOM): http://www.autcom.org
- The Individuals with Disabilities Education Act Amendments of 1997: http://www.ed.gov/offices/OSERS/Policy/IDEA/index.html
- Learning Disabilities Association of America: http://www.ldanatl.org
- Mandatory Child Abuse and Neglect Reporting Overview: http://www.smith-lawfirm.com/mandatory_reporting
- Midwest School Social Work Council: http://www.midwest-ssw.org
- National Center for Learning Disabilities: http://www.ncld.org
- The National Institute for Trauma and Loss in Children (TLC): http://www.tlcinst.org
- No Child Left Behind: http://www.ed.gov/nclb
- Special Education Resources on the Internet: http://seriweb.com
- U.S. Department of Education: http://www.ed.gov

Journals
- *Children & Schools*, NASW Press
- *School Social Work Journal*, Lyceum Books

Books
- *School Social Work: Theory to Practice*, by Lynn Bye and Michelle Alvarez (2006, Thomson Brooks/Cole)

Policy
- School Truancy and Dropout Prevention. In *Social Work Speaks*, 7th ed. NASW Policy Statements, 2006–2009
- School Violence. In *Social Work Speaks*, 7th ed. NASW Policy Statements, 2006–2009

Standards
- NASW Standards for School Social Work Services

Credentials
- NASW Standards for School Social Work Services: www.socialworkers.org

Professional Associations
- National School Social Work Association of America (SSWAA): http://www.sswaa.org/
- Midwest School Social Work Council: http://www.midwest-ssw.org
- School Social Work Association of Arizona: http://www.sswaaz.org
- Colorado School Social Work Association: http://www.csswa.org
- Florida Association of School Social Workers: http://fassw.org

- School Social Workers Association of Georgia: http://www.sswag.org
- Indiana School Social Work Association: http://www.insswa.org
- Iowa School Social Work Association: http://aea16.k12.ia.us
- Kansas Association of School Social Workers: http://www.kassw.org
- Kentucky Association of School Social Workers: http://www.kassw-ky.org
- Michigan Association of School Social Workers: http://www.masswmi .org
- Minnesota School Social Work Association: http://www.msswa.org
- School Social Work Association of Missouri: http://www.sswam.org
- Nebraska School Social Work Association
- New Jersey Association of School Social Workers: http://www.njassw.org
- North Carolina School Social Workers Association: http://www .ncsswa.org
- Ohio School Social Work Association: http://www.osswa.org
- Wisconsin School Social Workers Association: http://www.wsswa.org

Appendix A: Comparative Fields of Practice

	Addictions	Aging	Child Welfare	Criminal Justice	Domestic Violence	Health	Homeless Services
Core Functions	Case management Assessment and diagnosis Group, family and individual counseling	Case management Psychosocial assessment Family services Home visits	Psychosocial assessment Family and children services Home visits Case management	Counseling Legal advocacy Family court Mediation	Crisis intervention Safety planning Counseling Group work	Psychosocial assessment Family and individual counseling Case management	Case management Crisis intervention Psychosocial assessment
Settings	Inpatient Outpatient Residential	Hospital Long-term care facility Senior center	Public child welfare agency Foster care or adoption agency School	Court Correctional facility Advocacy organization Legal services	Domestic violence shelters Outpatient mental health clinic Hospital emergency room	Hospital Community health center	Shelter Food bank Street and mobile unit
Education	BSW for entry-level/ residential programs MSW for hospital and outpatient position	BSW for entry-level case management, senior centers, nursing homes MSW for hospital position	BSW for caseworker position MSW for supervisor level	BSW for probation and some correctional settings MSW for more advanced positions	BSW for shelters and hotlines MSW for outpatient mental health and hospital positions	BSW for community-based case management MSW for hospital and outpatient counseling	BSW for many positions MSW for supervisory level
Specialty Credential Available	YES (NASW addictions credential)	YES (NASW and national) Geriatric case manager certification	YES (NASW)	NO	NO	YES (NASW)	NO
Factors Influencing Job Market	Strong growth expected, particularly as an alternative to incarceration programs	Strong demand expected; workforce turnover and low salaries continue to be a problem	Continued demand expected; high workforce turnover continues to be a problem	Strong growth expected	Continued demand expected	Strong growth expected, particularly in community health settings	Demand for services expected to grow, particularly because of the economy and the rise in veteran population

	International	Mental Health	Military	Palliative and End-of-Life	Private Practice	School Social Work
Core Functions	Humanitarian work Data gathering Advocacy	Psychotherapy Assessment and diagnosis Case management Group, family, and individual counseling	Case management Psychosocial assessment Crisis intervention Individual and group counseling Family services	Case management Psychosocial assessment Family services Individual counseling	Psychotherapy Diagnosis Group therapy Marital/couples counseling	Case management Group, family, and individual counseling Community liaison
Settings	International setting Domestic organization involved in global issues	Inpatient and outpatient mental health center Day program Psychosocial club	VA hospital Military center Veterans' assistance organization	Hospital Hospice Long-term care facility Homes	Private office	School
Education	BSW for some overseas positions MSW for more advanced practice	BSW for case management positions MSW for clinical positions	MSW needed for most VA positions BSW for case management entry-level positions	BSW for some hospice work MSW needed for advanced positions and hospitals	MSW	An MSW is often required to be a public school social worker; some rural counties with a social worker shortage may be more likely to hire a BSW
Specialty Credential Available	NO	YES (NASW)	NO	Yes (developed jointly by the National Hospice and Palliative Care Organization [NHPCO] and NASW)	YES (NASW)	YES (NASW)

(Continued)

(Continued)

	International	Mental Health	Military	Palliative and End-of-Life	Private Practice	School Social Work
Factors Influencing Job Market	Greater professional interest in the field, with more educational opportunities being developed	Continued growth expected	Demand for services expected to substantially increase because of the impact of the wars in Iraq and Afghanistan	Expected growth in this area due to increase among older population and improved medical technology	Continued demand expected	Continued demand expected

Appendix B: Useful Internet Sites

American Board of Examiners in Clinical Social Work (ABE)
http://www.abecsw.org
This organization sets national social work practice standards.

American Association of Spinal Cord Injury Psychologists and Social Workers
http://www.aascipsw.org
This organization has the mission of recognizing the contribution of social workers and psychologists in advancing the care of persons with spinal cord injury.

Association of Baccalaureate Social Work Program Directors (BPD)
http://www.bpdonline.org
BPD is the main organization that focuses on undergraduate social work education. This Web site has a wealth of information about undergraduate social work.

Association for Community Organization & Social Administration
http://www.acosa.org
This Web site is a wonderful resource for social workers about community organizing and social policy.

Association for the Advancement of Social Work with Groups (AASWG)
http://www.aaswg.org
Social work's premier group work organization.

Association of Oncology Social Work (AOSW)
http://www.aosw.org
The Association of Oncology Social Work is a Web site dedicated to social work services for people with cancer and their families.

Association of Social Work Boards (ASWB)
http://www.aswb.org
This organization regulates licensing and has information about exams, study guides, and national licensing laws.

Council of Nephrology Social Workers (CNSW)
http://www.kidney.org/professionals/CNSW/
Information, including salaries and career options, for nephrology social workers.

Council on Social Work Education (CSWE)

http://www.cswe.org/CSWE/

This is the sole accrediting organization for social work educational programs. It provides information about schools of social work, conferences, and policy initiatives.

Fried Social Worker

http://www.friedsocialworker.com

This Web site is a great humor resource with lots of funny social work jokes and an excellent section on burnout.

Information for Practice

http://blogs.nyu.edu/socialwork/ip/

A state-of-the-art blog about current developments and news relevant to social work practice.

Latino Social Work Organization (LSWO)

http://www.lswo.org

This is a professional association dedicated to issues related to Latino social workers; it is focused on the recruitment and retainment of Latino social workers.

Mental Health Social Worker (MHSW)

http://mhsw.org

This Web site features current news from many different sources related to the field of mental health and social work.

National Association of Black Social Workers (NABSW)

http://www.nabsw.org/mserver

This is a professional social work organization for social workers of African descent.

National Association of Puerto Rican/Hispanic Social Workers (NAPR/HSW)

http://www.naprhsw.org

A professional association for Puerto Rican and Hispanic social workers, this Web site has job ads and many resources.

National Association of Social Workers (NASW)

http://www.socialworkers.org

This is the professional association for the profession and provides a wealth of information. This Web site will link you to local state chapters.

National Organization of Forensic Social Work (NOFSW)

http://www.nofsw.org

This is an excellent resource for information about forensic social work.

National Network for Social Work Managers

https://www.socialworkmanager.org

An excellent Web site for issues in social work leadership and management.

New Social Worker Online

http://www.socialworker.com/home/index.php

This Web site provides an excellent resource for social workers. Among its many features is *The New Social Worker* magazine, which can be accessed for free online, job listings, and a discussion forum.

North American Association of Christians in Social Work

http://www.nacsw.org

This is a professional association for Christian social workers.

Rural Social Work Caucus

http://www.marson-and-associates.com/rural/

This Web site provides information about rural social work, including a directory of funders that give grants to rural social work projects. It also has a listserv that one can join.

Social Work Access Network (SWAN)

http://cosw.sc.edu/swan/index.html

This Web site, developed and maintained by the University of South Carolina, provides an excellent directory of useful social work Web sites, publications, organizations, and other information.

Social Work Examination Services (SWES)

http://www.swes.net/home.html

This is a recognized and well-established publisher of social work exam prep books and materials.

SocialWork.com

http://www.socialwork.com

An excellent Web site for social work job opportunities.

Social Work Job Bank

http://www.socialworkjobbank.com/site

This is an excellent online career center for social workers and is a collaboration between the *New Social Worker* magazine and SocialWorker.com.

Social Work PRN

http://socialworkprn.com/

An employment agency for social workers with locations across the United States.

Social Work World

http://pages.prodigy.net/volksware/socialworkworld/index.htm
This is a fun and user-friendly Web site with basic social work information, including jobs and a discussion listserv.

Society for Social Work Leadership in Health Care

http://www.sswlhc.org
This is the Web site for the leading organization about social work in health care.

Society for Spirituality and Social Work

http://ssw.asu.edu/portal/research/spirituality
This Web site provides up-to-date information about trends in spirituality and social work.

References

Abramson, J. S., & Mizrahi, T. (1996). When social workers and physicians collaborate: Positive and negative interdisciplinary experiences. *Social Work, 41*, 270–281.

Administration on Aging. (2007). *A Profile of Older Americans: 2007*. Washington, DC: Author.

Alexander, R. Jr. (2008) Criminal Justice Overview. In T. Mizrahi & L. E. Davis (Eds.-in-Chief), *Encyclopedia of social work* (20th ed., Vol. 1, pp. 470–476). Washington, DC, and New York: NASW7 Press and Oxford University Press.

Allen-Meares, P. (2008). School Social Work. In T. Mizrahi & L. E. Davis (Eds.-in-Chief), *Encyclopedia of social work* (20th ed., Vol. 4 pp.3–7). Washington, DC, and New York: NASW7 Press and Oxford University Press.

Altilio, T., Gardia, G., & Otis-Green, S. (2007). Social work practice in palliative and end-of-life care: A report from the summit. *Journal of Social Work in End-of-Life & Palliative Care, 3*(4), 68–86.

American Psychiatric Association. (2000). *Diagnostic and statistical manual of mental disorders* (4th ed.). Washington, DC: Author.

Auerbach, C., Mason, S., & LaPorte, H. H. (2007). Evidence that supports the value of social work in hospitals. *Social Work in Health Care, 44*(4), 17–30.

Beder, J. (2006). *Hospital social work: The interface of medicine and caring*. New York: Routledge.

Beitchman, P. (2005). The 50-year evolution of social work in community mental health. *Currents of the New York City Chapter of NASW. 49*(6), 4, 15.

Berger, C. S., Robbins, C., Lewis, M., Mizrahi, T., & Fleit, S. (2003). The impact of organizational change on social work staffing in a hospital setting: A national, longitudinal study of social work in hospitals. *Social Work in Health Care, 37*(1), 1–18.

Bernabei, S. (2005). Regarding the recent reform to the Rockefeller drug laws: Don't be fooled by the tinkering. *Currents of the New York City Chapter of NASW. 49*(5), 6, 7, 12.

Beyond Shelter. (n.d.). *Housing first: Ending family homelessness*. Retrieved April 10, 2009, from http://www.beyondshelter.org/aaa_initiatives/ending_homelessness.shtml

Bureau of Labor Statistics. (2008). *Occupational outlook handbook, 2008–09 edition*. Retrieved November 14, 2008, from http://www.bls.gov/oco/ocos060.htm

Casey Family Programs. (2009). *Our work*. Retrieved January 10, 2009, from http://www.casey.org/OurWork

Casey Family Programs. (n.d.). *Institutional racism and disproportionality*. Retrieved April 11, 2009, from http://www.casey.org/OurWork/Disproportionality/InstitutionalRacism.htm

Center for Workforce Studies. (2007). *More money—less money: Factors associated with the highest and lowest social work salaries*. Washington, DC: National Association of Social Workers.

Child Welfare Information Gateway. (2008). *Child abuse and neglect fatalities: Statistics and interventions*. Retrieved January 2, 2009, from http://www.childwelfare.gov/pubs/factsheets/fatality.cfm

Children's Aid Society. (n.d.). *The orphan trains*. Retrieved April 11, 2009, from http://www.childrensaidsociety.org/about/history/orphantrain

Children's Aid Society. (2008). *History*. Retrieved February 13, 2009, from http://www.cassd.org/index_files/History.htm

Cisikai, E. (2008). End-of-Life-Decisions. In T. Mizrahi & L. E. Davis (Eds.-in-Chief), *Encyclopedia of social work* (20th ed., Vol. 2 pp. 127–132). Washington, DC, and New York: NASW7 Press and Oxford University Press.

Cohen N. L., & Marcos, L. R. (1990). Law, policy, and involuntary emergency room visits. *Psychiatric Quarterly, 61*(3), 197–204.

Colleen, M. G. (1998). Preserving end-of-life autonomy: The Patient Self-Determination Act and the Uniform Health Care Decisions Act. *Health & Social Work, 23*(4), 275–281.

Coltoff, P. (2005). Social work and voluntary child welfare services: Innovation and anticipating future needs. *Currents of the New York City Chapter of NASW, 49*(7), 1, 8.

Cowles, L. F. (2008) Health Care: Practice Interventions. T. Mizrahi & L. E. Davis (Eds.-in-Chief), *Encyclopedia of social work* (20th ed., Vol. 2, pp. 328–332). Washington, DC and New York: NASW7 Press and Oxford University Press.

Cox, J. (1999). The role of social work in policy practice. In J. G. Daley (Ed.), *Social work practice in the military* (pp. 165–174). New York: Haworth Press.

Correctional Social Work. (2006). In *Social work speaks* (7th ed.). NASW Policy Statements, 2006–2009. Washington, DC: Author.

Council on Social Work Education. (2007). *Statistics on social work education in the United States: 2004*. Alexandria, VA: Author.

Daley, J. G. (Ed.). (1999). *Social work practice in the military*. New York: Haworth Press.

Davis, L. V. (1996). Domestic violence. In *Encyclopedia of social work* (19th ed., pp. 780–789). Washington, DC: NASW Press.

DeAngelis, T. (n.d.). *Social workers help military families*. Retrieved January 10, 2008, from National Association of Social Workers Web site: https://www.socialworkers.org/pressroom/events/peace/helpFamilies.asp

Domestic Violence Courts Program Fact Sheet. (2008). Retrieved January 15, 2008, from New York State Division of Criminal Justice Services Web site: http://criminaljustice.state.ny.us/ofpa/domviolcrtfactsheet.htm

Dulmus, C. N. & Roberts, A. R. (2008) Mental Illness: Adults. In T. Mizrahi & L. E. Davis (Eds.-in-Chief), *Encyclopedia of social work* (20th ed., Vol. 3 pp. 237–242). Washington, DC and New York: NASW7 Press and Oxford University Press.

Ehrenreich, B. (1971). *The American health empire: Power, profits, and politics*. New York: Random House.

End-of-Life Care. (2006). In *Social work speaks* (7th ed.). NASW policy statements, 2006–2009. Washington, DC: Author.

Erlenbusch, B., O'Connor, K., Downing, S., & Phillips, W. S. (2008). *From foreclosure to homelessness: The forgotten victims of the subprime crisis*. Retrieved December 10, 2008, from The National Coalition for the Homeless Web site: http://www.national-homeless.org/housing/foreclosure_report.pdf

Family Violence Prevention Fund. (n.d.). *Get the facts: Domestic violence is a serious, widespread social problem*. Retrieved December 15, 2008, from http://endabuse.org/content/action_center/detail/754

Freeman, E. M. (1995). School social work overview. In *Encyclopedia of social work* (19th ed., pp. 2087–2099). Washington, DC: NASW Press.

Garber, D. L., & McNelis, P. J. (1995). Military social work. In *Encyclopedia of social work* (19th ed., pp. 1726–1735). Washington, DC: NASW Press.

Gaudiosi, J. A. (2006). *Child maltreatment 2006*. Washington, DC: U.S. Department of Health and Human Services, Administration for Children and Families, Children's Bureau. Retrieved April 11, 2009, from http://www.acf.hhs.gov/programs/cb/pubs/cm06/cm06.pdf

Gibelman, M. (2001). *What social workers do*. Washington, DC: NASW Press.

Globerman, J., Davies J. M., & Walsh, S. (1996). Social work in restructuring hospitals: Meeting the challenge. *Health and Social Work, 21*, 178–188.

Glusker, A. (n.d.). *A student's guide to planning a career in international social work*. Retrieved June 10, 2008, from University of Pennsylvania Web site: http://www.sp2.upenn.edu/~restes/isw/chapter52.html

Green, R. G., Baskind, F. R., Mustian, B. E., Reed, L. N., & Taylor, H. R. (2007). Professional education and private practice: Is there a disconnect? *Social Work, 52*, 151–159.

Hanson, M. (2001). Alcoholism and other drug addictions. In A. Gitterman (Ed.), *Handbook of social work practice with vulnerable and resilient populations*. New York: Columbia University Press.

Harris, J. (1999). History of army social work. In J. G. Daley (Ed.), *Social work practice in the military* (pp. 3–19). New York: Haworth Press.

Healy, L. M. (2008). *International social work: Professional action in an interdependent world*. New York: Oxford University Press.

Healy, L. M. (2008). International Social Work: Overview. In T. Mizrahi & L. E. Davis (Eds.-in-Chief), *Encyclopedia of social work* (20th ed., Vol. 2, pp. 483–488). Washington, DC, and New York: NASW7 Press and Oxford University Press.

Holliman, D., Dziegielewski, S. F., & Teare, R. (2003). Differences and similarities between social work and nurse discharge planners. *Health and Social Work., 28*, 224–231.

Hooyman, N. R. (2008). Aging Overview. In T. Mizrahi & L. E. Davis (Eds.-in-Chief), *Encyclopedia of social work* (20th ed., Vol. 1, pp. 88–96). Washington, DC, and New York: NASW7 Press and Oxford University Press.

Jenkins, J. L. (1999). History of navy social work. In J. G. Daley (Ed.), *Social work practice in the military* (pp. 23–27). New York: Haworth Press.

Kaplan, K. O. (1995). End-of-life decisions. In *Encyclopedia of social work* (19th ed., pp. 856–867). Washington, DC: NASW Press.

Landsman, M. (2001). Commitment in public child welfare. *Social Service Review, 75*, 386–419.

Lieberman, D. S. (1995). Child welfare overview. In *Encyclopedia of social work* (19th ed., pp. 424–432). Washington, DC: NASW Press.

Lincoln, A. (Saturday, March 4, 1865). Second Inaugural Address.

Litz, B. T. (n.d.). *The unique circumstances and mental health impact of the wars in Afghanistan and Iraq*. Retrieved January 10, 2008, from National Center for Post Traumatic Stress Disorder, U.S. Department of Veteran's Affairs Web site: http://www.ncptsd.va.gov/ncmain/ncdocs/fact_shts/fs_iraqafghanistan_wars.html

Louisiana State Board of Social Work Examiners. (1998). *Guidelines for child custody evaluations*. Retrieved April 11, 2009, from http://www.labswe.org/child.htm

Manske, J. E. (2008). Veteran Services. In T. Mizrahi & L. E. Davis (Eds.-in-Chief), *Encyclopedia of social work* (20th ed., Vol. 4 pp. 255–256). Washington, DC and New York: NASW7 Press and Oxford University Press.

Mental Health (2006). In *Social work speaks* (7th ed.), NASW Policy Statements, 2006–2009. Washington, DC: Author.

Miller, J. G. (1995). Criminal justice: Social work roles. In *Encyclopedia of social work* (19th ed., pp. 653–659). Washington, DC: NASW Press.

Mitton, J. H. (1999). Trends in domestic violence. *Journal of DuPage County Bar Association*. Retrieved July 15, 2008, from http://www.dcba.org/brief/febissue/1999/art10299.htm

Mizrahi, T., & Abramson, J. S. (2001). Collaboration between social workers and physicians: Perspectives on a shared case. *Social Work in Health Care, 31*(3), 1–24.

Mizrahi, T., & Berger, C. (2001). The impact of a changing health care environment on social work leaders: Obstacles and opportunities in hospital social work. *Social Work, 46*, 170–182.

Mullender, A. (1996). *Rethinking domestic violence: The social work and probation response*. New York: Routledge.

National Alliance to End Homelessness. (2008). *Veterans*. Retrieved May 10, 2008, from http://www.endhomelessness.org/section/policy/focusareas/veterans

National Association of Social Workers. (n.d.). *Issue fact sheet: Mental health*. Retrieved October 10, 2008, from http://www.socialworkers.org/pressroom/features/issue/mental.asp

National Association of Social Workers. (n.d.). *School social work*. Retrieved April 11, 2009, from http://www.socialworkers.org/pressroom/features/issue/school.asp

National Association of Social Workers. (1992). *Standards for social work case management*. Retrieved April 11, 2009, from http://www.socialworkers.org/practice/standards/sw_case_mgmt.asp

National Association of Social Workers. (2008). *Standards for social work practice in palliative and end-of-life care*. Retrieved April 11, 2009, from http://www.socialworkers.org/practice/bereavement/standards/default.asp

National Center on Addiction and Substance Abuse at Columbia University. (2000). *2000 Casa national survey of American attitudes on substance abuse VI: Teens*. New York: Columbia University.

National Coalition for the Homeless. (2008). *Why are people homeless?* Retrieved April 11, 2009, from http://www.nationalhomeless.org/publications/facts/why.html

National Hospice and Palliative Care Organization. (2008). *Advance directives*. Retrieved April 11, 2009, from http://www.caringinfo.org/AdvanceDirectives

National Institute of Mental Health. (2008a). *Post traumatic stress disorder*. Bethesda, MD: Author.

National Institute of Mental Health. (2008b). *Statistics*. Retrieved October 10, 2008, from http://www.nimh.nih.gov/health/statistics/index.shtml

National Law Center on Homelessness and Poverty. (2007). *Annual report*. Retrieved April 11, 2009, from http://www.nlchp.org

National Poverty Center, University of Michigan, Gerald Ford School of Public Policy. (2006). *Poverty in the United States*. Retrieved April 25, 2008, from http://npc.umich.edu/poverty

New York City Chapter of NASW. (2005, May). *Focus group with social workers in the field of aging: Overcoming mistrust and isolation to save lives*. Retrieved April 11, 2009, from http://www.naswnyc.org/OvercomingMistrustandIsolationToSaveLives.htm

New York State Department of Education, Office of the Professions. (2004). Education Law: Article 154, Social Work. Retrieved April 12, 2009, from http://www.op.nysed.gov/article154.htm

Olson, B. (2008). The case for inclusion of sexual orientation and gender identity/expression in school district harassment and violence policies. *NASW–School Social Work Section Connection*, 2, 3–5.

Ozawa, M. N., & Law, S. W. (1993). Earnings history of social workers: A comparison to other professional groups. *Social Work*, 38, 542–551.

Pecora, J.P. (2008). Child Welfare Overview. In T. Mizrahi & L. E. Davis (Eds.-in-Chief), *Encyclopedia of social work* (20th ed., Vol. 1, pp. 270–277). Washington, DC, and New York: NASW7 Press and Oxford University Press.

Price, J. (n.d.). *Findings from the national Vietnam veterans' readjustment study*. National Center for Post Traumatic Stress Disorder. United States Department of Veteran's Affairs. Retrieved January 10, 2008, from http://www.ncptsd.va.gov/ncmain/ncdocs/fact_shts/fs_nvvrs.html?opm=1&rr=rr45&srt=d&echorr=true

Rahia, N. K. (1999). Medical social work in the U.S. Armed Forces. In J. G. Daley (Ed.), *Social work practice in the military* (pp. 107–120). New York: Haworth Press.

Rennison, C. M., & Welchans, S. (2000, May). *Intimate partner violence* (Bureau of Justice Statistics special report). Retrieved December 10, 2008, from http://www.ojp.usdoj.gov/bjs/

Rizzo, V. M., & Abrams, A. (2000). Utilization review: A powerful social work role in health care settings. *Health & Social Work*, 25(4), 264–269.

Rizzo, V., & Rowe, J. (2006). Studies of the efficacy of social work services in aging with a focus on cost outcomes: A review of the literature. *Research on Social Work Practice*, 16(1), 67–73.

Rosenberg, J., & Rosenberg, S. (Eds.). (2006). *Community mental health: Challenges for the 21st century*. New York: Routledge.

Ross, J. W. (1996). Hospital social work. In *Encyclopedia of social work* (19th ed., pp. 1365–1376). Washington, DC: NASW Press.

Sackman, B. (2005). Importance of MSW's in community-based aging services. *Currents of the New York City Chapter of NASW, 49*(7), 3, 10. Retrieved April 11, 2009, from the NASW New York City Chapter Web site: http://www.naswnyc.org/ImportanceofMSWsInCommunity-BasedAgingServices.htm

Sánchez, J. R. (2003). *Social worker providing leadership in municipal system: An interview with José R. Sanchez, CSW, ACSW*. Retrieved April 11, 2009, from http://www.naswnyc.org/SocialWorkinHealthCare.html

Seebohm, P., Henderson, P., Munn-Giddings, C., Thomas, P., & Yasmeen, S. (2006, February). Power to the Community. *Mental Health Today*, 31–34.

Sherman, M. (2008, January/February). Trauma and the military family: Responses, resources, and opportunities for growth. *Social Work Today, 8*(1), 36.

Soska, T. M. (2008). Housing. In T. Mizrahi & L. E. Davis (Eds.-in-Chief), *Encyclopedia of social work* (20th ed., Vol. 2, pp. 389–395). Washington, DC, and New York: NASW7 Press and Oxford University Press.

Stone, R., Reinhard, S., Machemer, J., & Rudin, D. (2002, November). *Geriatric care managers: A profile of an emerging profession research report*. *AARP*. Retrieved December 15, 2008, from http://www.aarp.org

Strolin, J. S., McCarthy, M., & Caringi, J. (2005). *Causes and effects of child welfare workforce turnover: Current state of knowledge and future directions*. Retrieved April 11, 2009, from the New York State Social Work Education Consortium Web site: http://www.ocfs.state.ny.us/ohrd/swec/pubs/Future%20Directions.pdf

Substance Abuse and Mental Health Services Administration, Office of Applied Studies. (2008). *Results from the 2007 National Survey on Drug Use and Health: National findings* (NSDUH Series H-34, DHHS Publication No. SMA 08-4343). Rockville, MD: U.S. Department of Health and Human Services.

Suppes, M. A., & Wells, C. (2008). *The social work experience: An introduction to social work and social welfare* (5th ed). Upper Saddle River, NJ: Allyn and Bacon.

Talent, S. H., & Ryberg, R. A. (1999). Common and unique ethical dilemmas encountered by military social workers. In J. G. Daley (Ed.), *Social work practice in the military* (pp. 179–203). New York: Haworth Press.

Tanielian, T. (2008). *Invisible wounds of war: Psychological and cognitive injuries, their consequences, and services to assist recovery*. Santa Monica, CA: RAND.

U.S. Department of Education. (n.d.). *No Child Left Behind, Subpart 2: Elementary and secondary school counseling programs*. Retrieved February 1, 2009, from http://www.ed.gov/policy/elsec/leg/esea02/pg68.html

U.S. Department of Health & Human Services. (1999). *Mental health: A report of the surgeon general—Executive summary*. Rockville, MD: U.S. Department of Health and Human Services, Substance Abuse and Mental Health Services. Retrieved April 11, 2009, from the Surgeon General Web site: http://www.surgeongeneral.gov/library/mentalhealth/pdfs/ExSummary-Final.pdf

U.S. Department of Health & Human Services, Administration on Children, Youth and Families. (2008). *Child maltreatment 2006*. Washington, DC: U.S. Government Printing Office.

Van Wormer, K., & Davis, R. D. (2008). *Addiction treatment: A strengths perspective*. Pacific Grove, CA: Thomson Brooks/Cole.

Volland, P., & Sisco, S. (2005). The aging imperative: Preparing the social work labor force. *Currents of the New York City Chapter of NASW, 49*(7), 3, 10.

Wilt, S., & Olson, S. (1996). Prevalence of domestic violence in the United States. *Journal of the American Medical Women's Association, 51*(3), 86–92.

Whitaker, T., Weismiller, T., & Clark, E. (2006a). *Assuring the sufficiency of a frontline workforce: A national study of licensed social workers* (Special report: Social work services for older adults). Washington, DC: National Association of Social Workers.

Whitaker, T., Weismiller, T., & Clark, E. (2006b). *Assuring the sufficiency of a frontline workforce: A national study of licensed social workers* (Special report: Social work services for children and families). Washington, DC: National Association of Social Workers.

Whitaker, T., Weismiller, T., & Clark, E. (2006c). *Assuring the sufficiency of a frontline workforce* (Executive summary). Washington, DC: National Association of Social Workers.

Whitaker, T., Weismiller, T., Clark, E., & Wilson, M. (2006d). *Assuring the sufficiency of a frontline workforce: A national study of licensed social workers* (Special report: Social work services in behavioral health care settings). Washington, DC: National Association of Social Workers.

Whitaker, T., Weismiller, T., Clark, E., & Wilson, M. (2006e). *Assuring the sufficiency of a frontline workforce: A national study of licensed social workers* (Special report: Social work services in health care settings). Washington, DC: National Association of Social Workers.

Index